TRAPPED IN THE NET

THE UNANTICIPATED CONSEQUENCES OF COMPUTERIZATION

Gene I. Rochlin

PRINCETON UNIVERSITY PRESS

PRINCETON, NEW JERSEY

Copyright © 1997 by Princeton University Press
Published by Princeton University Press, 41 William Street,
Princeton, New Jersey 08540
In the United Kingdom: Princeton University Press,
Chichester, West Sussex

All Rights Reserved

Library of Congress Cataloging-in-Publication Data

Rochlin, Gene I.
Trapped in the net : the unanticipated consequences of
computerization / Gene I. Rochlin.
    p. cm.
Includes bibliographical references and index.
ISBN 0-691-01080-3
ISBN 0-691-00247-9 (pbk.)
    1. Computers and civilization. 2. Electronic data processing—
Social aspects. 3. Computer networks. I. Title. II. Title:
Unanticipated consequences of computerization.
QA76.9.C66R62 1997 96–41003
303.48'34—DC20 CIP

This book has been composed in Palatino

Princeton University Press books are printed on
acid-free paper and meet the guidelines for permanence
and durability of the Committee on Production
Guidelines for Book Longevity of the
Council on Library Resources

Seventh printing, and first paperback printing, 1998

http://pup.princeton.edu

Printed in the United States of America

10 9 8 7

TRAPPED IN THE NET

To Alexander, Andrew, and Bradley

FOR WHOM ALL OF THIS WILL BE ANCIENT HISTORY

Contents

Preface   xi

Acknowledgments   xv

1.
Introduction   3

Prologue   3
Enter the Computer   5
Compliance and Control   7
The Structure of the Argument   11
The Structure of the Book   13

2.
Autogamous Technology   15

Introduction   15
A Brief Historical Essay   16
Operating Systems   23
The Dynamics of Growth   29
The Hegemony of Design   32

3.
Networks of Connectivity: Webs of Dependence   35

Introduction   35
From Anarchy to Networks   38
The Interconnected Office   46
Conclusion   48

4.
Taylorism Redux?   51

Introduction   51

The Search for Managerial Control   53
The Deskilling Controversy   61
Expertise Lost   67
Heterogeneous Systems   69
Conclusion   71

5.
Computer Trading   74

Introduction   74
Markets and Exchanges   76
Automating Markets   82
Conclusion   88

6.
Jacking into the Market   91

The Demise of Barings P.L.C.   91
Trading in Cyberspace   94
Global Markets   99
Conclusion   105
Epilogue   106

7.
Expert Operators and Critical Tasks   108

Having the Bubble   108
Pilot Error   112
The Glass Cockpit   115
Air Traffic Control   119
Industrial and Other Operations   123
The Computer in the Loop   125
Conclusion   128

8.
Smart Weapons, Smart Soldiers   131

Introduction   131
Industrial War   132
Techno-Industrial War   135
The Postwar Transition   137
Quantity versus Quality   140
Trading Tooth for Tail   144
Conclusion   147

9.
Unfriendly Fire — 150

Introduction — 150
A "Reasonable Choice of Disaster" — 152
The USS Stark — 154
Tragedy over the Persian Gulf — 156
Conclusion — 166

10.
The Logistics of Techno-War — 169

Introduction — 169
The Gulf War — 171
Redefining Effectiveness — 182
Computers and the Transformation of War — 184

11.
C³I in Cyberspace — 188

Introduction — 188
The Ways and Means of Modern Warfare — 191
Moving toward Cyberspace — 199
The Virtual Battlefield — 202
Conclusion — 207

12.
Invisible Idiots — 210

Introduction — 210
Standardization and Slack — 212
Virtual Organizations in a Real World — 214
Conclusion — 216

Notes — 219
Bibliography — 265
Index — 285

Preface

WHEN I bought my first "personal" computer, it was definitely My Computer. With 64K of memory and one floppy disk drive, it really could not do very much. But it was an icon, a real computer of my very own. Several generations of development later, I am writing on a desktop machine comparable in power to the mainframes of only a decade ago. But it is now only my computer; the sense of elite possession has dissipated. To my sons, my students, and most of my younger colleagues, only a few large, superpowerful mainframes are ever referred to as capital "C" Computers; the machines they own and work on are strictly small "c" computers—capable and necessary appliances, but far from having the mythic overtones I still carry over from my experiences in the earlier days of computing.

At home and at work, small, compact electronic digital computers have moved more rapidly through the stages of development, deployment, and social incorporation than any major technological innovation in history. That much is widely recognized. What is less widely understood are the consequences of having moved so quickly to depending on computers and computerized networks for the performance of a wide range of tasks, critical and mundane.

The span of activities subject to computer control now ranges from international fund transfers to supermarket checkouts, from spacecraft controls to automobile warnings; there is even a proposal for guiding the blind via computer-coordinated and interpreted transmissions from computer-controlled Global Positioning Satellites. Yet the rapidity of consequential social and political change is rarely noted. Increasingly, business, social, and even personal rules and structures are being altered to better comply with the formalities and restrictions of computers and information systems.

Are the computers therefore taking over the conduct of human affairs? Not directly, in the traditional sense of runaway robots or insane mainframes. But they are reshaping our world and our lives through the long-term and indirect effects they exert on social and organizational forms and through the new kinds of dependencies that are thereby created.

What I call the "computer trap" has four parts: the lure, the snare, the costs, and the long-term consequences. The lure is obvious—the promise of modern computer "technology," which each year seems to offer increasing computing power and connectivity at decreasing cost, ever more powerful and adaptable tools with simpler and more human-centered interfaces. The snare is what usually ensues. Once heavily invested in the use of computers to perform central tasks, organizations and individuals alike become heavily invested in and irreversibly committed to the new capacities and potentials.

The costs are varied and have been pointed out by many. Computerization creates a whole new set of institutional dependencies, including a dependency on the manufacturers of hardware and software that often seems to border on pathology in the scramble to keep up with the incredible rate of change. It also has direct costs that may well be underestimated. A decade ago, Paul Strassman, seeking to explain why the widespread introduction of automation and computers had not resulted in any noticeable increase in the productivity of the American economy since the beginning of the 1970s, noted that most of the newly acquired power was being absorbed by administration and management.

As of this writing, economic productivity has remained flat for twenty-five years, the longest such period in America in this century. And the search for explanations as to why the computer "revolution" has not resulted in the anticipated gains has been expanded on, most recently by Thomas Landauer, who sets out in great detail the consequences for organizational as well as personal learning and for institutional stability in the face of overly rapid change, poor software design, and insensitivity to users.

What have been less frequently discussed in the focus on economic indicators and short-term effects on performance and productivity are the long-term, unintended, and frequently unanticipated consequences that flow both from increased dependence on computers and computerized systems and from the secondary effects that follow as the direct and indirect costs of that dependency. These are the subject of this book. The short-term and direct consequences that I discuss tend to be effects on regulation and the regulatory environment, occupational skills, operational reliability and safety, and managerial roles and responsibilities that are likely to result in long-term and indirect costs. Of particular interest are those that are likely to follow from the interactive reconstruction of organizational and social forms, and from changes in the modes and means of representation, political and economic as well as social.

Because this work is empirically grounded in research on organizations that manage safety-critical tasks, I pay particular attention to the potential loss of experiential knowledge as operations are increasingly computerized. The enduring myth is that extensive computerization and networking will distribute power as well as information and technical capability more evenly through industry, offices, bureaus, and the society at large. Virtual communities and virtual organizations are being promoted as flexible, adaptive, and empowering forms. What I see instead, in personal life, in business, in markets, and in the military, is the substitution of data-scanning for information-gathering, of rules and procedures for learning, and of models and calculations for judgment and expertise. In short, the replacement of art with artifice.

It is neither my intent nor my purpose to argue that the introduction of computers and computerized equipment is in itself a bad or disruptive thing. There are many places where the introduction of computers has enabled human beings to better cope with and manage an increasingly complex world, and there are many things that can be better done with computers than by hand. But in the rush to computerize, to automate, and to network, relatively little attention seems to have been paid to evaluating the consequences of submitting that particular realm of human activity to rapid and ofttimes radical technical change. This book attempts to take a step in that direction.

Acknowledgments

THIS book had its origins in a John Simon Guggenheim Memorial Foundation Fellowship in 1986–1987, during which a great deal of the conceptual framework was developed. Much of the research on military organization and emerging military doctrines was supported by a John D. and Catherine T. MacArthur Foundation Individual Fellowship for Research and Writing in International Security in 1987–1988. There is no way I can express my gratitude to either of these foundations for the time and space their support provided for thinking and reflecting on what was then still a dynamic and often turbulent time of technical change in computing and networking. Other kinds of support were provided by the Institute of International Studies, both intellectually and through funding of field work overseas, and by the Institute of Governmental Studies, which provided me not only with office space but with a hospitable, supportive working environment. The research on highly reliable organizations that underlies a great deal of the work on organizational analysis and operator expertise was supported in part by Office of Naval Research contract N-00014-86-k-03123 and National Science Foundation grants SES-8708804 and SES-8911105.

My thanks also to the managers of air traffic control centers, and of several nuclear power plants and the utilities that own them, to senior officers who facilitated our entry into the U.S. Navy, and to the many operators who shared their workspace, their time, and their thoughts with us, often for long periods, with grace, courtesy, and hospitality. They seemed at the time to share many of the concerns expressed in this book, and I hope they do not find that they have been misrepresented.

There is no way that I can adequately express the degree to which I am indebted to my colleagues on the organizational work, in particular Todd R. La Porte, Karlene Roberts, and Paul Schulman, who provided an atmosphere of continued excitement and stimulation throughout the project. Our work is not yet done, and I hope that this volume will contribute to it some modest value added. Without the skills and insights of Alexandra von Meier, my student, colleague, and compatriot in much of the field work, much of what is subtle and indirect in the data on operators would have been missed entirely. The military analysis would have been impossible without the expert knowledge and advice of Chris C. Demchak on matters organizational as well as professional; her help in the field and on the autobahn in Germany was indispensable. Members of the Berkeley Global Stability Group, particularly Ernst Haas, provided the kind of intellectual support and reflective criticism that one always hopes for but rarely finds in academia. Janet Abbate and Paul Edwards were incredibly generous in sharing their own unpublished work, as well as their unpublished manuscripts, as was Kären Wieckert, to whom I also owe a very special debt for her encouragement, advice, insight, and willingness to read and argue about various chapter drafts. And, finally, I am eternally grateful to Anne Middleton, with whom life is a constant exchange of housework, humor, advice, intellectual support, and penetrating and detailed criticism of both concept and writing. All of these friends and colleagues have helped make this a better book; the responsibility for its shortcomings and failures are mine alone.

Berkeley, California
May 3, 1996

TRAPPED IN THE NET

1.

Introduction

Prologue

This morning I got a call from a computer. The local telephone company had just repaired a defective line, and its computer was calling me to ask how satisfied I had been with the service. Somewhat amused by the role reversal, I dutifully punched the buttons of my touch-tone phone when requested, evaluating the promptness, efficiency, and quality of the work done. Only after I hung up did I realize that the reversal of roles had only been symbolic. It didn't matter whether I called the computer or it called me. In either case, I have learned to adapt my behavior to comply with the electronic menu, to conform to the specifications of a machine.

As the electronic digital computer and the networks it supports become ever more deeply embedded as constituent elements of life in modern industrial societies, stories about the frustrations and problems of dealing with computers, from automated voice mail to airline reservation systems, have become increasingly common. But even when really amusing, such stories generally deal with the roughness of the human-machine interface and the inherent inability of preprogrammed, automated systems, however clever, to deal effectively with the variety and unpredictability of human beings.

There are other, more consequential stories that are hardly ever told. When my travel agent was unable to book a flight that I wanted because her flexibility and range of choice were subordinated to the nationwide Sabre system, and the local airline office could not because it was blocked by arbitrary but firmly programmed rules, I was able to do so on my own by calling the frequent flier desk of the airline and speaking with a young woman to whom the booking computer was an accessory and an aid, not a confining and superordinating system.[1]

When the library at my university installed a bar-coded checkout system for books, they also put into place a supermarket-like inventory control system that automatically identifies books not recently checked out and sends them to storage. But university libraries are not supermarkets, university collections are not used in the same way as public libraries, and not all scholarly fields are equally time-bound, or heavily populated. One of the unintended consequences of the new system is that many important books in the more leisurely or esoteric fields of traditional scholarship (e.g., medieval studies) were moved to a remote warehouse, where access was difficult and the chance of finding them by walking the shelves remote.[2]

When my wife could not find a particular journal series on medieval English indexed on the library's elaborate computer system, she was told that the index was purchased from a commercial supplier, who tended to correlate the depth and detail of indexing with the laws of supply and demand. This privileges users in engineering and the sciences over scholars of literature and history, whose demand is smaller and less coherent in space or time.

These examples illustrate the long-term and indirect costs of preprogrammed automation and computerized efficiency. The more powerful a data management program, the greater the requirement that data be entered in certain specific and structured ways; what does not fit must be reshaped or discarded. The more structured the data entry, the more confining the rules and possibilities for searching. The larger and more established the database and its rules, the more difficult to modify or extend them. Eventually, the machine's rules reign.

The adoption of computers to organize, manage, integrate, and coordinate a wide variety of human activities has greatly augmented human capabilities and increased the scope and connectivity of human activities. But at what cost to resiliency and adaptability? Office networking allows considerable interactive flexibility, as do market transfer systems, electronic banking, and the Internet, but the requirements for compliance and strict adherence to standards and protocols are stringent. Just-in-time industrial systems offer great flexibility in manufacturing, but, as was discovered in the recent Kobe earthquake, they are essentially inoperable if the electronic system that coordinates and schedules the required network of tightly coupled activities is damaged or destroyed.

Enter the Computer

The argument of this book is that the complacent acceptance of the desktop "personal" computer in almost every aspect of modern life is masking the degree to which computerization and computer networking are transforming not just the activities and instruments of human affairs, but also their structure and practice. As they become familiar, indeed ubiquitous components of appliances, communication, work processes, organization, and management, computers are increasingly regarded as no more than exceedingly capable and complex tools. And humans seem always to regard what they have made as something that they can therefore control.[3] That our history has been shaped by the form and use of our tools in ways totally unanticipated by their inventors is, as always, conveniently forgotten.

It is not surprising that the ordinary person hardly pauses to reflect on the rapidity and scope of the transformation of social structures and culture that are resulting from the widespread acceptance of the digital computer. There seems to be little doubt about the value of collecting and indexing more information than any one of us could possibly scan, let alone digest, in a lifetime; of instant and virtually unimpeded global communication; or of automating difficult and complex industrial operations. Modern societies have made a totem of their hardware, cloaking dependence by transforming what it is necessary to own into what it is merely desirable to have, and disguising the imperatives of compliance as no more than a set of operating rules.

As the computer has passed from novelty to ubiquity, one of the most identifiable characteristics of its reconstruction of the human world has been a flood of accompanying propaganda that verges on adoration. Newsstands are filled with magazines tutoring us on the latest trend in software, the most appropriate hardware, the latest modes of interconnection, while newspapers report with breathless earnestness the new levels of empowerment to be reached with the technological breakthrough of the week. Their idols, and perhaps ours, are the visionaries of Intel, of Xerox PARC and Apple, of Lotus and the Internet, who pulled the digital computer out of their technological temples and onto the desktop. And floating above it all, you find the techno-metaphysicians in search of a larger, more profound meaning to it all: the Tofflers and their "third wave" and the "informatic society,"[4] Bruce Mazlish and the "fourth discontinuity,"[5] and the wizards of the world of artificial intelligence in peripatetic pursuit of a machine "who" really thinks.[6]

The remarkable clockwork automata of the eighteenth century were capable of inspiring a fascination bordering on awe in a mechanical age when even the human body was regarded as perhaps little more than an elaborate machine.[7] And in a later age of electronics and information, so were the huge mainframes of the early days of computing—remote, forbidding, and, perhaps, capable of taking over human societies through their superior intelligence and calculated rationality.

The early fear of computers was focused on the idea of large, discrete, immensely powerful thinking mechanisms, run by mysterious engineers in white coats, capable of becoming autonomous decision makers if not closely watched and supervised, and possibly of acting through our centralized and hierarchical institutions to take control of human affairs. What was not anticipated was that simplified robots would be employed everywhere as standard production machines, and that smaller, cheaper, more flexible, and more adaptable electronic digital computers—more powerful and more intricately networked than their inventors could ever have imagined—would be common tools in every business and office, moving into almost every school, and familiar, if not present, in almost every home.

Large, centralized computers are now on their way to becoming specialized rarities, and it is the movement of smaller, more adaptable, and far less expensive "computers" onto desktops and into increasingly smart "machines" (seemingly harmless and hardly remarked upon) that is becoming the agent of transformation, altering not only the range and scope of decisions and choices but the methods and processes by which they are made.

Of even greater importance is the rapid growth of interconnecting networks of communication and information, created by the new capabilities and supported by them, which are bypassing both the structure of centralized institutions and the controls, internal and external, that developed to direct, manage, and regulate them.

What makes the process so elusive to characterize and difficult to analyze is that the conquest of human decision processes and procedures is taking place through the transformation of the means and representation of interaction rather than through the more direct and potentially adversarial processes of displacement of authority or assertion of control. Indeed, some of the harshest critics of traditional industrial societies, of the "modernist" vision of industrialization and development, are found among the enthusiasts of modern computerization and networking, arguing that individual computing is not just a useful, but a *necessary* resource, an indispensable tool not just for dealing with the forbidding complexity of modern society but also as a means for gaining access to the explosive growth in human knowledge.

The consequences of the increased social reliance, and, in many cases, dependence, on computerized information systems, computerized data processing, and computer-aided decision making are therefore likely to be neither direct nor obvious. There is no sign that computers are, in the sense of directly controlling our lives, "taking over" the conduct of human affairs either autonomously or as agents of human organization. Instead, they are creating patterns of reliance and dependency through which our lives will be indirectly and irrevocably reshaped.

Compliance and Control

For the greater part of this century, the search for efficiency and rational organization of space and time was the essence of modernity. Synchronicity, the rational ordering and coordination of work by planning and authority, was to be established through the planning of work and the formal centralization and hierarchical ordering both of the workplace itself and of its management and administration. The gains in efficiency from coordinated production and standardization and rationalization of the workplace were set against the presumably wasteful and disorganized artisanal and small-shop experience of the past. Efficiency losses caused by alienation, deskilling, and lack of flexibility and adaptability were by comparison judged to be small. The first, mainframe computers were admirably suited to that environment and, if anything, increased the centralization of administration, management, and control.

The introduction of the small digital computer, whether as a dedicated mid-frame for business or as desktop personal computers and individual workstations, was promoted as a form of electronic liberation from the powerful and centralized computer center. One of the most persistent arguments for social benefits of the introduction of computers and computer-aided machinery revolves around the argument that the personal computer is an instrument of social (and perhaps political) democratization, a means for providing a flexible, adaptable work environment more like the historical assemblage of craft workers that made up early factories than the mega-production lines of mid-century.

But historical artisan and craft production took place in an environment in which information was difficult to obtain and slow to propagate. The introduction of the computer into business and industry also provided the firm with far greater capacity to gather, order, and disseminate information, almost without practical limit. The era of the free-standing personal workstation lasted only a few years before the usual arguments for efficiency, coordination, and synchronization led to their interconnection, creating networks whose connectivity and flexibility far overshadow the simple hierarchical structure of the mainframe. As a result, it is now possible to control and coordinate process and production without imposing the static and mechanized form of organization of workplace and administration that so characterized the synchronistic approach.

What the computer transformation of business and industry has done is to maintain the appearance of continuing the trend toward decentralization, to further reduce the visible hierarchy and formal structures of authoritarian control while effectively and structurally reversing it. Instead of the traditional means of formalization, fixed and orderly rules, procedures, and regulations, the modern firm uses its authority over information and network communications to put into place an embedded spider web of control that is as rigorous and demanding as the more traditional and visible hierarchy. Because of its power and flexibility, the new control mechanism can afford to encourage "empowerment" of the individual, to allow more individual discretion and freedom of action at the work site, and still retain the power to enforce the adjustments that ensure the efficiency of the system as a whole.

If democracy truly depends upon free and ready access to information and unfettered interpersonal communication, the social effects of recent developments in computer networks have indeed been democratizing, in the sense of empowering individuals to make better judgments and arrive at better decisions—at least for those with sufficient training, experience, and education to use them for social development, interaction, and personal growth rather than for conversation and entertainment. But the unit of analysis for this argument is the individual, and the social context is one in which the individual has the power to put the information, and the communication, to effective use.

If democracy is instead defined in terms of power, of the balance between individual autonomy and centralized coordination, the results are at best mixed. In the personal and traditional (public) political realms, the computer is a potentially useful tool, both for avoiding coercion or deception by others seeking power and for enabling better action by groups as well as individuals. But the myth of democratizing technologies developed first and foremost for the introduction of "intelligent" machines into the workplace has been applied more forcefully for the introduction of computers than for any other historical case. Promoters argue that both workers and managers will have better information, more autonomy, more flexibility, and greater control.[8]

This is neither a unique claim nor a modern one. The historical record of the introduction of new techniques, and new technical systems, into factories, offices, and other workplaces is full of parallels that suggest that the democratizing claim is frequently made, and the democratizing effect does indeed frequently manifest itself during the early phases of introduction. But the democratizing phase is just that, a transient phase in the evolution of the introduction of new technology that eventually gives way to a more stable configuration in which workers and managers find their discretion reduced, their autonomy more constrained rather than less, their knowledge more fragmented, and their work load increased—with an added burden of acquiring and maintaining a larger and more complex body of required knowledge.

Whatever the initial distribution of power or authority, redistribution rarely diffuses any of it to those at the bottom of the organizational hierarchy. The price of increased worker autonomy has always been either to contract and forego the protective net of insurance and retirement that support regular employees, or to accept new rules that strictly bound and shape the range and character of the new domain of "autonomous" behavior. As computerization penetrates business and other organizations, those rules and bounds are increasingly imposed by technical rather than operational cadres, by middle managers more skilled in computers than in practice and by designers external to the firm.[9]

Those who are trying to defend the boundaries of human expertise and integrative judgment in operation and process are increasingly challenged by a new breed of neo-Taylorists who seek to automate everything in sight in the name of reliability, efficiency, and progress. But because it is difficult in an era that equates rationality with calculation to defend those apparently nonfunctional parts of the work experience from which expertise is synthesized, or the types of indirect and difficult-to-quantify inputs that create and sustain cognitive integration, the outcome of introducing computers into a complex task environment cannot be fully predicted in advance and is not really well and completely understood.[10]

When (and if) they are carefully and sensitively introduced, computers can greatly augment the use of human capabilities. They can perform partial integration of data, simplifying the display of information. They can master and simplify many kinds of complexity and deal with them routinely. They can also release operators, pilots, market analysts, and managers from the time-consuming chores of daily, repetitive tasks, freeing their time to deal with more challenging and pressing matters. If such uses can remain stable over time, people will eventually learn to incorporate them into their cognitive and representational frames and become comfortable, even expert, in the new working or social environment.

But the nature of computers, and of their use, makes it unlikely that the environment will remain stable, particularly as computers become more deeply embedded into the structure of operations and decision making. Computers not only create new potentialities and new options; they also allow for the creation and maintenance of new linkages and new domain boundaries, which in turn create new modes and degrees of interconnectivity and response that create new sets of problems. The complexity and demands both of immediate tasks and of their linkage to other tasks increases, as does the interaction with social and political environments that give them meaning and structure. Moreover, because computers are inherent promoters of efficiency, and because the people who run the organizations and activities in question are constantly seeking to improve it, the tendency to tighten coupling, to reduce slack and time of response, also tends to increase.

These effects are almost certain to increase the difficulty of acquiring experiential expertise by complicating and confusing the processes of cognitive integration by which difficult and complex tasks have always been managed.[11] If present and recent past experience is any guide, one response to the increasing difficulty of human control will be attempts to insert computers even more deeply and thoroughly into the process, thus creating a reinforcing feedback loop.

At first, such trends were highly visible, and in some cases they could be arrested, reversed, or at least examined. But the more deeply the computers become embedded, the more they shape and frame the representation of the work to be performed, the more subtle and hard to identify these effects will become.

The Structure of the Argument

I began the inquiry that led to this book with a direct question: *Are* the computers taking over? As I pursued it, it became clear that the answer, or answers, are far more complex and indirect than I first realized. If the question is put in the classic and traditional sense of loss of human autonomy and technical determinism, the answer is certainly no. Computers are not intelligent, they are not autonomous, and they would not know how to run human affairs even if they could comprehend them.

However, in the subtle and more indirect sense of having infiltrated a wide range of human activities in ways that we have not appreciated, and with consequences we have yet to understand, the answer may well be, yes. They have already taken over in communications, in finance and banking, in the military, in the cockpit, and, increasingly, even in industry. But taking over in this context is measured in terms of growing dependency, growing vulnerability, and, more importantly, by socially constructed adaptations and responses that make it difficult to imagine the shape of modern society without them.

Whether what is occurring is or is not "revolutionary" in its implications, it is clearly of considerable social and political importance because of the cumulative, and probably irreversible, reconstructions of social organizations, social formations, and even social systems that are taking place. What I argue is that the changes are being driven by short-term goals for presumptive short-term benefits, balanced against short-term costs, with little guidance or understanding of the long-term costs and consequences.

The argument proceeds on three levels, interwoven to various degrees through the chapters that follow. The first is concerned with the direct effects of the introduction of computers into communication, information, and networking, areas where the technical progress of the past few years would simply have been impossible without the introduction of computers as constituent elements. It deals primarily with the origins and means of changes in capability and connectivity.

The second level explores the ways in which the new technical capacities and opportunities have interacted with the social and organizational environments in which they have been put to use to socially construct new organizational forms, and new types of behavior, while eroding or deconstructing others of long standing, thereby transforming structure as well as function. Just as the mechanization of work transformed its meaning and representation, moving the worker from the producer of goods or services to being the operator of production machinery, the process of computerization is causing one more step of removal, from being the operator of a machine or process to being the controller and manager of the computer that actually operates the machine or controls the process. It is, in the deepest sense, a reconfiguration of the representation of work, whose consequences are still being explored.[12]

The third level is an exploration of longer-term systemic and societal implications, following the question of loss of expertise and experiential knowledge from the factory floor to the cockpit of a commercial airliner, and from the floor of the stock exchange to the command of military forces. The last two are particularly interesting because they stand at the verge of virtual reality, of conflict in "cyberspace," a universe defined and bounded by interactive electronics. The cyberspace the military is exploring is that of electronic warfare, surveillance, and control, in an environment where failures and errors are very consequential in the very real world. That of the stock market is one of computerized interaction and trading in concepts and symbols rather than rockets and missiles, but can be equally consequential in its own domain.

The Structure of the Book

Following a brief introductory chapter, chapters 2 and 3 review the history of personal computing and of interactive networking, with a particular emphasis on social formations and embedded purpose, leading to a consideration in chapter 4 of the implications for the emergence of new modes of organizational control, indirect and diffused instead of direct and centralized, but with overtones of Taylorism and scientific management nonetheless.

Chapters 5 and 6 explore the world of financial markets and computerized trading, which has been penetrated most rapidly by computerization and seems closer to the promise of virtual reality than any other economic sector. Chapter 7 pursues further the problem of loss of expertise, particularly in safety-critical applications such as air traffic control and airliner cockpits.

The next four chapters explore computerization in another leading-edge technical sector, militaries and military technologies. Chapter 8 sets out in brief the history of military computerization, while chapters 9 and 10 identify some of the problems that have been found in the field and relate them to similar problems that might occur in civil society if and when it becomes similarly committed to computerization of operation and control. Chapter 11 is a reflection on the movement toward virtual organizations, using as a case study the military's pursuit of war in cyberspace.

Taken together, these chapters paint a picture of computerization that is spreading rapidly in the large, that promises distributive benefits while insisting that costs are local and capturable. Computers are becoming accepted not just as useful, but as necessary, not as exotic and remote objects, but as the appliances of everyday life. What results is a structural paradox. The lack of concern over whether computers are "taking over," the acceptance and embedding of the computer as a constitutive technical element of social as well as industrial systems, seems also to imply the casual and often uncritical acceptance of structural and representational transformations that follow.

In *The Second Self*, Sherry Turkle provides a revealing example of her supplying children with a smart "Say it" machine that was programmed to complete a ten-word playback cycle even after the machine had been turned off. The children were not amused. As Turkle points out: "The 'Say it' bug contradicts our most basic expectations of a machine. When you turn the switch to 'Off,' machines stop. The cliché response to people's fears about computers 'taking over' is that you can always 'pull the plug.' "[13]

But can we? As computers become more deeply embedded, as an increasing number of social functions and activities come to depend structurally as well as functionally on the power of computers, there is no way that we can pull the plug, at least not without incurring substantial costs.

This growing and irreversible commitment to the computer as an essential building block of modern society is not limited to the specialized uses and users familiar to the case studies of this book and so many others. Deeply embedded computerization is not limited to the military, or to specialized industrial enterprises or financial markets. It is already difficult to imagine American society without computerization; soon it will be nearly impossible. And when new representations of what it means to be and act in society are constructed, the computers will be built right in.

If this results in highly complex, safety-critical systems that fail in unforeseen ways; markets whose movements seem arbitrary and uncontrollable; businesses in which authority is spread everywhere but responsibility localized nowhere; military systems that demand compliance with preprogrammed assumptions to fight effectively; and organizations and systems of every type that can no longer function effectively if the computer or network goes down, we will indeed be caught in the computer trap.

2.

Autogamous Technology

Introduction

In his learned and lucid book, *Autonomous Technology*, Langdon Winner argues that the historical theme of technology-out-of-control misplaces and disguises human responsibility for outcomes by assigning to artifacts instead of people the processes of volition and choice.[1] The social and institutional processes that have shaped and controlled the introduction of computers into a wide range of social and organizational settings are no more autonomous than any other. However, they do seem increasingly to be driven not by the needs and demands of users, or of society at large, but by an internal dynamic that originates in and is sustained by the industry and its "designers"—those people who specify how and where computers will be used, with what hardware, and with what software and interface. Progress in electronic digital computing is not an autonomous process, but it has increasingly become an autogamous one—self-pollinating and self-fertilizing, responding more and more to an inner logic of development than to the desires and needs of the user community.

The computer industry is not like traditional industries in which the normal course of events once maturity is reached is incremental evolution and struggle for market share on the margin. The companies that drive and dominate the computer industry market, and the people they hire, are committed to innovation and change, to rapid market growth and new products. Lacking any new breakthrough or killer application that would create a body of user demand on the scale of the spreadsheet, they race with themselves, and each other, to create new variants and add more gadgets. As each generation of hardware gets faster and more powerful, each generation of new software more than consumes the incremental gains, driving users to search for even newer and more powerful machines, and so on ad infinitum.

How did this come about? There are few answers in the existing literature, for the question is rarely asked.[2] I do not presume that I can fully address it here; that would require, at the minimum, not just an extension, but a reformulation of the present theory of the development and evolution of large technical systems.[3] The social history of electronic digital computing and networking does provide some data and a few examples that may prove useful for the future development of a more comprehensive analysis. It also provides the essentials for understanding how the later interconnection of computers to form computerized networks of immense capacity and scope was able to so easily impose on the newly decentralized web of users elaborate sets of standards and rules that would severely limit their discretion and choice even as it was being promoted as a means for opening up the world.

A Brief Historical Essay

The history of computer hardware is in itself fascinating, and important. Without the incredible pace of hardware development, miniaturization, and decreased cost that followed the introduction of solid-state electronics, there would have been no computer revolution, and the social and political effects on which this book focuses would never have been possible. But hardware in itself cannot be an agent for change. In the case of the computer, coevolution with software made the difference; despite market-driven races to develop faster and ever more powerful hardware, and despite fierce and often nasty competition between suppliers of software to capture market share through specific features, it is the nature of the application, not the machine, or the programming, that attracts potential users.

As with nuclear energy and a number of other fields that had once been the subject primarily of scientific inquiry and discourse, the development of the electronic digital computer was greatly spurred by the Second World War. Although the purposes were at first narrow and specialized, the concentration of the research community and the comparatively huge resources given to it were to form the foundation of the postwar effort, with continuing governmental support. The government also continued to support the initial development of programming languages and other fundamental software that became central in remaking computers into general-purpose analytical tools, electronic successors to Charles Babbage's dream of a generalized "difference engine."[4] Over time, the capabilities were transferred for use by developers and government agencies, and then for large, central firms doing considerable government business.[5]

Those who got their start in one or another of the early military projects, or consulted for them, eventually moved out into private industry in search of uses, applications, and markets. But the military roots remained, and it was not until the 1960s that commercial markets grew large enough to support a fully independent industry. As the computer revolution picked up speed, entrepreneurs and just plain technical enthusiasts moved in, and most of the hardware and software now in common use was developed specifically for commercial applications. Much of what remains of direct government support is focused on the formulation of specific equipment and specific software for dedicated purposes.

But the U.S. government continues to see the development of advanced computer techniques as having important implications for national security (i.e., military) purposes, and therefore remains heavily invested in supporting fundamental, forefront research, particularly in high status areas such as artificial intelligence. This also has consequences. The community of government-supported superstars, often far removed from real users or immediate needs, continues to shape the attitudes of programmers throughout the entire industry both by example and by its ability to shape the goals and beliefs of the social universe in which designers live and work.[6] And that universe in turn was formed and shaped by the history of the industry.

The Age of the Dinosaurs

The first large, digital computers were hardly more than electric realizations of Charles Babbage's difference engine (and many were barely electronic). Their purpose was primarily to perform huge calculations rapidly and accurately (i.e., what they computed were numerical results, such as firing tables for large artillery and naval guns), and the operation of each was done through a tedious and usually quite idiosyncratic process of setting up a calculational program through the setting of an enormous number of switches and patches.[7] In those early days, progress was measured largely by increases in the size and capacity of the machines. As it was widely believed that the total social demand for computers at this scale was for no more than a few dozen, or a few hundred, machines—large, expensive, and run by in-house experts—there was no particular reason or economic motive for the development of general, nonproprietary software or simplified front ends for operation.

The invention of the transistor and the creation of the integrated circuit caused a major reorganization and redesign of the nascent industry. Smaller, faster, more reliable, and with much simpler requirements for power and cooling than their vacuum-tube predecessors, machines using solid-state circuitry revolutionized every aspect of electronics from simple radios to the most complicated computers. In only a few years, the huge, ungainly machines that gave off enormous quantities of heat, and whose time of continuous operation between failures might be measured in hours, or at best days, were completely superseded by solid-state, integrated-circuit machines that were inherently faster and far more reliable.[8] The failure rate of the first solid-state computers was orders of magnitude smaller than that of their vacuum-tube predecessors.[9]

Because of their size, cost, and complexity, the commercial manufacture of the first mainframe computers was a task not to be entered into lightly. The field soon came to be dominated by a few large firms, including a preexisting corporate giant—IBM—that gained knowledge from government contracts and access through the reputation and experience it had gained from dominating the market of electromechanical office equipment. IBM controlled half the market by 1955, only two years after its entry, and more than 65 percent by 1965, when the business had become known as "IBM and the Seven Dwarfs."[10] Although other companies continued to compete, it was IBM that determined the course of development.

The situation as of the mid-1960s has been neatly summarized by Larry Roberts.

> In 1964 only large mainframe computers existed, each with its own sepa-
> rate set of users. If you were lucky the computer was time-shared, but
> even then you could not go far away since the terminals were hard-
> wired to it or connected by local phone line. Moreover, if you wanted
> data from another computer, you moved it by tape and you could forget
> wanting software from a different type of computer.[11]

Such standards as existed for moving data about were mostly set by
IBM, which had adopted its familiar accounting technology, the
Hollerith punched card (modeled in turn on the cards used for more
than a century to program Jacquard looms), as a method for providing
input.[12] Even the later development of magnetic storage and standardized programming did not free users from being tied by their computers and terminals to a set of very restricted environments.

Technical and systems evolution had gone down the same socio-
historical path as the classic infrastructure technologies of the early
part of the century, with one important exception. Although expansion and growth were still controlled by managers who judged them
by actual performance and real returns, the large, centralized, computer centers that emerged, and still dominate many companies and
government organizations, seemed forbidding, remote, and, with
their cadre of experts speaking arcane languages, sometimes threatening. The combination of the isolation of the centers with the presumed
power of computers they operated became a focal point for a public
that increasingly felt that technical change was threatening loss of
control in "modern" societies. As such, they became the obvious target of manifestations of social concern about the future, in forums
ranging from editorials to popular art.[13] What few people realized
was that the mainframes were dinosaurs, soon to be almost completely displaced except for specialized purposes such as running
huge, complex mathematical models.

What did survive, however, was a rather unique social-organizational legacy, the creation and empowerment of a small cadre of hardware and software designers and highly trained operators whose special skills and special languages isolated them from the rest of the
organization and left them free to pursue their own design and developmental goals.[14] Given the cost of the new computer centers, and the
need to justify both their existence and their budgets, these internal

desires were always subject to rather strict limitations. But the precedent of autonomy and control had been set.

Small Is Bountiful

Progress in the semiconductor industry, driven in part by the search for defense-related applications, proceeded at a ferocious pace that has not yet let up; every year, components continue to get smaller, cheaper, faster, and more complex.[15] During the 1960s, solid-state circuitry had progressed sufficiently to significantly lower the costs of entry into the burgeoning computer market, triggering a second developmental wave that was to carry the computer industry far from its megalithic beginnings in less than a decade. Although IBM continued to exploit the decreasing size and cost of solid-state circuitry to improve and expand mainframes, a new entrepreneurial firm, Digital Equipment Corporation (DEC), chose to avoid competing with IBM by producing a line of "mini" computers—small but powerful laboratory and business machines that did not require specially prepared and conditioned rooms. Eventually, the minicomputers were to become small enough to actually be placed next to a desk, or even on top of one.[16] More to the point, they were to expand the community of programmers to include a large number of people independent of both hardware manufacturers and large, centralized computer operations.

Because the DEC machines were particularly flexible and powerful, and because DEC welcomed participation and involvement from the research community, their machines quickly became popular in laboratories and universities.[17] With the introduction of UNIX™, an adaptable and open operating system that had been developed by AT&T's Bell Laboratories and widely disseminated for a nominal fee, DEC/UNIX systems and networks became ubiquitous in research laboratories, universities, and, eventually, classrooms across the country.

Mainframes were fine for grinding out big, difficult calculations; as a means for communication, the new art of text processing, or performing simpler tasks, they were at best clumsy. The relative openness and transparency of the UNIX system, the power and simplicity of the high-order programming language (C) that had also had been developed at Bell Laboratories and in which it was coded, and the incredible facilitation of interpersonal networking, at first at individual sites and then among them, created expectations and demands in the community of sophisticated users that could not be easily fulfilled by centrally controlled hierarchical computer centers and large, powerful mainframes.

The social consequences were profound. Intelligent, mathematically skilled, eager to make use of the newly accessible power of computing in their laboratories and even classrooms, and devoted to the new means of access and communication, the new community accepted as part of the cost their own lack of control over system development. Although participation by users in system and interface design had raised expectations about devolution of control and decentralization of authority that were very much at odds with the mainframe tradition, it also paradoxically reinforced the ceding of control over system and evolution and development to those who were physically in charge of the computers. If DEC had a new machine, or if Bell Labs or its own computer center had a new release of or improvement on UNIX, it was the computer center and not the user community who dictated when and where it would be installed or adopted.[18]

The long-term, probably unintended, but possibly deliberate, consequence was the emergence of a community of programmers who demanded respect, and even acquiescence, from the user community at large, while insisting on their own independence and autonomy from large companies and organizations, including, at times, those who owned and operated the facility at which they worked. This complex of behavioral patterns, added to and reinforced by the tradition of autonomy that characterized the mainframe computer centers, are a legacy of the origins of digital computing that persists to the present day.

Building the Home Computer

While researchers back East were concentrating on the minicomputer transformation, an eclectic collection of electronic tinkerers were working in garages and workshops around the San Francisco Bay Area on something even smaller. Many had dropped out of major computer corporations to pursue the dream of a computer that was entirely one's own,[19] often overlaid with a libertarian philosophy that blended

the radical and communitarian thought that emerged during the up-
heavals of the 1960s with the traditional American dream of the independent small business entrepreneur.[20] Of necessity, the resulting machine would have to be relatively small, simple, and inexpensive; easy
to maintain and upgrade; and convenient to program and operate.

In 1971, a small Silicon Valley company called Intel announced the
result of two years of research—an integrated circuit that put the essentials of a computer on a single chip. Christened the *microprocessor*, the
Intel chip was fully programmable despite its small size. The micro-
chips seemed destined to the arcane world of pocket calculators until,
in 1974, Ed Roberts decided to build a computer kit.[21] When the Altair
hit the market in 1975, the response was almost frenzied. The following
year, 1976, was the *annus mirabilis* of the microcomputer transformation. From Silicon Valley and its surroundings flowed the commercial
realizations of the intelligent video display terminal and the miniaturized floppy disk, the first standardized bus, BASIC, CP/M, the first
programming languages for microcomputers, Electric Pencil, the first
microcomputer word processor. And linking them all together was the
Homebrew computer club, the irreverent, anarchic, thinktank of the
new industry.

The third wave of computing emerged from what was quite literally
a garage operation in California, when Steve Wozniak designed the
Apple I, primarily to impress the club.[22] The Apple I was hardly more
than a circuit board, but its successor, the landmark Apple II of 1977,
was the prototype of every desktop machine. Using a keyboard for
input instead of toggle switches, with a video display system instead
of blinking lights, and with a small, flexible (floppy) magnetic disk for
storage, it is as recognizable to the modern user as a Model T—to
which it might be aptly compared, for the widespread adoption of the
Apple II and the word spread by its dedicated users reconstructed the
meaning and image of electronic digital computing.

Given that DEC and others had already appropriated the term minicomputer for their now midsized models, the Apple and its descendants came to be referred to by the somewhat inappropriate appella-
tion of *microcomputers*, perhaps because of the microprocessors that lay
at their heart. The most familiar term in use today, however, is the one
that IBM appropriated in 1981 for its first ever desktop computer—the
personal computer, or PC. At first, the person in question was far more

likely to be a computer professional or dedicated hobbyist than a typical office worker or member of the general public. The hardware was nice enough, but what was it for?

Operating Systems

In the world of mainframes and minicomputers, the proprietary nature of operating systems was to some degree compensated for by islands of standardization in programming software, some promoted by the government and some by business and corporate interests.[23] Having been deliberately developed outside of those worlds, software and operating systems for the first personal computers were even more chaotic and idiosyncratic than the machines themselves. At one time, for example, almost every manufacturer, including those who had standardized on the same Intel chip and the same underlying operating system, used a unique format for floppy disks. Exchange of software and data between users was a trying and often frustrating experience—when it could be done at all.

As with the historical cases of automobiles, electricity, and telephones, increasing acceptance and use was accompanied by a demand for standardization. Over time, two primary standards emerged—that of Apple computer, closely tied to and integrated with its own hardware, and the more open system that serves not only the descendants of the first IBM PC, but the world of clones that now dominate the microcomputer market.

Of Mice and Menus

In the early 1970s, a group of researchers at the Xerox Palo Alto Research Center (PARC) was pursuing a vision of the future of computing that was radically different from that of IBM or DEC.[24] The market niche that Xerox had originally sought to penetrate was the growing market for powerful, specialized desktop computers, primarily graphic workstations for the growing sector of electronic computer-aided graphic design (CAD). At Xerox PARC, the basic unit of computing was therefore taken from the outset to be the individual user

workstation. The researchers at PARC were encouraged to break with
the notion that the computer user community was a narrow and
highly specialized one. Whatever they developed had to remove, or at
least greatly reduce, the burden of learning and memorizing long lists
of commands in order to master the system.[25]

The PARC researchers sought to provide users of desktop computers with an interface that featured simplicity of organization and command to mask the growing complexity of operating systems and software. The traditional command-line and character-based interface of
the early machines was leading to ever more arcane and elaborated
sets of commands as machines and programs evolved in capability
and sophistication. Manuals grew thicker and more complex; a whole
secondary industry grew up around publishing books to supplement
the traditionally horrible manuals. Particularly in commercial applications, organizations found themselves once again driven to hire professional programmers to master the software.

The solutions proffered by the PARC crew are now legendary. The
Alto, completed in 1974, but not marketed commercially until 1977,
had the first production bitmapped screen, now familiar to every computer user, instead of the character-based system used by the old video
terminals.[26] It had an interactive, video-oriented menu interface and a
graphic pointing device to move around in it. And it was the first computer ever advertised on television (in 1978). Although Xerox never
marketed it effectively, and only a few thousand were ever sold,
the idea of a bitmapped screen capable of doing graphics instead of a
character-oriented one that was the video equivalent of a teletype was
very, very attractive.[27]

As Apple computer matured, it incorporated many of the features
developed at PARC, along with some of its staff and many of its attitudes. The mice-and-menus approach that became the characteristic
signature of the Apple Macintosh line was created by a cadre of devotees who regarded the old method of input by keyboard and character
as totally archaic and impossibly linear. To optimize performance and
speed, and provide a consistent, iconic, graphically oriented interface
required a very sophisticated operating system, which was almost
completely shielded from the user. Indeed, until quite recently, Apple
ran the equivalent of a proprietary shop, refusing to divulge some elements of its hardwired code except to developers under very strict license agreements.

Apple's attitude toward users is familiar to those who followed the history of DEC, or of PARC. In principle, easily understood interfaces and sophisticated but user-invisible processing free users from the need to understand cryptic and arcane commands, or to learn much of the inner details of the machine. In practice, what it creates is an asymmetric dependency relationship, in which the designers and programmers are free to do what they feel is right, or necessary, and the user has little choice other than to accept it, and stay current with the latest version of software, or to reject it and drift down the irreversible path of obsolescence.

Apple's closed-system approach, defended by aggressive lawsuits against those attempting to market clones, protected its market niche, but also kept it narrow. Although Apple also benefited from the rapid growth of the 1980s, its base of loyal customers remained at about 10–12 percent of the total desktop market, with an even smaller share of the commercial and business sectors.[28] As a result, Apple finally opened its system to developers, generating the first Macintosh clones. But the relationship between users and operating systems remained the same. Moreover, it has spread into the other community of PC users, casting a long shadow over their dream of open and accessible systems.

Beyond the Command Line

Apple may have generated the vision of individual, personal computing, but it was the IBM PC of 1981 that was to spread that vision widely and carry it into the world of commerce and business. Instead of keeping the machine specifications closed and guarded, and writing its own operating software, as it had traditionally done for mainframes, the IBM personal computer division chose an open-system approach, making its hardware standards widely available and buying an open operating system (DOS) from an independent vendor, Microsoft.[29] Secure in the belief that IBM would dominate any computer market in which it competed, the company was willing to create a standardized market in which independents could develop programs and manufacture disks without having to acquire special licenses or sign nondisclosure agreements, for the sake of faster and more expansive growth.[30]

The rest, as they say, is history. The standardized, reliable PC with its new operating system, carrying the respected logo of IBM, was welcomed into homes and offices with an eagerness that no one in the industry could ever have imagined. Within only a year, the term "PC" had entered the common language as the generic term for a desktop microcomputer. Sales soared, and by 1983, *Time* magazine had a computer on its cover as the "machine of the year." Within a few years, PC systems with MS-DOS and standardized disk formats and software had created a whole new market, pushing CP/M and other competing systems aside. Small, entrepreneurial companies either adapted or found their market share shriveling to a narrow and specialized niche.[31]

Over time, the story acquires an ironic twist. As the PC market expanded, IBM failed to keep up with the cutting edge, either in perceived performance or in price. The open architecture of the PC and the easy license requirements of DOS made possible the rapid worldwide spread of PC "clones" that reduced not only IBM's share of the market but its position as market leader and standard bearer. What did become standard was Microsoft's DOS, in all of its variants, and, later, not only its own line of specialized programs, but a visual interface, Microsoft's Windows™, that replicated in purpose, if not precisely in detail, the mice-and-menus approach of the Macintosh.[32]

In 1981, when you said PC, you meant IBM. By the 1990s, the future development of PCs was largely in the hands of Intel, maker of the continually evolving line of processor chips that lay at the heart of the machine, and Microsoft, maker of operating systems and software. The evolving interactive complex of Intel chip code and DOS (and Windows) operating system was, in principle, still open, as it had been from the outset, but the gradual layering of sophistication and complexity required to make use of the new capabilities made other developers de facto as dependent on Microsoft's system programmers (and Intel's hardware plans) as they were on Apple's.

With each new release of Windows and the new wave of software to accommodate it, PC users grew more remote from and unfamiliar with what was once an operating system of remarkable transparency. Moreover, as Microsoft grew larger, the development and release of new versions of its operating system software no longer seemed coupled to user demand at all. What users wanted were fixes for existing products; instead, they got new ones, as often as not bundled in auto-matically with their new hardware, which of course was required to make full use of the new software. It is clear that there is a feedback loop running between Intel and Microsoft, but it is not clear that end user demand has any real place in it.[33]

Whatever the rhetoric of individual freedom, autonomy, and "em-powerment," users are increasingly at the mercy of those who design and set the standards of the machines and their operating systems. There are now basically only two important standardized operating systems for individual desktop systems in common use, each with unique, and standardized, input-output and disk operating subsys-tems.[34] And although they still claim to represent the two opposing world views of personal freedom and the individual entrepreneur ver-sus corporate conformity and the multinational corporation, both the interfaces and the outcomes are converging rapidly.[35]

As the systems grow more complex, the dependence of users on a network of subsystems of design, programming, maintenance, and support to keep their machines and operating systems current and functioning continues to increase. As recently as a few years ago, many users still continued to try a little bit of programming, if only for the excitement. But the structure of Apple's System 7, or Windows 95, is as inaccessible to most users as it is invisible, and as far beyond their ability to influence or control as it was in the days of the mainframe computer centers.

The Search for the Killer App

Good hardware and a good operating system make for a smoothly functioning machine, but the question of what the PC was actually for remained open. What really spurred the market for personal comput-ers, Apples as well as PCs, was the advent of the first "killer" applica-tion, the spreadsheet. Spreadsheets allowed serious business and cor-porate users to do financial and other modeling and reporting on their own individual computers rather than going through centralized data processing and information services, while being simple enough so that even relatively unsophisticated home users could build numerical models or balance their checkbooks on it. And they could graph the results, automatically. The resulting surge of user-driven demand was unprecedented, almost completely unexpected, and has not been repeated since.

Word processing was an interesting task to perform on a computer, but not fundamentally different from what could be done (at least in principle) with whiteout, scissors, and paste. Once graphics were included, the spreadsheet was a nearly perfect expression of what you could do with a computer that you could not do without it; it combined the computer's specialty, memory and calculating power, with the most powerful and most difficult to replicate power of the human mind, the ability to recognize and integrate patterns. Once users discovered it, they became committed; once committed, they became dependent on it; once organizations became dependent on it, they demanded compatibility and continuity, firmly locking the existing Apple and IBM/DOS standards in place.

The irony of the Homebrew club is that the success of this anarchic collection of independent thinkers and libertarians created a bottom-up demand for de facto standardization whose results were not much different from those traditionally imposed from the top down by large, corporate manufacturers. Without the hardware being developed by the club, spreadsheets would never have been developed, and the market for microcomputing would never have expanded so rapidly.[36] Programmers and companies have been searching ever since for the next "killer app," an application so powerful, and so attractive, that it will cause another boom in the market similar to that experienced in the early 1980s.

Meanwhile, success has locked the systems in place. Users demanded interchangeability and interoperability, as well as compatible disks. Just when the industry was in its major growth phase, providing immense amounts of capital for innovation and change, computer user magazines were using full compatibility as a major benchmark for evaluating new programs and new machines. With no dramatically new application on the horizon, and no reasonable way to reconstruct systems at the basic level, innovation and ingenuity, which remain one of the prime cultural values of the programming community, seem to have turned into a race for features instead of real capabilities. The greatest irony of all is that it is now the features, and not the applications, that are driving the machines not only to greater power and complexity, but to greater uniformity and standardization.[37]

The Dynamics of Growth

The historical process of interactive growth and expansion that characterized earlier technical systems such as the railroads or the telephone can be described as the interplay between two realms of activity: the scientific and technical exploration of physical and engineering possibilities on the one hand, and the managerial innovation and social imagination of entrepreneurs, operators, and even regulatory authorities on the other.[38] The balance shifts with time, between the search to exploit new capabilities and the effort to develop the equipment to follow up new opportunities, but in almost every case the nature of the interplay is relatively clear, even when causality is disputed.[39]

Broadly speaking, every large technical system has followed the familiar logistic curve, with market penetration beginning slowly during the period of development of techniques and markets, rising rapidly during the exciting period of social acceptance and deployment (often referred to as *diffusion*), and then flattening out as markets saturate. Social and economic change is small in the beginning, but although direct social change is likely to be greatest during the period of most rapid adoption when the rate of diffusion is highest, there is some dispute as to whether economic gains are also most rapid at this time or tend to occur at some later time after the growth curve has started to flatten out. Paul David, for example, argues that maximum returns from new techniques occur only after they have a chance to mature, and claims that we are still ten or twenty years from realizing the productivity gains from digital computing.[40] Others argue that using such traditional gauges as net capital investment or comparisons with traditional industrial machinery underestimates the maturity of fast-moving sectors such as the computer industry, and that the lack of productivity gains cannot be attributed to "immaturity."[41]

The difference between computers and computerized equipment and hardware such as electric motors, dynamos, chemical processes, and production machinery is not trivial. When the rate of change in the introduction of traditional technical-industrial innovations slows, markets saturate, and entrepreneurs and others seeking rapid profits and high rates of return turn elsewhere, as do the interests of the cutting-edge engineering community. The maturing industry is left with slow-growing, if predictable, sales, and comparatively small incentive for further innovation.

The experience with the adoption of computers, however, has been markedly different. Sales continue to expand rapidly even in markets that are numerically saturated; although the rate of diffusion has been high, there have been no apparent gains in productivity; although more and more workers have computers, few people feel that they have really mastered them; although we know more and more about what they can do, we seem to know less and less of what the consequences will be. Nor does there seem to be any way to determine whether some of those consequences are unintended, if perhaps deliberate, attempts to keep sales up in a mature system, the result of turbulent growth in the period of maximum innovation, or reflect a state of technical immaturity despite high market penetration.[42]

It is not sufficient to claim that computers are different because of the special character of their capabilities, or unique because of their importance in fostering social development and/or change. There have been other technical changes of equal importance, ranging from the printing press to television, from the moldboard plow to the harvester combine, that were in their own way just as unique, just as path-breaking, and just as important for social change, yet still fit the traditional models of diffusion and deployment pretty well. But in each of these cases, the process of adoption and diffusion was governed by use and not by design, by measurable and demonstrable gains rather than future promises.

Logistic analysis of market penetration is not well suited for analyzing rapid growth accompanied by substantive structural change, particularly when adaptation and learning are as demanding and intellectually challenging as that of personal and office computing. The familiar S-shaped curve of adoption and diffusion is not based on a dynamic model at all, but on a quasi-static one. The only social dynamic measured is market penetration as a function of time. The internal dynamics of adoption and diffusion, including stock replacement, evaluation of gains, and learning both how to operate the equipment and how to put it to productive use, are omitted—which is equivalent to saying that they come to equilibrium in times short compared with the rate of growth. Moreover, the model assumes that major processes of innovation and technical change take place before the period of most rapid growth—indeed, it implies that finding the right configuration is what triggers it.

The assumptions that there will be only modest technical change during the rapid growth phase, and that in any case the processes of individual and organizational learning are fast and responsive enough to provide continuous adaptation during the period of diffusion and adoption, are primary, and crucial, for understanding why the case of computing is different. Learning, too, tends to follow a logistic curve. There is very little gain at first for a large investment of time; eventually, enough basic knowledge has been accumulated to allow for rapid gains (the "steep" part of the learning curve). Once mastery is gained, further improvement again requires a fairly large investment of time and energy.

The implicit assumption of the traditional diffusion model is that people, and organizations, are dynamically capable of learning to make use of railroads, or telephones, or data banks, fast enough to accommodate and to understand reasonably well the state of the technical system at any time, even during the period of rapid growth. As a result, demand growth is governed by evaluation of real and well-understood costs and benefits. Growth in demand in turn invites competition and opens new markets, stimulating innovation and change, which in turn triggers another round of learning and adoption.[43]

None of these assumptions appears to hold very well, if at all, for the recent dynamic of development and deployment of small, powerful digital computers, particularly in smaller offices and businesses. Only in a few specialized markets are new developments in hardware and software responsive primarily to user demand based on mastery and the full use of available technical capacity and capability. In most markets, the rate of change of both hardware and software is dynamically uncoupled from either human or organizational learning logistics and processes, to the point where users not only fail to master their most recent new capabilities, but are likely to not even bother to try, knowing that by the time they are through the steep part of their learning curve, most of what they have learned will be obsolete.[44]

Logistic analysis, like other traditional economic tools designed to measure growth and expansion of traditional markets, is an equilibrium tool, based, among other things, on the assumption that it is user demand that drives change and growth, and not the community of developers, builders, and programmers. But there is no sign of equilibrium in the current race between hardware capacity and software demands; each generation of new software seems to easily consume the new margin of performance provided by faster and more powerful machines, providing only marginal gains in real performance while emphasizing additional layers of often useless embellishments.

The need to understand and accommodate the new variations and options, the new manuals and auxiliary programs, the new set of incompatibilities and exceptions, and even, in many cases, the lack of backward, interplatform or interprogram compatibility, keeps users perpetually at the foot of the learning curve and struggling to survive, let alone adapt.[45] The net result is growth beyond the logistic curve, saturation without maturity, replacement without obsolescence, and instant obsolescence built in to every purchase. As Landauer puts it:

> While the price per megathing has plummeted, the cost of computing has oddly stayed nearly constant. An equivalent machine today costs a fraction of what it did just ten years ago, but you couldn't buy one, and your employees wouldn't stand for it if you did. Instead you get one with ten times the flops and bytes at about the same price. The price of software has not dropped much either, partly *because* the hardware has become so much more powerful. It is now possible—and irresistible—to write very much bigger programs with many more features.[46]

Once invested in computerization, individuals and organizations seem to have acquired the Red Queen's dilemma, running as fast as they can just to stay where they are, ensnared by a technical system whose dynamic properties seem to be determined by factors beyond their reach. And, as I will argue further in the following chapters, staying at the low end of the learning curve can in itself be the source of long-term, unanticipated consequences.

The Hegemony of Design

The rapid diffusion of the personal computer that began in the 1980s was a classic case of interactive social change that reconstructed the computer industry as well as the social definition and context of computer use. What did not substantively change, however, was the gulf between the goals and culture of system and software designers and the needs and desires of the general user community. Landauer has expressed it well:

> Unfortunately, the overwhelming majority of computer applications are designed and developed solely by computer programmers who know next to nothing about the work that is going to be done with the aid of their program. Programmers rarely have any contact with users; they almost never test the system with real users before release. . . . So where do new software designs come from? The source is almost entirely supply side, or technology push.[47]

Landauer's book contains numerous examples, ranging from proposals for "heads up displays" to project instrumentation on automobile windshields to the case of the mainframe designers who refused to talk to operators for fear of being distracted by them.[48] The argument may seem a bit overstated to make a point, but even within the industry, interviewing end users and taking their needs and desires into account is still considered remarkable.[49]

Why do designers act this way? That none of the authors read or cited here provides a satisfactory explanation is not surprising. Most of those who have pointed out the problems, including Landauer, are not really outside the community of developers and designers at all. They are dissidents within it. For all the extensive research that has taken place on users and user communities, there has been almost no systematic research done on designers and the community of design.[50] There is a growing reform movement based on the notion of user-oriented or user-centered design, which does at least accept as a founding principle the need to find out what it is that users want, or need,[51] but it is not clear how widespread an effect this has outside the circle of thoughtful critics. And even participatory design has been criticized for being as much a normative design model as the ones it sets out to critique, a way to give users power over designers without asking what the formal context is.[52]

Designers and users come from different communities, they work in different environments and different organizational contexts, they have different goals and different means. And, for reasons that emerge partially from the history described earlier and partially from the different contexts of design and use,[53] the special knowledge possessed by designers gives them a privileged position in the dialogue.[54] Users can have input, and even give advice, but generally from a subordinate position. As will be discussed in chapter 7, the question of user authority, or real user control over *whether* new techniques are introduced (rather than how), is rarely raised as a realistic option. And that, too, has long-term consequences for operability, reliability, and performance.

Another, perhaps more difficult, question is why users continue to put up with this. Arguments based on differences in power or status do not fully explain what happens to individuals, or in smaller organizations. To some extent, the more general willingness to accept the rash of technical tweaking and exciting but nonproductive applications and embellishments as a sign of progress is a social phenomenon, not that distant in its sociology and politics from the long-standing American relationship with that other icon, the automobile. But that still does not fully explain why there are so few pockets of resistance where old machines running old software that does the job perfectly adequately are maintained and used, or why corporate and business users appear to be even more vulnerable to the argument for new hardware and software than individuals.

If there is an explanation at all, it must lie with collective social behavior. Plausible causal factors range from simple desire to stay at the cutting edge of technology (without being able to have much input on defining it) to fear of losing ground to the competition if they have even a small marginal advantage. In some markets, and for some industries, that might make sense. In many, perhaps most, it does not. Instead, what seems to provide the impetus at the moment are the demands of new systems for computer interconnection, for global as well as local networking. The mainframe provided a central store of information and a central means of communication that was lost in the fragmentation of one computer for every user. For many firms, the first result of the desktop revolution was the replacement of an integrated and manageable computer system with an idiosyncratic collection of individual pieces of relatively isolated machinery. As will be discussed in the following chapter, it was the subsequent development of networks that provided both an impetus and a means to recapture users and rerationalize the technical variance of offices and businesses.

3.

Networks of Connectivity:
Webs of Dependence

Introduction

The installation and networking by research libraries of computerized catalogs and their associated powerful search and retrieval tools has been promoted by librarians, and by library schools, as a user-empowering technology. Instead of having to go to the library and physically search the drawers of card files, or wander the stacks and shelves, anyone needing to find an item can work in their office, or at their home, at their own convenience and on their own schedule. The ability to search by keyword, by title, or by subject has no parallel in the linear world of 3×5 cards impaled on brass rods in neat arrays in their wooden drawers. Moreover, the search can be extended to link other libraries that may have what you want even if your own library does not.

So far, so good. The computerized library search system at my own university was eagerly welcomed by faculty and students alike, even for those who are working inside the library (on some days there are lines waiting for a turn at the terminals). And even Berkeley, with one of the largest university libraries in the world, does not and cannot own everything in print. Networked library software opened the world for searches. The benefits were clear. There were, however, some unexpected costs.

Last year, my wife went to a group meeting about a new "information technology" soon to be available through the campus computer network. The claim was that these new search methods would be vital tools for scholars seeking access to journals and other information not available through the campus library computer system and its links to other networks. The demonstration turned into a scholarly mini-rebellion. Visual presentations were rated by most of the group as scholar-hostile. Keyword searches were trying.[1] There were no help screens. "Hits" were listed in a frequency table using algorithms that were opaque and could not be modified. There was no way to scroll back through the screens of data other than restarting a search.

Gopher and other Internet-access tools were considerably better, but lacked any convenient means for doing layered keyword searches. Even the new visually oriented interfaces such as Mosaic and Netscape were not rated any more highly by the audience, who found the organization of the material opaque and the structure totally mysterious. The interface rules, complete with check boxes, mouse-selected icons and mouse menus, buttons, and hypertext links were considered to be more of a distraction and an annoyance than an aid to use.[2] And for those in the audience still working in DOS, the nongraphical interface was incredibly clumsy.

As might be expected from the argument of the preceding chapter, the response of those giving the demonstration was to place the burden on the prospective users. Because the network was nationwide, its protocols and software were fixed. Adapt to the system and its rules. Learn the interface. Get a bigger, faster, computer, or a Macintosh (they are cheap). Work in the office over the Ethernet, or get a high-speed modem or even faster link at home. In short, there was no choice but to comply.

As pointed out by Nicholson Baker,[3] there was more at stake here than efficiency or modernization. The enthusiasm with which librarians are discarding their catalogs once their computerized systems are up and running can only be explained as part of a deliberate reconstruction by the librarians of representation of a library. Across the country, library schools are becoming schools of "information science." As Baker notes, the hated cards continue to carry the image of Marian the librarian—female, mousy, graying, old-fashioned, and probably single. The technomodern image conveyed by the librarian as programmer and expert computer consultant is quite different.[4]

At one library after another, the rooms that once housed the card catalogs are being replaced with study tables or computer terminals. The cards are being burned, shredded, turned into cereal boxes or electrical insulation, and even used as decorations and wall coverings. The computer record was to be the master record. It took a while for the implications of that to sink in. It took even longer for us to realize that the ultimate fate of the card catalog itself was destruction. Once the task of transferring the information to the computerized data base was complete, the catalog was to be destroyed.[5] But the information that the cards once contained is not necessarily all in the computer. Retrospective conversion of catalogs is expensive, and many of the country's finest research libraries, including mine, have not been able to pay to have all of the information on each card put into the database.[6]

What was also lost with the card catalog was respect for a certain way of looking for information that was, for many of us, a well-developed and efficient research skill. With experience, the card catalog was a flexible instrument of incredible versatility. Computerized data searches, on the other hand, are inherently structured. The first search might be refused (too many entries), or result in a dump of thousands of listings; an attempt to narrow it can be an exercise in frustration that would try the patience of Job.[7]

It is said that we increasingly live in an information society. With powerful desktop computers, CD-ROMs, and global networking, each of us now has potential access to much more material than any single human being can be expected to read, let alone to master in a lifetime—even within one's own discipline, field, or special area of interest. With this has come a new form of anomie and alienation "information anxiety" that is already spawning a cottage industry in techniques for restoring confidence that one's own limited range of knowledge and skill still counts for something.[8]

It is the network and not the computer that created this trend. Networking has increased the availability and accessibility of data by orders of magnitude: by one recent estimate, the Internet already makes available to even the casual user several million megabytes of online, public data—a digital "encyclopedia" roughly a thousand times the length of the *Encyclopedia Britannica*. It would take more than a decade of continuous operation via a high-speed modem operating at 28,800 baud to download this data, even if one had a place to store it.[9]

But this aspect of networking, however challenging, still lies within the domain where computers are only substituting for what humans cannot do very well—data storage and processing. The dimension that mattered, and surfaced indirectly during the meeting, was the degree to which one of the major social costs of networking was loss of user autonomy and control over the means and processes of access. No wonder the librarians felt empowered. Instead of providing the traditional service of ensuring access to the community on demand, they were now managing a vital and necessary resource. Whether they liked to admit it or not, the information specialists were defining, shaping, and, in some ways, controlling user behavior through standardization of process and procedure.

Circling out from this example are others that have become nearly invisible to us through their familiarity: the airline reservation systems used by almost every travel agent; box office and ticket reservations; and, less visible to the public but increasingly central to business and commerce, the public and private nets that foster financial trading and markets, inventory control and purchasing, and just-in-time and other management strategies designed to increase efficiency by eliminating the need to carry or manage inventories. Networks, it seems, are everywhere. The computer or terminal on your desk, at home or at the office, is not just a means for giving you access to the world of networks, but also a means for the networks to impose on you the standards for hardware, software, and behavior required to make them accessible and (presumably) useful.

In the days of the mainframe, computers were seen as carrying forward the original purpose of information technology as a means to maintain and improve the centralization of task and functional hierarchy that had created so many of the great industries of the century.[10] But reducing fragmentation while keeping the benefits of individual workstations required the development of effective, reliable, and standardized local networks, tying independent users into an interconnected web that could be resubjected to central control. That parallel story has three main threads that converged in the 1980s into the web of connectivity that most computer users now take for granted.

From Anarchy to Networks

DARPA Builds a Net

The Defense Advanced Research Projects Agency (DARPA), formed in 1958 (as ARPA) to develop the basic research needed to promote the development of advanced technologies for defense applications, was the fountainhead of many of the subsequent developments in computers and computing.[11] Over the years, DARPA gradually became the lead agency for federal funding for most mathematics and computer-related research. Among the projects it supported during the 1960s were the first experiments in timesharing, project MAC at MIT and a joint Bell Laboratories–GE multiplexed computer system (Multics).[12] Although Multics ultimately failed, it strongly influenced the design of future operating systems, particularly with regard to incorporating timesharing as a fundamental attribute.[13]

DARPA was also interested in the development of computer networks for reasons that have profoundly shaped their subsequent evolution. The first was to allow the more efficient interconnecting of what were then relatively independent and mission-dedicated, defense-oriented computing centers.[14] Until that time, the only way to connect was analogous to a telephone call; the computers established a dedicated link and transmitted back and forth along it. This was relatively inefficient because data transfer rates were slow compared to the speed of the machines. It was even less efficient for a timeshared machine because of the lack of coordination between the availability of the machine and that of the link.

The second purpose of DARPA was to use the net as an early experiment in "hardening" the U.S. communications system against the possible ravages of nuclear war by building a decentralized network that could continue to function even if parts of it were damaged.[15] The underlying assumption therefore was that any single link in the network was unreliable; the communications links would have to be redundant and passive. As a result, the burden of managing the transmission of information was to be placed on the senders and receivers.

Proposed solutions for meeting the technical implementation requirements while meeting these objectives quickly converged on the notion of transmitting packets of information that contained within them a code indicating how the packet had been assembled, by whom, and for whom it was destined. To allow for redundancy and multiple channels, and to prevent tying up any one line for the long time needed to send a sizeable message at telephone speeds, some method would be needed to interleave them. The best way was to break up each message into small packets, each marked with an ID code that also indicated what part of which message it belonged to. What was then required was a method for implementing the idea technically, a means for switching between packets. Indeed, such a method, if successful, could also be applied to increase the carrying capacity of existing long-distance and transcontinental telephone service, which at that time was still largely restricted to transmission over cables of limited capacity and bandwidth.

With the idea firmly in hand, DARPA funding resulted in the first packet-switching experiments at MIT, and the subsequent development of the technology for packet-switched computer communications.[16] It also funded the basic research into packet "collision control" that made possible the development of effective packet-switched communication. The experiments were so successful that DARPA moved almost immediately to standardize both hardware and protocols and put a system into place.[17] By 1973, a nationwide system, ARPANET, was fully operational. The next step was the development of a set of "protocols" or rules for network transmission. The resulting combination of IP, the Internet Protocol, which standardizes the way in which the address of the potential recipient is coded, and TCP, the Transmission Control Protocol, which performs both the function of reassembling the packets into a coherent sequenced message at the far end, quickly became a de facto standard (TCP/IP) still in use today.[18]

In addition to achieving the primary goals of developing a robust and decentralized network whose performance was nearly independent of the source machine, DARPA's network initiative had several unanticipated spinoffs that would have a profound influence on the future of computer networking. Many of the Bell Laboratory staff who were to design UNIX had worked on DARPA projects. Robert Metcalfe, the principal designer of Ethernet, came from Project MAC, carrying with him the same goals of a universal, flexible network. And because most computer research institutions at that time were DARPA funded, and therefore entitled to use the ARPANET, it provided them with continental electronic mail, file transfers, and other services via a nearly invisible and instantaneous web of interconnection that became the standard to which other research communities aspired.[19]

Decentralized Centralization: UNIX

The Bell Telephone Laboratory was famous for its opposition to centralized and hierarchical organization. Researchers were used to moving around freely, exchanging and sharing information and their latest results. When DEC made available its first minicomputers, the staff eagerly adopted them, and set about transferring to their new UNIX system some of the ideas about connectivity that had been developed in the Multics project. As a result, UNIX was designed from the outset to timeshare, while presenting to the network of independent users the appearance that each was operating his or her own machine.[20]

But that was still not enough to satisfy the Laboratory community. Suppose one had a memo, or data, or a program, that one wanted to communicate to or share with another. The solution was to allow the transfer of files between users—what looked like sent "mail" was in reality a direct internal copy from one account (subdirectory) to another.[21] As the laboratory acquired more independent machines, each with its own system, it also seemed natural to interconnect them without at the same time subjecting them to centralized control. The importance of that small step cannot be overstated. It changed the relationship of users to computers completely. Instead of seeing themselves as part of a hierarchical tree under central control, the representation to the users was that of a distributed horizontal network.

When the UNIX-DEC combination was made available to colleges, universities, and research laboratories around the country, the new groups quickly moved from being passive recipients to active co-developers. In particular, the Computer Systems Research Group at the University of California at Berkeley had a set of expectations about connectivity that were not yet matched by the capability of existing systems. With contributions from other centers, the Berkeley group developed a complete package of built-in networking and communications capabilities that greatly fostered network communications between as well as within the various centers, and between them and other federally funded laboratories.

Networking was the outcome that the Berkeley group had been supported by DEC and government grants to pursue. The unanticipated, and, in the long term, perhaps the most socially important consequence came from the seemingly trivial and relatively simple extension of the network to make the computers easily accessible via telephone from anywhere on or off the campus. Within a few years, even those parts of the university community that were furthest removed from concern or interest about the future of computers or computing had become computer literate and connected.[22] A whole generation of budding academics and political and business leaders in training was not only raised on the experience of easy, direct access to powerful computing abilities, and each other, but on the idea that the potential uses of the new methods of connectivity had yet to be fully explored.

Ring around the Laboratory

Researchers at Xerox PARC took an entirely different approach. Although at least as interested in intercomputer connectivity as their predecessors at the Bell Labs had been, their dedication to stand-alone workstations meant there was no central computer to carry the communications processing load. Nor could they follow the UNIX approach, since the users really did each have a completely dedicated and independent machine. How then to build a local-area network (LAN)? In existing LANs, the management of communications traffic was handled by the central processor essentially along the lines of traffic flow control. Without a central node or machine, the flow of signals would become an unidentifiable jumble.

The elegant solution the PARC researchers ultimately developed in the mid-1970s was distribution of the traffic control functions across the network. Through this method, individual machines are all connected to a single, high-capacity loop, the Ethernet, which carries many simultaneous messages around and around past all the terminals as interleaved packets of information, each with a code to identify the sender and the intended recipient. Common circuitry and software installed at individual workstations watches the packets coming by, picking off the ones destined for it (and removing them from the loop). When a machine needs to transmit, it waits for gaps in the sequence to transmit output; if two machines try to "talk" at the same time, and scramble the result, each waits a small, random interval and tries again.

Ethernet was more than a technical triumph, it was a complete break with the historical tradition of computer "centers." The assemblage of Ethernet-interconnected, independent, graphics-oriented workstations at Xerox had no center, and no central coordination other than the standardization of software and protocol. Even the system administrator had to log on as an individual user, with considerable powers of access but no authority over the individual stations. Ultimately, the system developed to the point where users could actually gain direct access to programs and files on each others' computers. Whether by design or by accident, the resulting network of equivalent users had permanently displaced the mainframe-derived hierarchy as a model for organizing interactive computing.[23]

In 1974, 90 percent of computer sales were mainframes. A decade later, just before the explosive growth of home computing began, minicomputers already had a 20 percent share, and microcomputers had 35 percent. At least part of that growth was the result of the new capacity for networking. "The 1980s marked the passage from an era of large, centralized computer installations to a world in which vast numbers of more inexpensive machines, distributed widely among users, are tied to one another and to a shrinking number of specialized, centralized computing resources."[24] And as the networks grew from local to regional to national, and, eventually, to international, so did the possibilities—and the potential implications.

Internet

Nowhere are the alternatives of a networked future more thoroughly or imaginatively explored than in the pages of the journal *Wired*, an eclectic blend of technical detail, New Age spiritualism, and futuristic hype that has become the semiofficial voice of the libertarian wing of the computer culture. The common vision portrays a fully interconnected society where the networking of individuals has undermined the power of existing firms, institutions, and governments and destroyed or bypassed their instruments of hierarchy and central control, replacing them with more open and democratic global social communities that are self-organizing, self-regulating, and self-empowered.[25] And the means for this freedom and empowerment is to be the Internet.

This point of view has been subject to a number of pointed critiques, most recently and notably those of Stoll and of Turkle,[26] and I will not repeat them here. Nor do I directly address such issues as advertising and commercial use, censorship, and encryption, which are now being so noisily contested. Rather, I confine myself to the question of whether and how the Internet has contributed to or affected the processes of standardization and control described earlier.

Almost any user in the United States with a telephone line and a modem (and many other users at sites in Canada, Europe, and even the Far East) can now log on to a worldwide communications network almost as easily as making a telephone call, using a standardized protocol and a method of addressing that is as unique and unambiguous as a telephone number.[27] Through the nearly global system of interconnection provided by the Internet, a number of remarkable services are provided, ranging from simple, international electronic mail to the ability to log on directly to remote computers and search or transfer files, to actual sharing of data and databases.

Even within the user community, the Internet has often been described as organized anarchy. Self-organized would perhaps be a better term. The Internet (which is distinguished from various other forms of internets by its capital "I") is an institution without a real organization, a network of networks, a formal entity with characteristics that are any moment described almost entirely by those of the units that band together to form it. Its existence is predicated entirely on the desire of its participants to perpetuate it; its standardization and coordination are driven entirely by the requirements to adhere to a common set of rules and protocols.[28]

The Internet came into being almost by accident.[29] In 1983, ARPANET was split into two networks: ARPANET was retained as the name for the research network, while the military part with controlled access became MILNET. When NSFNET was created in the late 1980s, it was intended to retire the ARPANET entirely. Instead, however, it was replaced with a defense research internet, which fully took over its functions in 1989 when ARPANET was officially disbanded.[30] Meanwhile, the set of interconnected networks using the TCP/IP standard, and the NSFNET design of chained communications links, had grown to the point where ARPANET was no longer needed as the backbone of the system, a function that has since been taken over by commercial networks.

Internet has grown exponentially. When it started there were about fifty connected networks. In 1981, there were about two thousand individual users and 213 host computers. By 1989, there were more than five hundred networks connected, and some tens of thousands of computers. By 1993, more than eleven thousand separate networks were being linked, interacting through more than 1.5 million host computers, and still growing.[31] The number of individuals worldwide who now have access is difficult even to estimate, but it is certainly in the tens of millions.

Given the increasing power of computers, it was not long before even users on LANs or other closed systems using strictly local software and protocols were able to spare the extra computing power to implement protocol translation.[32] The resulting additional layer of interface via specified "gateway" computers continues to provide increased access to the Internet every year through an incredible variety of means.[33] Users without direct access to their own gateways can subscribe through electronic mail or bulletin boards at costs in the tens of dollars per month; small companies can pay larger fees to link distant offices or services; larger companies can even find very high speed services whose monthly costs may amount to many thousands of dollars.[34]

The ability of users to educate, to communicate, to share, and to find extended networks of other people with the same interests and opinions was and remains unprecedented, even if the quality of that interaction is debatable. The emergence of the World Wide Web, a set of hypertext Internet sites with standardized protocols and a common hypertext markup language, imposed a de facto standardization. With that development, and the emergence of standardized interfaces such as Mosaic and Netscape, the Internet moved toward becoming a commercial service as well as a personal one, and a formal source of information instead of an informal one. Many libraries, newspapers, and even companies now provide access via Web pages. For a few, it is already the primary means of supplying information to customers (other than by very slow physical mail—commonly known to net users as snail mail).

The protocols required for global connectivity, particularly those with graphic interfaces and multimedia mixes of text, sound, and pictures, place even greater demands on hardware and software than did LANs and limited networks, and require more standardization and compliance. As the global network becomes more functional for business, and more commonly used as a database and source of commercial as well as informal information, it will further extend the range and scope of forces compelling convergence of equipment and software, and, given present experience, it will add another layer of pressure to the drive for faster, more powerful machines.[35]

The Interconnected Office

The original networking of users to single, large centralized computers required extensive hardwiring, strictly limiting flexibility and the ability to work at home, or even at remote sites. The equally demanding requirements for maintenance and standardization resulted in centralized control by system operators. The introduction of the minicomputer did not much relax this condition. Although the minis were themselves interconnected, the individual users were really not. What appeared to be peer-to-peer communication was actually user-to-mini-to-mini-to-user, and still subject to considerable central control by the system operator(s).

This was fine in some circumstances, and still is. But in the 1980s, most of the growth in business as well as personal computing was in the direction of stand-alone machines, open systems, and user control over software. This did not sit well with managers in many organizational settings.[36] In addition to the isolation of workers, "sneaker-net," the carrying of floppy disks back and forth between machines, was a system of limited efficiency and questionable reliability. Although connectivity through the mainframe had been clumsy and inefficient, the central system had the advantage of enabling electronic communication and data flows between and among users. A generation of managers had been brought up on the idea that the information revolution was a means for restoring managerial control.[37] The fragmentation of machines and software left no mechanism for managers to improve the coordination and integration of their work.

The first wave of office interconnection was almost as anarchic as the first wave of computerization. Companies, and even individual units within them, were free to assemble a network in any way they liked. Over time, many competitive systems emerged. Some were basically intercommunication packages restricted to specific types of machines, others were actually operating systems of their own, capable of using any one of a variety of interconnection hardware. In some businesses and offices, there were several interpenetrating, sometimes overlapping systems that were only marginally compatible with each other. Even an organization with nothing but standardized PCs might end up with a heterogeneous array of LANs that were only partially compatible and rarely interoperable.[38] Connecting from one organization, business, or unit to another became a major headache. The only real standard that emerged was the choice of Ethernet as a de facto wiring standard.[39]

The proliferation of desktop computers and local networks threatened to decentralize office tasks and office structure as well. As the work done over networks became more central to the organization's function and purpose, there were increasing demands to integrate the LANs and bring their administration under central authority. Moreover, the increasing capabilities of both workstations and network hardware made it possible to interlink the LANs within any organization, assembling them into a single, larger network. Over time, the two historical approaches converged. As central computers grew more powerful, the effects of system load diminished. As LANs grew more powerful, and more complicated, they increasingly required the presence of a full-time management information system (MIS) staff to keep them running efficiently. As office integration continued, many of the LANs were assembled into larger nets managed by a central mainframe or minicomputer.

Over time, the network began to become the central functional element in the office or business, operating central software and communicating various pieces of critical information to and from databases, data management systems, and other programs of major importance. Given the original history of information technology as a method for integration and control, it is therefore not surprising that the choice of information technologies, including communications and design as well as individual workstations and their software, became tightly meshed with the design of the networks, and the whole package became a design choice and not just an enabler for organizational performance and change.[40]

Almost independent of size, scope, and purpose, one organization after another moved to centralize information systems purchases and establish organizational or corporate standards, and to replace ad hoc and disorganized management of idiosyncratic LANs with network management under the control of management, usually through a dedicated MIS staff not that different in their power and approach from that of the traditional centralized computer center. The paradox was nicely put in an article in *Infoworld*: "In order to construct the flexible, interconnected systems business demands, a fair amount of centralized control must be exercised."[41] Freedom and empowerment, it seems, are available only at the price of increased technical and user conformity with specifications, protocols, and software established by those who create and implement the net.

Most recently, large firms have been adopting a new language, "intra-net," to describe a networking system that is either entirely internal, or connected to the global Internet only through specified gateways, and with traffic that is not only controlled, but often carefully monitored. In addition, many firms that do continue to provide Internet access are now being offered special software that monitors the net access time and usage of every user, and may be expanded to scan messages as well.[42] Were workers ever under more control than this?

Conclusion

In its early days, the automobile was also considered by many as having the potential to foster a "revolution" in American society.[43] Like the computer, the automobile continues to nurture the mythic dimensions of autonomy and personal freedom. But that freedom lives mostly in the world of advertising, where vehicles are pictured on mountaintops instead of in traffic jams. What is not advertised are the costs and demands of the network of roads, highways, and the other elements needed to make the automobile useful. It is through the network and not the vehicle that the automobile has irreversibly transformed modern societies. And if the future dream of an intelligent highway is realized, user independence and autonomy will be further sacrificed for the sake of efficiency, mediated and ruled by yet another computerized network.[44]

Where computerization differs is that the computer, whatever its iconic status, is fundamentally a constitutive and not a productive element, a tool and not an end product. It defies comparison with almost any previous technical artifact, even the telephone or the automobile, not just because of the uniqueness of its capabilities (and limitations), but because the process of computerization embeds them doubly in the structure of modern societies. As structural elements, computers determine the shape and the function of the computerized networks that are increasingly displacing traditional means for the provision of necessary social and business services. And the networks themselves are becoming deeply embedded as essential elements of the organizations and institutions that now perform them.

As is the case with library information specialists, MIS specialists and others in charge of developing the new capabilities and exploring the means and techniques for developing new means and modes of control must be thoroughly familiar with the rapid pace of technical development that characterizes the field. They are among the most avid and motivated readers of the vast body of magazines, special newsletters (many dedicated solely to information technology managers and MIS specialists), and other literature that emanates from the computer design community, and the most likely to attend conventions and demonstrations of the latest hardware and the latest variants of software. Even when they specifically promote the need to involve end users in decisions, it is, with very few exceptions, done from the perspective and context of design, and not of use.[45]

The return of managerial control in a new, decentralized guise via the design and standardization of networks therefore suggests an organizational explanation for the shift in the balance of authority and power back to the designers after the brief era of end-user liberalism that both complements and reinforces other explanations based on more general social or psychological phenomena. MIS specialists and managers in charge of information systems for organizations, ranging from the largest corporations or government agencies to the smallest business, were hired not just to manage and maintain existing systems, but to help design and install new ones to increase organizational performance and efficiency—in other words, to act also as designers.

What gives this meaning and relevance are the parallels between the effects that the first wave of computerization—the automation of tools—had on the industrial work force and those that are taking place through the second wave—the networking of information systems—in the service and business sectors. In its initial phases, the microcomputer revolution seemed to offer the possibility for a social reformation of the workplace, restoring to users and workers some of the power and autonomy that had been lost with the decline of craft work and craft skills in the era of mass production and standardized office work. At first, owners and managers were prepared to accept independence and some degree of anarchic self-organization as the price of capturing the promised returns in productivity and efficiency. But control of information technology remained as central to the purposes and goals of management as ever,[46] and it was only a matter of time and technical development before means were found to reassert it. The goals, the intentions, and the consequences are not unique to computers or computerization, but defined and shaped by the historical evolution of scientific management in the twentieth century, as discussed in the following chapter.

4.

Taylorism Redux?

Introduction

The previous chapters pointed out the degree to which desktop electronic computers and widespread interconnection by local as well as national and global networks have become accepted as constitutive elements of modern life. Many of the short-term consequences and problems are well known and widely discussed. But this process has been under way for only a short while, and there is little basis for systematic understanding of the nature and implications of the long-term changes that will ensue as computers and networks begin to transform the structure as well as the practice of social, economic, and political life. Such long-term consequences as have attracted widespread attention and public debate have centered on the Internet and other systems of global telecommunications and information, and have focused on arguments as to how, or whether, they will transform the personal and social worlds of individuals.[1]

The substantive transformations already taking place in economic, business, government, and other social and political organizations are attracting far less notice, even though their long-term consequences are equally uncertain, and probably more significant. Existing organizations, from small businesses to government agencies, are changing both their structure and their practice in response to the opportunities and challenges of computerization, often with little or no attempt to understand the possible long-term effects.

In the 1960s, new technologies of computerized electronic control provided a new basis for the organization of production. The replacement of craft with production work at the turn of the century had transformed the representation of work, gradually moving the worker from being the direct creator of a product to one who operated a machine. The new introduction of process-control machinery, numerically controlled machine tools, and, eventually, production line or process computerization, transformed the representation once again, moving the worker one step farther back, from being the operator of the machine that did the work to supervising the controls that operated the machine that did the work.[2]

As computerization developed further, specification of output was increasingly incorporated into the machine by computerizing it. The first automated machinery incorporated only process into the machine; what was actually to be done was trained into the worker. The second generation removed even that discretion, preprogramming action as well as process into the machinery, or, more properly, into the computer that now operated the controls that guided the machinery.

As computers grow more powerful and networks more extensive, these processes are no longer confined to factories and production, but are extending into the world of knowledge-based work, including that of designers and managers themselves, creating entirely new forms of organizations in which managers do not manage and supervisors do not supervise; rather, they, too have become the operators of computers that supervise, and manage, through pre-programmed algorithms and models.

The widespread acceptance and use of the earlier revolutionary techniques for information and communication, the printing press and the telephone, not only transformed the social as well as the economic sphere, but also resulted in the invention of entirely new businesses and organizations entirely based on the new capabilities. Whether one believes that computerization amounts to a "third-wave" social and political revolution of equal importance or not, the new power of computers and computer networking is already making possible the creation of entirely new forms of technical systems whose possibilities and risks are not yet fully understood.

In order to understand these effects, and to relate them to the existing literature on the direct effects of workplace computerization and delocalization, much of which has traditionally focused on the skilling and deskilling of workers, it is necessary first to review briefly some of the relevant literature on the effects of automation and computers on business and management. Much of it tends to be normative or exhortative. But there is also a growing body of analytic work that seeks to address the problems and consequences of the widespread introduction of computers into knowledge-based as well as production-oriented segments of the economy, and seeks to explore the importance of increasing functional differentiation, spatial decentralization, and automation of program as well as task on the role and structure of management.

The Search for Managerial Control

The management and business literature has long pointed out that the tremendous gains in efficiency and productivity that resulted could not have been captured without the developments in information technology that took place in the latter half of the twentieth century.[3] The state of coordination and integration of early industrialization has been described as a piecemeal aggregation of individual jobs performed by skilled workers trained largely through apprenticeship.[4] Standardization was lacking, diversity reigned, and comparing the output of two workers was at best trying. It was interconnection and communication via the telegraph, and more important, the telephone, that made possible the expansion of the span and scope of managerial control.

There are striking parallels between early forms of industrial organization and the early state of desktop computing in business prior to the development of standardized methods of networking. In early attempts to convert collective workplaces into factories, work was more often divided by product or subassembly than by task, and increases in efficiency as the industrial revolution took hold were sought through the partitioning of labor, narrowing the scope and definition of the individual task, de-emphasizing the importance of "craft" skills, and turning workers into "productive units."[5] The genius of Henry Ford was to integrate these into a single productive machine via the assembly line, a method that could be applied to nonmanufacturing firms only with the creation of networks of communication equally hierarchical and equally susceptible to central design and control.

The increase in control and communication in turn both fostered and facilitated the formation of the large, vertically integrated companies and corporations that have dominated industry and business, socialist as well as capitalist, for most of the century.[6] But without a theory of management to implement them, it is likely that none of the new techniques would ever have been put to productive use. And the first of these theories, developed around the turn of the century, was the school of scientific management, the first, but not the last, to try to apply rational principles of science and engineering to social organization.

Scientific Management

As the creation of large factories or industries that employed large numbers of people to perform tasks by rote on a piecework basis shifted the emphasis from the skilled worker to the simple laborer, the more ambitious, motivated, and intelligent were quick to note that income and social mobility were increasingly associated with soft jobs such as management and sales rather than physical work, however skilled.[7] Intelligence and experience were therefore leaving the plant and shop floor even before the first wave of task specialization and standardization narrowed the scope of individual tasks. Those who remained, or who replaced the ones who left, had few incentives to work any harder than was necessary. The new managers, lacking either work experience or a set of reliable measures against which to measure performance, were aware of the decline in morale, and, frequently, the decline in productivity that followed, but found it difficult to devise or enforce measures to increase efficiency in the face of worker recalcitrance.

It was in this context that Frederick W. Taylor was moved to introduce the principles of what he called "scientific" management, derived at first largely from the application of production engineering. As an engineer, Taylor believed that if rational rules and tight control replaced previous disorderly and informal modes of plant organization, management would be better able to combat labor problems such as soldiering and low motivation among workers.[8] Many of Taylor's methods have become famous (or infamous); some, such as time-and-motion studies, were widely adopted. But others were too strict, or too mechanical, and Taylor had only moderate success in getting firms to adopt his means and methods.[9] What did flourish was his agenda, with its underlying precepts of rational modeling and analysis and its emphasis on finding the correct organizational form for any business or activity.

As later critics have pointed out, the growing movement toward scientific management that resulted was more of an ideology than a management system in the modern sense.[10] What was sought was the "one best way" to organize, to coordinate and rationalize not only to reduce conflict within the plant, but also to eliminate all forms of possible discord or disorderliness throughout the entire firm or industry. To the Taylorists, an ideal employee not only did what she was told, but stayed strictly within designated boundaries and task specifications. These in turn were set by managers using superior knowledge and rational methods of analysis.

The principles of Taylorism were never more clearly in evidence than when Henry Ford extended them to develop the first assembly line.[11] In the classic "Fordist", model, individual tasks are sequenced together tightly by mechanical means (the line) whose underlying structure and purpose is the increase of productive efficiency. Costs are lowered by reducing slack (available but normally unused resources), buffering capacity (resource storage space between or among different tasks to allow for uneven output rates), and skill duplication; this was made possible by providing central sources of data and coordination, removing the need for interworker negotiation between and among various steps.[12]

In the classic mass-production plant, increased production was achieved not only by dividing and specializing tasks, but by pre-processing away into the mechanisms of control much of the information contained in the final products.[13] The plant was indeed "automated" even before the era of the digital computer.[14] Given that not all products are equally adapted to these strategies, items to be manufactured were therefore increasingly selected, and designed, according to the ease with which they could be subjected to the new techniques of mass production.[15] Moreover, because sunk costs in a plant were high, every effort was made to reduce the variance between one product, or one generation of a product, and another. In effect, the range of consumer choice was being shifted from the end user to the designer.

The Taylorist ideology and approach were not confined to industries that mass-produced "hardware" such as automobiles or washing machines, with their simple structures and standardized outputs, or to offices that performed a narrow range of simple tasks. The growing sophistication of process at the end of the nineteenth century had resulted in a major internal reorganization of industries whose output was now based largely on scientific and engineering knowledge. In the electrical and chemical industries, for example, the entire means of production was radically revised to coordinate with the shift in emphasis from practical to formal knowledge.[16] These firms sought not only to improve and monitor the individual performance of more highly skilled workers, but also a means to eliminate the wasteful duplication of skills, particularly obsolete ones.

The principles of Taylorism coincided neatly with this agenda, as one of the aims was to remove the control the craft guilds had heretofore retained through their monopoly on experiential knowledge and expertise.[17] As craft procedures became increasingly reduced to formally codified individual tasks, craftsmen were to be eased out and replaced by less skilled workers performing a limited range of standardized and simplified procedures.[18] As the workplace was socially reorganized to separate the organization of work from its execution, management was also to be reorganized along formal lines, using bureaucracy and technical infrastructure as a means of coordination and control.[19]

The Deconstruction of Craft

Although traditional mastery had disappeared with the craft guilds, the importance of tacit knowledge had not vanished. The more complex the plant and process, industry or enterprise became, the more important was the role of those who could maintain an integrative view of operations and react quickly to situations without pausing to break them down and analyze then one step at a time.[20] Almost every plant or business has had a story equivalent to "old Mike" on the plant floor, who could tell a boiler was going to break down by the way it sounded, "old Harry" in management, who seemed to be able to smell how a certain change would affect sales, or "old Eloise" in accounting, who was the only one who could predict accurately whether operations were to be profitable that quarter.[21]

The period of the "old hand" is often remembered with some nostalgia, and considerable fondness, but such people were rarely well rewarded either for their value to the firm or for making their knowledge available to those who sought to codify and formalize it. What they lacked was the status and power to defend themselves as independent sources of authority and variation in an increasingly standardized work environment. The scientific management movement's claim to be able to embed their knowledge and judgment into plant and process design carried with it the implication that "old so-and-so," however quaint, was no longer central to efficient and reliable operation.[22]

To compensate for the loss of broadly skilled workers with integrative knowledge of plant and process, more elaborate and detailed models of work and task were created; control was asserted by increasing the direct, line authority of foremen and other intermediate managerial classes, under the assumption that better data and information would continue to ensure smooth integration.[23] As the transition from skilled to standardized labor proceeded, more and more oversight was demanded for process reliability, which in turn increased organizational complexity and the need for managerial coordination. Despite its absence from traditional measures of productivity, the extensive bureaucratization, with the attendant increase in office and managerial staff it required, was now seen as necessary and productive, rather than as an expensive and wasteful consumer of resources.[24]

Gradually, those who had risen into the white-collar technician class from the plant floor began to be displaced by professional engineers, whose understanding of management practices and objectives, coupled with knowledge of the principles and general theory of their field, was considered more important than detailed knowledge of any particular plant or process.[25] As engineers became more professionalized, their familiarity with operational details decreased; as processes became more sophisticated, the range of competence of individual workers was a decreasing fraction of the whole, and as management became a rationalized profession, preference was increasingly being given to those with formal education and training.[26] And just as the shift in importance to the plant of machinery rather than workers elevated the status, and importance, of those on the technical staff who designed and specified the production machinery, so did it elevate the status of those who were responsible for formal design and organized plant flows.

Open Systems

The Taylorist agenda, strongly opposed by organized labor, was widely resisted in the 1920s.[27] What was emerging instead was a greater emphasis on cooperation and social rewards, aided and augmented by changes in the training of the growing and increasingly professionalized cadre of middle managers. During the 1930s, the work of Mayo and of Barnard emphasizing social roles and group norms completed the agenda of social transformation. Instead of viewing workers as isolated productive units, the organization was viewed as a primarily cooperative, socially integrated enterprise.[28]

In contrast to the mechanistic and class-ridden approach that had characterized the Taylorist movement, and even its more humane Fordist sequel, the underlying premises of moral purpose and social cooperation were based on nurturing worker interaction and personal growth, emphasizing the importance and purpose of rationalizing the performance of the organization rather than of the individual. Managers now sought to legitimate their right to command, and to control, through a variety of social processes such as communication, cultivation of loyalty, worker identification, and plant and office culture.[29] Scientific management based on mathematical analysis and rigorous model-building was replaced with a social approach whose methods, however clear, could never be divorced from the human performance of managers.[30]

As tasks, goals, structures, and social interactions grew more complex, organizations came increasingly to be visualized not as self-contained entities, but as "natural" or "open" systems interacting strongly with their environments.[31] But the acknowledgment of the role of uncertainty and the imperfection of models did not much impede the organizational search for as much certainty and predictability as possible. The literature on management continued to focus on rational, closed-system models, emphasizing the importance of formal planning, goal-setting, and the search for control rather than adaptation and negotiation.[32] Increasing the control and efficiency of use of information therefore remained as much of a concern to business managers as it was at the turn of the century. Until the Second World War, however, there were few means for systematically addressing either.

Socio-Technical Tools

Not all of the important developments made during the war were technical. There were a number of complex analytic problems to be solved, such as optimal strategies for hunting submarines, or the allocation of interdependent resources, that resulted in the development of two quantitative socio-technical tools of considerable significance. Although confined during the war primarily to specific military tasks of highest salience, the importance for business and other more general applications of both operations research, with its focus on mathematical strategies for optimization, and systems analysis, as a means for formal analysis of complexity, was perceived from the outset.[33] Those who created and developed these tools were eager to find broader, more general applications. They sought to provide a rational and quantitative means for analyzing a wide variety of social phenomena, including business management, often in close conjunction with theoretical developments in information theory and computing.[34]

In the 1950s, operations researchers and their descendants began to move into industry and business as advisors and consultants, leading to two currents that have shaped contemporary management science. On the theoretical side, the dominant human relations model of management was to be overtaken by the new systems school in the mid-1960s, complementing the rational-actor and decision models being developed by Simon, March, Cyert, and others.[35] On the practical side, as the systems perspective moved into the business schools, managers skilled in quantitative analysis and systems thinking moved from the periphery to the center of the discipline, aided by the expansion and availability of computers to perform the calculations.

The transfer of these formal analytic techniques to the business world reinvigorated the movement for quantitative scientific management, fostered and augmented by the rapid development of automated equipment and data processing techniques. The new agenda differed from the old in a major expansion of the scope of analysis; instead of treating the firm as a series of isolated, interacting operations to be integrated from the top, it was now visualized as a single, complex, interrelated pattern of activities, to be analyzed, coordinated, and optimized as a whole.[36] At first, progress was slow. What was clearly needed were more and better data, and more comprehensive, less costly means for gathering, storing, and processing them.

The mini- and microcomputer revolutions provided the material and the means. Increased computer power and availability enabled the creation of far more elaborate models and techniques than had ever been imagined, aided and augmented by the availability of relatively simple applications for model-building and parametric adjustment. At the same time, the growing "informating" of the workplace by the introduction of computers for operational and process control was not only generating much more data about performance than had been possible before, but was offering the option of making it available online, in real time, as well as storing it in huge amounts for later analysis.[37]

In a volume prepared as the report of the Management in the 1990s program organized by MIT's Sloan School of Management, Michael S. Scott Morton, the director of the project, laid out the dramatic changes that were expected:

> Information technology has important general-purpose power to manip-
> ulate symbols used in all classes of work, and therefore, as an "informa-
> tion engine," it can do for business what the steam engine did in the days
> of the Industrial Revolution. It goes beyond this, however, as a technol-
> ogy that permits one to manipulate models of reality, to step back one
> pace from the physical reality. Such an ability lies at the heart of IT's
> capacity to alter work fundamentally.[38]

Others were even more enthusiastic. In the view of Davidow and Malone, for example:

> Computers can gather most information more accurately and cost-effec-
> tively than people, they can produce summaries with electronic speeds,
> and they can transmit the information to decision-makers with the speed
> of light. Most interesting for our purposes is that, frequently, this infor-
> mation is so good and the analysis so precise that an executive decision
> is no longer required. . . . Anyone restructuring a company that does not
> take this new employee empowerment into account is not dealing with
> the future but is merely streamlining the past.[39]

What would be required was not only a recognition of the differences that would be made in the way work was done but in the way it was coordinated, an overhaul of management structure and strategy to accommodate the new possibilities and incorporate them into systematic new means for integration and control.

The Deskilling Controversy

Although much of the historical focus of the debate over workplace automation and the presumed deskilling of workers was on industrial production, similar changes were taking place in other sectors over roughly the same time period.[40] The general decrease in the fraction of product costs attributable to labor and the growing importance of non-manufacturing industries, businesses, and other forms of regulatory or administrative organizations in the economy drew increasing attention instead to the softer tasks of desk workers. The introduction of magnetic check coding and automatic tallying equipment into banks, for example, had effects on the structure of employment that were not that different from what had been observed in industries such as manufacturing.[41] Some occupations were more affected than others, but the pattern was consistent.

> About 80 percent of those jobs initially taken over by computers were defined as clerical/bookkeeping. One of the most severely affected operations was that of the highly skilled bookkeepers. This job, traditionally the ladder upwards in banks, had already been partially undermined by the use of bookkeeping machines and tabulators. The impact of computers proved devastating. There was a 50 percent reduction in the number of bookkeepers from 1960 to 1965, and the remaining jobs became more routine and less skilled. By [1970] the job had virtually been eliminated.[42]

By the 1980s, much of the work of performing transactions also became computerized; now the tellers themselves were threatened unless they could convert to computer operators. Long considered a traditional venue for employment, banking replicated in two decades a century of industrial history, moving a large part of its work force two steps back from contact with the actual work.

There were similar stories throughout the economy. Automation of inventory and stock control, price totaling, and invoicing were among the first processes to become extensively computerized. Supermarket checkers went from ringing up prices by hand to electronic cash registers to bar-coded prices, to complete bar-code checkout automation—now frequently including a direct computer link to credit card or bank account. Both inventory and access control in many high-technology firms use bar-coded access cards and computers to keep track of who is where, as my university library does to charge out and track books. Operators answering order phones follow preprogrammed sets of responses on their screens—if they have not been completely replaced by programmed voice mail.

Because of the traditional focus on labor, and in particular industrial labor, a great deal of the analysis, and the debate, concerning the introduction of advanced computers continued to focus on the traditional problems of worker power and the value of labor, extending the argument about deskilling and reskilling in the workplace. The most powerful and direct statement of the deskilling hypothesis in the new context of workplace automation was that of Braverman, whose influential work set the terms of the ensuing debate.[43] Braverman also argued that the introduction of new "technology" deskilled workers, but he concluded that the main source lay not in the changing relation between workers and their machinery, but in the increased control by management that was being made in the name of technical efficiency.[44]

This was clearly an argument that could easily be extended to office and other white-collar work—including management itself.[45] Some analysts and business gurus are even predicting that the advent of machine intelligence and other quasi-intelligent techniques will do for knowledge workers (such as managers, administrators, and other professionals, including, presumably, designers) what earlier and less sophisticated office computerization did for transactions processors (such as clerks and keypunch operators).[46] Although the argument for replacement may be a bit exaggerated (and technically too optimistic), it is much more plausible when rephrased in terms of increased control of the workplace.

By the 1970s, many of the new class of "scientific managers," trained in and completely familiar with increasingly powerful computerized tools and methods, were using their quantitative skills to move up the management ladder.[47] The attitudes of many of those responsible for the design and implementation of the new systems had decidedly Taylorist resonances, among them the notion carried over from science

and engineering that there is one best way to perform any task, including a managerial one. As deeply ingrained, and more operationally
important, was the associated belief that excess capacity, the "slack"
that provides a buffer against uncertainty or unexpected events, is
wasteful, and that new forms of electronic integration can replace organizational buffers as well as inventories by implementing the equivalent of the tightly managed and controlled flows of "just-in-time"
strategies.[48] These were to be accomplished by the "leveraging of expertise," which translates in practice into preprogramming the
workplace through rigorous standardization and adherence to formal
models.

The advent of the personal computer in the 1980s and the accompanying dramatic increase in the capabilities and power of all forms of
computing equipment allowed these designers and other experts to
extend the use of their tools and techniques into all levels of the firm,
from the shop floor (when there is one) to the office of the CEO,[49] resulting indirectly in reconfiguration of the historical flow of information in the firm. Whether what results is or is not characterizable
as "automation" in the traditional sense, new computerized techniques for managing communication, information, and operation are
"informating" the workplace, generating vast bodies of new data and
information.

In historical, centralized, hierarchical forms of organization, the
span and scope of managerial control were strictly limited at any level.
Much of the position and power of middle managers lay in their role
as collectors, processors, and forwarders of information up the chain.[50]
The interconnected computerized workplace provides a means for an
unprecedented degree of penetration across and through the lines of
authority. Managers at all levels, including the most senior, can now
collect and process data directly, not only overseeing the work of subordinates but actually monitoring it. They can bypass their subordinates, or work around their peers, by communicating directly with
anyone in the firm and by checking the work of anyone over whom
they have formal authority. In short, and depending on your perspective, managers can now oversee work directly, intervene, micro-
manage, or interfere, even in tasks and processes for which they have
no particular expertise or formal training, and in cases where the
blame for adverse consequences will be placed elsewhere. Teasing out

the potential long-term and indirect consequences of this form of informal operational networking runs as a continuous and major thread through the case studies and analysis of the following chapters.

The Informated Workplace

Many elements of the changing workplace, both as reported by empirical research and as analyzed by the growing business literature on computerization, seem uncomfortably close to the goals and aspirations of the classical Taylorists.[51] Just as Taylorism eliminated a generation of craft workers, or converted them, plant automation threatens a generation of machine operators unless they are willing and able to acquire the skills (and attitude) needed to work with automated equipment.[52] It was the principles of Taylorism that created the typing pool and the single-purpose clerical worker. The same principles seem to have created the full-time word processing specialist, or data processor, and may work in the future to create their managerial equivalent.

In her study of workers ranging from blue-collar manual labor to white-collar international banking, Zuboff bypassed the traditional, machine-oriented debate over deskilling in favor of a more intellectually oriented framework centered on the definition of work as a representation of the body in labor.[53] In her work, she found evidence that the "informated" workplace was not so simply analyzed as the automated factory.[54] Workers did express concern over the loss of experiential knowledge, and of hands-on control of procedures and processes, but they also acknowledged that their own status and knowledge were in many ways improved.[55] Users had to acquire further training to put the new information to good use, but it was not at all clear whether the new systems gave them more discretion or less.[56]

There were also striking indications of the continuing search for central control. Zuboff found several instances where the manager's view of the intended result was centralization of control in order to reduce uncertainty and allow for syncretic planning of all operations.[57] A survey of plant managers conducted by the Honeywell Corporation found that "almost without exception, the 'technology ideal' reported by plant managers was having one screen in their office from which they could operate the entire plant."[58] Another study cited found that information systems "are indeed being used to reproduce the logic of scientific management—top-down control and the centralization of knowledge—more comprehensively than ever before."[59]

As noted in chapter 3, these are effective means for exerting control through compliance rather than hierarchical authority, allowing for formal decentralization while ensuring that the range of significant deviance from central plan and intent is narrow. Such tactics have a long history of success in social and political affairs.[60] It is therefore not a complete surprise that in other studies on the introduction of computers, particularly into businesses and other service-oriented organizations and bureaucracies, users do not see computerization as resulting in either an increase of direct central control or in the displacement of status and authority that many analysts had predicted.[61] The question remains as to whether the accompanying increase in the information flows and connectivity that textualizes the work environment actually empowers workers or only enculturates them, whether there are operational gains in status and autonomy or only a new means for continuing the drive toward managerial oversight and control that first nurtured the Taylorist movement.

What is clear is that similar tendencies and trends are at work up and down the scale of employment, from the lowest production or clerical worker to at least the middle levels of management and engineering. According to Zuboff, the historical categories of blue collar ("acting on") and white collar ("acting-with") are both disappearing as computers are introduced. The blue-collar worker is increasingly an operator or monitor of an automated process; the white-collar worker is personally isolated but technically integrated into an automated office or enterprise.

If this tendency continues over the long term, operators and managers will be deprived of both the context and the meaning of action. What will emerge in the future is a world of work in which operators have evolved into "operatons," placed in a job that seems to require human judgment and human action, but so bounds and circumscribes what they can and cannot do that there is no room for discretion, let alone perfection of skill. Managers will have co-evolved into "manageroids," looking human, acting human, but having no real autonomy or control, and no discretion to evaluate or deviate from the plans and programs of their organizations. This is indeed a bleak vision, not just for workers but for the societies that depend on the products and services they provide and the organizations they staff.[62]

Those who reject the preceding argument as a simplistic critique of a neo-Taylorist strawman argue instead that computerization can enhance and expand the universe of work. The skills required to make effective use of computers are often of a higher order, engaging workers (and managers) more fully, making better use not only of their education but also of their innate capacity. More important is the "textualization" of the new workplace into an environment where workers read and respond to abstractions of the process and manipulate abstracted symbols and controls, rather than observing and acting on or with the processes themselves. In this view, the increased knowledge of operations required to master the new work environment does in fact give workers more than a sense of having more status and increased control over their own work. In the long term, they have the means to realize both.[63]

Despite several heroic efforts to clarify arguments, premises, and evidence, the terms and findings of the debate over deskilling remain confused, and somewhat contradictory.[64] But is it in fact the central point at all? Some authors think not. Hirschhorn has suggested that the focus on deskilling and reskilling in the workplace confuses integration with discretion, blurring the distinction between reconfiguring the breadth and scale of task and redefining its nature and scope. The distinction he makes between skill and function is similar to that made in other contexts by Zuboff:

> As workers are deskilled, their actions are narrowed and they become more integrated into the machine systems. In defunctionalization, on the other hand, the workers give up all execution functions and manual action and are fundamentally displaced from production. Displacement is hidden in semiautomatic systems, as workers lose execution functions but gain in control activity. . . . Mechanization narrows skills and coerces workers to commit their bodies, if not their minds, to the machine process. Post-industrial technology threatens to throw them out of production, making them into dial watchers without function or purpose. The problem of skills is dwarfed by the larger problem of fundamental identity and function.[65]

Although the specific notion of "defunctionalization" has also been the subject of some argument, Hirschhorn's description points directly toward the heart of the issue of the new transition.

Expertise Lost

One of the more remarkable accomplishments of human beings faced with situations of great complexity and difficulty is the ability of some to gain a mastery that is beyond even highly accomplished proficiency. Dreyfus and Dreyfus have characterized as "true expertise" that level of performance that is so rapid, so skilled, and seemingly so intuitive, that it cannot be attributed to rational, incremental accumulation of experience either through practice or through process.[66] Whether chess player or pilot, artist or race driver, a true "expert" can be defined as a person who has an acquired instinct for going straight to the solution, the knack for finding a correct path or action without having to pause to logically deconstruct and rationally analyze the problem.[67]

The usual terms used in rational and reductionist analysis of good performance of complex tasks—such as competence or skill—are usually characterized, and measured, in terms of the ability to construct or reconstruct a logically exhaustive deductive chain, and then proceed along it. What many call expertise is in this sense only proficiency, the ability of a well-trained individual to find the shortest path through the logical chain to a correct (or effective) solution. Workers can achieve these levels of performance through practice, through training, and even through simulation, since proficiency can be built through experience, repetition, and the accumulation of knowledge.

But rote learning without the discretion to try, and to err, cannot produce an expert. What is required is to test and experiment, to practice until the cognitive map of action becomes an integrated representation instead of a series of causally linked discrete steps. Consider, for example, photographer Peter Gullers, writing on the subject of expert judgment of light in photography:

> When faced with a concrete situation that I have to assess, I observe a
> number of different factors that affect the quality of the light and thus
> the results of my photography. Is it summer or winter, is it morning or

evening? Is the sun breaking through a screen of cloud or am I in semi-shadow under a leafy tree? Are parts of the subject in deep shadow and the rest in bright sunlight? . . . In the same way I gather impressions from other situations and environments. In a new situation, I recall similar situations and environments that I have encountered earlier. They act as comparisons and as association material and my previous perceptions, mistakes and experiences provide the basis for my judgment.

It is not only the memories of the actual practice of photography that play a part. The hours spent in the darkroom developing the film, my curiosity about the results, the arduous work of re-creating reality and the graphic world of the picture are also among my memories. A faulty assessment of the strength of the light and the contrast of the subject, the vibrations and tremors become important experience to be called upon next time I face a similar situation. All of these memories and experiences that are stored away over the years only partly penetrate my consciousness when I make a judgment on the light conditions. The thumb and index finger off my right hand turn the camera's exposure knob to a setting that "feels right," while my left hand adjusts the filter ring. This process is almost automatic.[68]

What Gullers describes as "right feeling" typifies the master craftsman in every field of human endeavor, from artists to politicians, from generals to metal workers, from athletes to theoretical scientists.[69] It has its mirror in those workers and operators who over time gained such familiarity with their work that much of what they knew had passed over into the realm of tacit knowledge.[70]

As will be discussed in greater detail in chapter 7, the pattern of response found in empirical studies of the introduction of computers into nuclear or chemical plant operations, or into other similarly knowledge-based and integrative tasks such as air traffic control or airplane cockpits, has been shown to be far more complex than that found in studies confined to the automation of assembly lines and other technically simple workplaces. What is being replaced, or displaced, is not the direct and tactile involvement of the worker, but tacit knowledge, in the form of expert judgment of the state and condition of operation of plant, process, activity, or firm, and the range of experiential knowledge that allows flexibility in interpretation of rules and procedures when required.

The problem of maintaining formal control is dealt with simply enough—in principle. If designers are clever enough, and their knowledge of the technical system detailed and thorough enough, computer controls can be preprogrammed to detect all possible variance and correct for it automatically. The job of the operator (or manager) in that case would be simply to monitor the automated process and make a report when and if any major deviation or other unexpected event occurred. That would probably suffice for a "jellybean factory,"[71] but would not be sufficient for a plant that depended on continuous processing, or for nuclear power plants or dangerous chemical facilities that needed to be under control at all times.[72] What would be, and is, expected is that the operators also be able to step in and take over if the plant enters a configuration not programmed into the computer; or if it goes down; or if they see any other deviation that they think might threaten process, production, or plant or public safety.

The question the operators have asked, of themselves and of management, is whether they will be able to maintain the necessary skills and expertise if most of their time is spent nurturing the computerized control system instead of actually running the plant. More to the point, how will their successors and replacements be trained, or gain expertise, without learning through hands-on operation? It is the same sort of question asked by machine workers displaced from direct control of their machines, but at a broader and more publicly consequential level. The irreversible loss of expertise is one of the more serious potential long-term and indirect costs of the penetration and acceptance of computers and computerization into the operation and control even of complex and critical tasks. Concern over the possible consequences is another theme that is pursued through the following chapters.

Heterogeneous Systems

I suggested earlier that the new computer-based information techniques were not only affecting existing technical systems but creating entirely new ones. Many of these may be no more consequential than the jellybean factory, and no more important. But in the past few years, new forms of technical systems have begun to appear that are created as heterogeneous assemblies of selected functions of pre-existing ones, and that depend completely on the capacity and capabilities of computers and networks for their function.

The most carefully analyzed case to date has been that of Eurotransplant, designed to provide an integrative mechanism for facilitating and coordinating the availability of human organs, surgical teams, and potential recipients.[73] The perishability and unpredictability of the supply mandates requires this to be done on very tight schedules and in real time. The technical core of the system is a central computer with an international database connected by modem and phone lines to a network of other desktop and minicomputers that contain local information about hospital admissions and records, potential transplant recipients, doctors and medical teams, etc., without requiring potential recipients to tie themselves to a hospital for fear that they may otherwise miss the opportunity, or allowing viable organs to deteriorate before recipients can be found and teams assembled.

Eurotransplant is a system with no infrastructure of its own other than the coordinating and data-managing computers. It draws on other existing multipurpose systems for rapid air and ground transport, database management, telecommunications, and physical facility readiness, all of which must be smoothly coordinated and integrated, often within a matter of minutes. In traditional large technical systems, failure of a coordination or control computer may shut down subsystems, but the main system continues to exist and, if well designed, to operate, even if at reduced capacity. But Eurotransplant is different. If coordination and integration fail, the subunits continue to function (indeed, they may hardly notice), but the overall system ceases to exist.

Because these new, heterogeneous networks have no primary infrastructure other than computer hardware and software, both of which are known in any case to have short productive lifetimes, sunk costs are very small. Even a minor innovation in computer hardware or software, or a new idea about putting existing capabilities to work, can lead to a new way of framing the networking potential, which in turn can be implemented with great rapidity by rearranging and reassembling the component elements. Thomas Hughes has characterized large technical systems as somewhat ponderous, possessed of a "momentum" that carries them forward even in the absence of external stimuli.[74] But many of these new systems will be nearly free of encumbering infrastructural and managerial "mass," enabling them to respond rapidly, radically, and perhaps unpredictably, to relatively small changes in integrative capabilities, problem definition, or representation.

As central elements of complex systems based entirely on networking, be they homogeneous or heterogeneous, computers are no longer simply auxiliaries, aids, or replacements for traditional ways of doing things. Because they are capable of storing enormous amounts of data and recalling them automatically, and carrying out remarkably complex and widespread actions in very short times, they create entirely new ways for other systems or individuals to take action. But to whom, or to what, are the coordinating systems and their designers, programmers, and operators accountable?

Who is responsible for supplying safe, reliable, just, or equitable performance of Eurotransplant? Surgeons? Pilots? Ambulance drivers? Can a computer programmer be sued for malpractice for a programming error? Is the hospital responsible if a perishable organ has been sent to the wrong place, or matched to the wrong potential recipient? Can a dispatch system be sued for incorrectly prioritizing ambulance calls, or a financial data trading system penalized if a transaction vanishes between sender and recipient? As the functions of the traditional vertical organizations that have dominated our thinking for the great part of this century are dispersed along and across the new networks of interconnection, we are hard pressed to locate, let alone improvise, means for ensuring accountability. This too is one of the threads that weaves through the following chapters.

Conclusion

The original information technologies, the telegraph and the telephone, made possible the emergence of the mass production–oriented, vertically integrated hierarchical organizations that dominated most of the industrial development of the twentieth century.[75] They enabled increasingly gigantic and differentiated firms to retain centralization and hierarchical control while expanding in scope and scale to a degree never before possible.[76] Although they may not be rendered as completely obsolete as the enthusiasts of the virtual corporation would have us believe,[77] the new techniques are transforming them again in ways that are as pervasive as they are subtle, dispersing function away from the central organization while also supplying a means to retain coordination and control. And just as the telephone and the telegraph not only made possible the emergence first of entirely new organizational forms, and then of wholly new services for which information technology was central, the new, computerized techniques are not just fostering change on present organizations and services, but creating entirely new ones.

The power of desktop computers, harnessed to the new techniques for global communication and networking, are making possible the creation of new types of large technical systems that are inherently transboundary where traditional ones were nationally or regionally oriented, differentiated horizontally across strong networks rather than vertically between weak ones, and organized around communications rather than hierarchies, with management and control diffused horizontally through the system instead of flowing up toward the top.[78] This is a major and important change.

Unfortunately, the present state of theory and analysis of either large, technically oriented firms or large technical systems in general does not seem adequate to the task of understanding the coming changes. Although the lure of computerization is clear, and the short-term costs and benefits are becoming increasingly well understood, the longer-term consequences for system performance, for the changing social and economic role of existing large-scale systems as they transform, and for the social, economic, and political structures and practices of the societies that depend on them, are still at best only dimly perceived.

Moreover, the tools and methods we have inherited and developed remain grounded in observation and analysis of the historical, hierarchical, vertically oriented institutions and organizations of the precomputer, prenetwork industrial revolution. It is not at all clear how appropriate they are for analyzing (let alone predicting) even the direct effects on social and industrial organization of the newly emergent, horizontally organized and network-coordinated forms that are coming into being, let alone for the more complex and difficult task of trying to understand the longer-term, larger-scale, more diffuse, and more general impacts.

The chapters that follow amount to a set of preliminary case studies bounded and defined by the preceding agenda, and set in contexts and situations where some of these indirect effects have already been consequential—along with some speculative inference on where they might be heading. The list of possibilities is long, and the ultimate consequences in some cases may be as hypothetical as the future capabilities that are promised. There is, however, one instance that already serves to illustrate and illuminate the range of emerging critical problems—the growing international network of trading in currencies, bonds, stocks, and other assets. As *The Economist* has put it: "How, in an age of computerized trading and borderless financial markets, can regulators ensure the efficient and fair working of a central market equally accessible to all investors big and small?"[79] That question will be taken up in chapter 5.

5.

Computer Trading

> He's merchant-bank Bertie, who sets off at 6:30
> ... [crowding], with thousands of others, into a
> shabby train or bus headed for the City of Lon-
> don. Then they all swarm through damp, grimy
> streets to their skyscrapers. To do what? To clus-
> ter in some of the world's most expensive office
> space, to stare at flickering screens and pore over
> pages of numbers, and to talk on the telephone to
> other disembodied voices about this deal and
> that price. Bertie's business has its ups and
> downs, though it is mostly a good one. But why
> does he do it in London?
>
> (The Economist, *1991*)

Introduction

Why in London indeed? Possibly because of the myth of the City as the
place where transactions take place, and the idea that markets are
made real and physical rather than enacted by his embodied presence.
Before 1986, stocks in London traded on the floor of the London Stock
Exchange, in a controlled and structured chaos of shouting, shoving,
sweating, and dealing, as they had since the nineteenth century. But in

October 1986, electronic trading came to the City of London with a "Big Bang." After several months of soul-searching and critical examination, operations on the floor were converted to electronic transactions.[1] The market became the International Stock Exchange, and the exchange floor itself ceased to be the focus, replaced as the real locus of transactions by glowing squiggles on thousands of computer screens.

What happened in London has been repeated, before and since, in other markets and on other trading floors, as computerized trading and computerized databases replaced the traditional methods of trading and settling accounts. Why pay the high rents of traditional business districts, or put up with the awful winter weather of London or New York, when one can set up a computer and a data link and trade from Bermuda, Belize, or the Bahamas—or Spain or the south of France (if one wants to keep European hours)?

In the process, the entire range of activities connected with financial markets, from simple interbank transfers to the creation of entirely new instruments that represent possible movements of indices rather than tangible worth, became delocalized. Although the process is far from complete, most of the trading has now shifted from such physical institutions as banks and market floors to the interactive networks originally built simply to interconnect them. No other major human activity has moved so quickly to the edge of "cyberspace."[2]

Becoming expert in market trading and analysis was once a craft skill, acquired by apprenticeship and experience. Whether trading in stocks, in commodities, in futures, or in money itself, the ability to anticipate market movements and trends was the substance and hallmark of success. But the power and influence of the old traders, and of their institutions, is waning. As more and more of the action takes place over the newly global computerized networks, both the influence of the traditional, hierarchically ordered firms and the power of the regulatory structures designed around them are diffusing horizontally across the net.

It may be acceptable to allow the City and Wall Street to continue as social rather than functional centers, while the real players sit at their remote computers, improving their models and machines in search of a more elaborate model or an improvement in response time that will give them an edge on their competitors in the net.[3] It will probably not be acceptable to assign the same course of evolution to either private or public regulators of market fairness and behavior. But even if it were, that would require monitoring and control of activities on the net, without hierarchical authority, by a new class of players sufficiently equipped and informed to allow them to enter on equal footing.

Markets and Exchanges

To those who trade in bonds, securities, and other financial instruments, rapid and accurate information has always had tangible value. New technologies for information and communication have been not only welcomed, but encouraged.[4] The telegraph, first demonstrated in 1844, was already being used by 1846 to make markets and to speculate in stocks. Price quotations from London were being published in New York papers only four days after the transatlantic cable was completed. In the 1860s, the exchanges developed a specialized information technology of their own, the stock ticker, and raced to upgrade speed and capacity. By 1880, there were over a thousand tickers in New York, and the New York Stock Exchange (NYSE), in the first example of regulation of new information technologies, acted to consolidate and integrate the distribution of information.

Wall Street was the first major consumer of the telephone and the electric light. The U.S. financial industry was the first major sector of the economy (after the telephone system) to make widespread use of electronic data processing and related innovations such as computer-readable cards and optical scanners; the now-familiar technology for magnetic ink character recognition was introduced as far back as 1958. Banks were among the pioneers in business use of the new capabilities of mainframe computers; by 1980, almost every bank had at least one computer, accounting for half of their capital expenditures other than for buildings.[5] It is therefore not surprising that financial institutions moved more quickly than most to make use of the new techniques for marrying information processing and analysis to the management and manipulation of large databases.

The need to make efficient use of the new information capabilities while still conforming to the understood rules for trading and for transaction settlement led to concentration and hierarchy. Activities were increasingly dominated by a few large and powerful firms, concentrated geographically, along with their less powerful cohorts, in relatively few locations such as Wall Street and the City. For the most part, the hierarchical distribution of power and influence among the financial centers, among the increasingly international firms, and between markets, firms, and national regulatory authorities was stabilized in the 1930s; although the distribution of power and wealth underwent radical changes through the Second World War and its aftermath, the structure itself changed little for fifty years.

Centralization was encouraged by structure and by intent. Information flows outside of financial capitals were too limited and often too slow to allow for much interactive trading, especially across national borders. Even when advances in communication technologies allowed for national integration, the information flowed in and out of the exchanges, to be acted upon by traders on the floor. And with the memory of the market collapse of the late 1920s constantly refreshed by reexamination and re-analysis in schools of business and economics, governments sought to keep markets nationalized and localized, so that regulators could ensure honesty, control economic fluctuations, and avoid overseas flights of capital and ownership.

From the 1950s to the present, the structure and behavior of markets were relatively stable, needing little more than regulatory trimming to encourage wider participation, particularly by small investors. But the recent rate of technological change has begun to create visible signs of upheaval.[6] As traders moved from mainframes and dumb terminals to faster and smarter mainframes and individual computers, increasingly rapid access was required to different sources and types of information. The direct effect was to make the market more active, and more volatile. The indirect one was to further increase trading in secondary instruments, such as futures, and to encourage the development of a host of new financial instruments that represented bets on the future movement of markets rather than the markets themselves.

By the mid-1980s, multiplexing and video switching made possible both consolidation of physical equipment and expansion of access to other sources. Satellite transmissions and digital data feeds made information accessible worldwide, increasing both complexity and the pressure to respond quickly. More powerful desktop computers fostered the development of sophisticated programs that further encouraged the expansion and activity of trading on secondary markets, and in derivative instruments. And, as will be discussed more fully in the following chapter, the eventual linkage within and between markets has created a global net of interactive trading capable of operating twenty-four hours a day, seven days a week.

Information and Centralization

What markets need to operate well and fairly are liquidity and efficient payment mechanisms.[7] Both of these have always required accurate, up-to-date information, at first to make sure that the posted value of stocks, bonds, and currencies was a good measure of the current performance (and presumably value) of the underlying industry or enterprise. In addition, getting more accurate or timely information has a special value to those seeking to play markets for short-term profit rather than invest in them.[8] Given the technologies available before the 1980s, these requirements tended to favor increased centralization, increasing the power and importance of the traditional exchanges.

The first collective approach was the "call" system, in which small numbers of traders gathered (often behind closed doors) to hold auctions. Unlike the system that preceded it, in which trading occurred informally and privately in bars and coffee houses, the call system encouraged market prices set by supply and demand. However, the call room was usually closed to outsiders. In Sydney, where the call system persisted into the 1960s, traders were locked in the call room, with no access to phone or telegraph, and all forms of the media excluded, until the call was over and prices established.

Closed systems provided few opportunities for small investors, and were too vulnerable to manipulation to encourage the entry of those not well socialized into the circle of traders. In an effort to open the system to the growing middle class, in 1871, the NYSE adopted the present "post" system, in which trading takes place on an open floor, and almost every other major exchange soon followed. Listed securities or futures are each assigned a specific floor area, or post, and buying and selling take place in auctions held at the posts on the spot. Trading is continuous and parallel, and traders have ready access to information. At first these were provided by telephones and telegraphs on the floor, and from public services such as stock market tickers, radio, and television. More recently, these have been augmented by computers and display terminals, providing access to a wide range of global information, to colleagues, and, in many cases, to the home office.

The manifest openness of the post system encouraged even relatively small investors to enter markets, greatly increasing the volume of trade and the pool of available investment capital. Moreover, the increased centralization that resulted provided more efficient and timely mechanisms for transaction settlements. When it became clear that a manifest demonstration of fair and equitable treatment encouraged further participation as well as being in the best interests of the majority of traders, centralized trading in concentrated financial centers also afforded a convenient means and venue for the expansion of government regulation.

The increased concentration of activity also created new opportunities for indirect manipulation of markets, through control of information flows or the misuse of inside information. After several identified abuses, preventing the exploitation of markets by insiders possessed of knowledge not yet made public became another motivation for regulatory intervention. Regulations were subsequently put in place to protect investors from false or misleading information and from the issuance of paper that had no underlying real value. Over the years, the relationship between markets and regulators became a symbiotic one, fostered and nurtured by the concentration of major activity in a few large sites, and by the desire of large, centralized firms to avoid public reprimand or punishment.

Although the system clearly was still subject to abuse (as in the recent junk bond scandal), the centralized exchange system, centrally regulated and centrally controlled, remained stable for more than fifty years, from the Great Depression through the 1980s. As volume grew, so did the ability to provide and analyze information. And as the techniques for managing and processing information became more powerful and rapid, that in turn spurred more frequent trading, further increasing the volume.

Electronic Trading

As access to up-to-date information broadened in the 1960s, large, institutional funds began to acquire their own analysts and in-house expertise, and to explore the notion of buying and selling directly rather than acting through (and paying high fees to) brokerage houses. But the brokers still had a monopoly on trading on the exchange floor, and the funds needed a substitute for the liquidity the exchange normally provided.[9] In 1969, seeing an opportunity to broaden its information services, Reuters created *Instinet*, an institutional network that allowed subscribers to make and accept offers electronically, and directly.

As its computers grew more capable, *Instinet* further broadened its growing services, providing at first a computerized system for matching buy and sell orders and finally, as exchanges themselves became computerized, a mechanism for placing and executing direct orders electronically, bypassing the brokers completely.[10] By the 1980s, electronic trading, at first offered only to institutional investors through vendors such as Reuters, was transformed by desktop computers and improved data systems into an electronic trading system that provided information and liquidity to anyone with access—and access itself broadened considerably as market deregulation came into vogue.

The final step toward breaking down the former hierarchical control of markets and trading came about in the 1990s as a combination of regulatory and technological innovation.[11] The deregulation of telecommunications removed the blocks once placed on the entry of telecommunications firms into the computer arena, and computer firms into telecommunications, just when powerful desktop computers connected to local, national, and global networks were becoming standard desk accessories in the financial world. The result was a functional merger of communications and data processing. The "data terminals" originally put on desks to display and process information could now manage and settle transactions as well.

Once electronic trading removed the monopoly of financial centers on information, liquidity, and settlement, and provided access to expertise and information dispersed across the network, the hegemony of the centralized institutions was broken. The electronic program trader staring intently into a computer screen is increasingly as important a market actor as the floor trader or the traditional expert with a line to a broker. The stock ticker spewing forth its yards of yellow tape is now a recorder of trading history rather than a guide to investment strategy.

It has also replaced the old set of problems and potential abuses with an entirely new set. Near-instantaneous trading has spawned a new breed of "paper entrepreneurs" who seek profit through exploiting small market shifts in currencies or interest rates, or through other methods of manipulation of corporate paper, reacting to such stimuli as changing political conditions or immediate news, or gossip, with little or no concern for the production of goods and services.[12] And nearly every firm engages in program trading or other forms of automated stock-index arbitrage, seeking to generate short-term returns from price discrepancies between markets.

Electronic trading has increased both the rapidity and the volume of large market movements—both by providing automatic responses and by removing the physical limits of executing trades on actual exchange floors.[13] Stability once depended on large investors with a vested interest in long-term performance and both the time and the resources to assure it. Ensuring market stability may now be moving beyond the scope of those who understand, or care about, the tangible part of economic activity, or the companies, industries, and institutions that constitute it.[14] Even in the market crash of 1987, large investors were able to stem the tide only with the help of massive intervention by regulators.

Traditional modes of regulation, both private and public, were designed to prevent gross manipulation by powerful people using their special accesses or special privileges to cheat, disinform, or misinform their peers and the investing public. They are likely to be far less effective against networks of program traders, freed of market floors, who can make nearly simultaneous moves in huge baskets, rather than as individual entities. The resulting increase in volatility would further discourage small investors, who already find it nearly impossible to enter the market effectively without also buying in to the new technology.[15]

Computers were introduced into centralized markets and exchanges to make them better informed and more efficient. The unanticipated secondary effect has been to render them increasingly obsolete. Control of markets is increasingly passing out of the hands of large institutions and dispersing into the network of computers and data links that make up an ever larger share of the trading volume. But the decentralization of markets, the dispersal of activity and deconstruction of centralized power, has not worked to the advantage of the general public. Instead, it threatens to remove from effective control both the mechanisms for market access and the means to regulate market behavior.

Automating Markets

When the "Big Bang" came to London in 1986, *The Economist* reflected on some of the implications and concluded that some of the resulting changes (most notably the sharp increase in index arbitrage) were in fact inevitable, now that technology allowed the kind of quick movements needed to make profits out of small, transient movements. Its conclusions, however, merit quoting:

> The fact is that none of the regulators knows exactly what the new techniques are doing to the markets. It looks likely that America's Security and Exchange Commission will soon mount a formal inquiry into the causes of September's mini-crash, which some have blamed on computer trading. Because the SEC has the power to demand documents from brokers, it may find out who did (and does) what and why. But for a fair verdict, wait to see how Wall Street's computerized investors handle a bear market.[16]

The answer was to arrive within the year. In September, the Dow Jones average fell by a then-record 87 points, and closed the week down 141. Analysts were quick to point out the role that computer-driven program trading had played.[17] Wild market gyrations during the third week of January 1987 were also blamed on the too-quick response of computer-driven program trading.[18] Although these events heightened concern about increased volatility in the press as well as in governments, none were prepared for the rapid decline that occurred in October 1987.[19]

The Crash of 1987

In August 1987, the Dow Jones average had risen to over 2700. A gentle decline that continued into the fall raised no alarm and little concern. Then, without warning, the Dow dropped by more than 95 points on Wednesday, October 14. On Thursday it declined by another 58. On Friday, the market was down by 60 points by 3:00 P.M., but still orderly. At that point, the bottom fell out. Swamped with sell orders, many from automatic trading programs, the Dow dropped another 48 points in the last hour.

The 108-point decline for the day (and 235 points for the week) made headline news. But far more important was the perception by traders that the market had become disorderly. Had the closing bell not intervened, program and automatic trading would probably have been joined by other, slower to respond, investors seeking to cut their losses, taking it down further. Other markets, however, were still active, and the response continued.

By late Sunday, markets in the Far East were already down sharply; London was down by 10 percent before the market even opened in New York. At the opening bell, NYSE's "state of the art" mainframe computer was already overloaded. Mutual funds began to try to dump stock to get out from underneath. And every program trader and automatic trading program sent only one message to the NYSE: Sell!

The result was chaos. The NYSE dropped by over 100 points in the first hour, and another 104 in the next thirty minutes. With electronic trading systems active, and transaction reports lagging, the market staged a series of rapid and seemingly unmotivated rallies and falls that blocked attempts by more seasoned traders to act.[20] This erratic behavior broke the confidence of many large traders and index arbitragers, who then opted to close down their high-tech systems and wait the market out. This removed the largest players from the market, and left the old-fashioned trading specialists on the floor of the exchange as the sole buyers struggling against the tide of automated selling programs.[21]

What followed was a disaster. By mid-afternoon, portfolio and fund managers began to dump large quantities of stock again, and the market went into free fall. As each automated program read the increasing rate of decline, it triggered its own emergency dump program, effectively adding to the wave of sell orders. Under the pressure of the tremendous volume, even the automated trading systems began to break down.[22] It became increasingly difficult to get accurate quotes, let alone to make transactions.[23]

By the closing bell, the Dow had declined a record 508 points to 1738. Moreover, market orderliness, fairness, and access had gone the way of stability. Individual buyers and small traders, seeking to step in and take advantage of the low quoted prices, could not get through. Neither could old-fashioned specialists seeking to stabilize the system, even large ones. Indeed, financial expert Felix Rohatyn thought the market came "within an hour" of total and complete disintegration.[24]

Tuesday morning, a combination of restrictions on program trading, and the withdrawal from the market by specialists trading in specific players, reimposed some semblance of stability. Around mid-day, the old-fashioned experts staged a bald-faced market manipulation. According to the *Wall Street Journal*, a "small number of sophisticated buyers," using very little cash, engineered a rise in the Major Market Index futures.[25] Automated trading programs read this as a clear signal to buy, and slowly but surely buyers returned. By mid-afternoon, in what may well have been another deliberate manipulation, they were joined by major corporations offering stock buybacks.[26] Over the next few days, program traders, faced with dire threats of severe regulatory interference, monitored their electronic trading more carefully, while large buyers continued to intervene selectively to stem prospective runs. Faith in the market was gradually restored, and with it the myth that prices were based on the underlying economy.

In a TV show analyzing the crash, many expert analysts blamed the exaggerated response largely on computerized trading programs, which kicked in at the first steep decline, turning what would otherwise have been only an unusually bad day into an automated panic, driven entirely by electronic transactions.[27] "The fundamentals of the market changed," said one analyst, "We became part of a computer instead of part of a system, and the liquidity in our marketplace was taken out of the hands of the professionals and run through a computer."

Neoclassical markets are supposed to measure the performance of the economic activities whose representative paper they value and trade. In the weeks that followed, regulators and major traders moved to restrengthen that legitimating myth. Supposedly adequate restrictions and restraints were put on program trading, particularly during large market moves—treating the symptoms rather than the disease. Public confidence was thereby restored. Over the next few years, the market moved generally up, eventually recapturing most of what had been lost during those frantic days. But in the new era of electronic networking and program trading, the decoupling between markets and real-world activities remain; markets have remained more volatile, and less predictable, since.[28]

Electronic Bulls and Bears

Finding itself at a loss to respond to public demands for better protection, Congress requested from the Office of Technology Assessment (OTA) a report on the growing role new communications and information technologies play in the U.S. securities market. The OTA report, whose title I have shamelessly borrowed for this section, set out in some detail the pertinent market mechanisms and methods, including options, futures, settlements, and market clearing, dealing with twenty-four hour, global trading in a separate report.[29] OTA found U.S. markets to be basically healthy, liquid, efficient, and fair.[30] But they acknowledged that the stress being caused by technological change not only affected market structures and procedures, but put a major strain on existing methods for regulation and oversight.

The direct impacts of technical change were clear. But they could not be easily separated from other, less direct factors such as the changing role of large investors.[31] These technological factors, arising from often indirect and seemingly contingent interactions between the social and technical dimensions of markets, are changing both rules and structures.[32] OTA suggested that this may be the most lasting effect of the integration of computers and information systems, but was unable to predict what the long-term outcomes might be.[33]

OTA made three main observations. The emergence of an interactive global economy makes it increasingly difficult to limit trading to those whose actions may be constrained by their involvement in the national economies that markets are said to represent. New modes of trading are fostering the development of global institutional investors with enormous resources and open access to national markets and exchanges. The changes that are made possible by the computerized means of interaction are seemingly radical, but still far from complete.

The regulatory situation was found to be far behind the pace of change. The two primary agents of federal regulation, the Securities and Exchange Commission (SEC), established in 1934 to regulate the primary exchanges, and the Commodity Futures Trading Commission (CFTC), established in 1974 to regulate commodity and futures markets, operate separately, with different goals, different means, and different objectives, even though securities, futures, and options markets grow increasingly interdependent because of the new technologies that link them.[34] Neither has either the jurisdiction or the authority to deal with trading across national borders, and neither is able to keep up with the rapid, nearly automatic trades made by computers over networks.

When program trading began, the major concern was that rapid execution of large orders could be transacted so quickly that small investors were simply locked out. What was not realized was that regulators might be locked out as well. There are already visible consequences. Some analysts have pointed out signs of manipulation by program traders, although they prefer to use less tendentious words, such as "persuasion," to describe their activities.[35] The question is, what are the prospects for maintaining regulatory control in the new environment?

In October 1987, experienced traders were able to intervene to stabilize the market when regulators could not. But their power, too, is waning. As skill with the computer and its models becomes more important than accumulated experience, power and influence are shifting to a generation of younger traders more familiar with electronics than trends, less concerned with preserving long-term market stability than with developing and mastering better, quicker models with which to outmaneuver the competition.

The increased rapidity of market action and reaction also requires constant attention, which will not only disadvantage the older generation of insiders but gradually shut out other traditional investors who still have to act through brokers instead of dealing directly with the electronic networks. It also presents enormous problems to regulators seeking to guarantee that the improvements in information and liquidity are not compromising the other central value of fairness that characterized the historical exchanges.

The only response thus far has been to seek ways to monitor the relation between information and communications networks and actual trading activities. Some markets have already moved to incorporate limited electronic after-hours trading systems rather than leaving themselves at the mercy of global traders working in the wee hours; even the traditional NYSE is beginning a phased program that will take it to full around-the-clock, global trading by the year 2000.[36] But the SEC has no real authority over financial information vendors or others who threaten to move a large part of the trading volume outside of regulatory structures.[37]

A more effective response would be to recognize that what is emerging is a radical and not an incremental transition. Although current trends to decentralization and deregulation have resulted in major changes in many industries, and will probably affect many more, what is happening to electronic markets may be the first important example of a structural reformation of industrial societies that goes beyond the near-chaos of postmodernism to something just as radically different from traditional, large, powerful firms based on vertical integration of functions and skills, but more systematically organized. The vertical modes of organization that once governed markets and trading will not fragment into disorder, but rather will progressively devolve their powers, and their roles, to more horizontal modes of organization and functional differentiation in which authority, purpose, and skill are widely dispersed and integrated by computer networks rather than bureaucratic hierarchies.[38]

Nasdaq's Very Bad Day

On Wednesday, July 19, 1995, technology stocks led American stock markets down, and then partially back up, in another of the dramatic roller-coaster rides that have marked the era of electronic trading.[39] The Dow Jones average was down by over 130 points before recovering to close down 57 for the day. Trading volume was the third highest ever, more than 480 million shares; phone lines were jammed and home-computer trading systems were almost locked out completely.[40] The invocation of program-trading circuit breakers and other mechanisms did manage to stabilize the Dow, and phone lines and switchboards expanded in the wake of the 1987 crash were for the most part able to handle the tremendous volume of calls. But the smaller Nasdaq Stock Market had a terrible, horrible, no good, very bad day indeed.[41]

Now the second-largest stock market in the United States after the NYSE, the newer Nasdaq has a higher proportion of the high-technology stocks whose trading drove the Wednesday activity. Lacking a traditional market floor, it also depends heavily on its new and powerful computerized system for handling trades. On Wednesday, July 19, the rocketing trade volume exceeded the computer's capacity, causing at first delays and later almost a complete halt in trading. Customers trying to shift to phone lines instead also overloaded the switchboard capacity of Nasdaq traders; many could not get through at all during the critical hours when the market bottomed out before starting its rise. It was not a repeat of October 1987, but it came uncomfortably close. It would seem that we are not yet quite finished learning all the lessons of the potential risks of computer trading.

Conclusion

Because markets trade in wealth rather than creating it, because what they deal in are symbols and promises rather than tangible goods, they have been able to exploit the new opportunities of computers, computerized databases and information systems, and computerized networks almost as quickly as the technical means have progressed. In the process, they have transformed the structure of the financial world in ways that were never anticipated. What started out as technical improvement and technical change quickly evolved into systemic, technological change, in the broadest sense, reconfiguring the institutions that developed and deployed them.

As computerized networks and powerful satellite communication links make markets accessible from almost anywhere on the globe, experienced traders with a vested interest in making and stabilizing markets are increasingly being displaced by a new breed of "paper entrepreneurs," computer wizards who depend on their computers

rather than experience, seeking to make short-term profits by antici-
pating small market movements rather than long-term ones by creating a pattern of stable investments, driving the market in response to
trading programs with little or no concern for the underlying economic activity.[42]

With access to rapid, accurate information and fast response times,
the opportunity to make many small profits by quick trading to capi-
talize on time lags, small movements between and among markets, or
rapid transactions in secondary instruments, is a tempting alternative
to the traditional processes of seeking sound investments. Why invest
large sums and wait for market movements in response to the comparatively glacial change in economic indicators when larger profits
can be made more quickly by investing in derivatives, or speculating
on future movements on margin?[43]

Thoroughly modern Bertie, sitting on a beach in Belize, may trade in
relatively real things, such as securities or money, in a variety of new
secondary instruments that exist only because the power of networked
computers makes trading in them possible, or even seek to profit on
minuscule differentials or time delays between markets separated by
continents. He does not need to submit to traditional exchanges, nor to
the trading restrictions imposed on national markets by exchanges or
governments.

The computerized networks of information and communication established to allow powerful, centralized, vertically organized firms
and banks to exert better control over financial markets are now transforming into networks of action, dispersing their power and decreasing their control. Over time, the large firms and banks may simply become convenient nodes for such physical inputs and outputs as are
required. Traditional government regulation was designed and implemented to impose order on the system through its leverage on these
concentrated nodes. As their importance decreases, so will regulatory
effectiveness.

To adapt, regulators would have to accept that they can no longer
regulate effectively from the traditional position of an outside authority, able to control a few large firms by rewarding good behavior and
punishing bad. To do so in the newly dispersed markets would involve a degree of intrusiveness and control that would be neither effective nor affordable.[44] The alternative would be to devise regulatory

structures adapted to the new circumstances. Horizontally rather than vertically oriented, these regulators would be charged with entering into the networks as co-equals, using people and equipment as sophisticated as those of the traders to monitor behavior by participation and involvement.[45] As with the case of the California Highway Patrol being visibly present on major highways over holiday weekends, their presence alone would have a considerable effect.

Unfortunately, no such entity is yet on the horizon. The coordination costs would be enormous, and so would the knowledge burden that would be imposed on regulators or other agents, who would have to become at least as proficient in the uses and misuses of the new technology as those whose behavior they are trying to identify and detect.[46] Such self-organization and self-regulation would require at least tacit acceptance by traders of the validity and legitimacy of both the rules and their enforcers. But that in turn would require the formation and maintenance of precisely those kinds of social exchange relations that characterized the traditional, centralized markets the new computerized trading systems are systematically deconstructing.

6.

Jacking into the Market

The Demise of Barings P.L.C.

In 1992, Barings P.L.C., a small, highly regarded British banking firm, hired one Nicholas W. Leeson, installing him in its small office in Singapore. Over the next few years, Mr. Leeson made a reputation as an expert trader over the global network, using his computer, and his computer programs, to make small but significant profits on tiny differences between the prices of financial instruments in Japan and in Singapore.[1] In January 1995, for reasons still not fully understood, Mr. Leeson abandoned the strategy of matching the prices of derivatives and began trading in them directly, making large purchases of futures on the Japanese stock market. These turned out badly, stimulating him to make further purchases in an effort to cover his losses and hedge his bets. But neither his purchases nor his strategies were very effective. By late February, he was threatened with margin calls, which would have required him to put up large amounts of cash to cover the options.

On Thursday, February 23, faced with possible exposure, he simply disappeared from Singapore, leaving behind him near contracts with a face value of nearly $30 billion and almost $1 billion in debts. The consequences were severe. Although highly regarded, Barings' capital did not exceed $500 billion. It had little choice but to declare bankruptcy and close its doors permanently.[2] The ripple effects were felt throughout the world's markets. Stocks fell sharply in New York, London, and Japan, but recovered somewhat when it was realized that the Barings loss would be contained. Institutional investors as well as traders expressed the need to exercise more caution, and more control. But no specific recommendations were offered.

The collapse of Barings illuminates the consequences of the institutional and structural changes that have overtaken financial markets. Before the advent of computer trading, no single person of any age would have had the access and power of Mr. Leeson, nor been able to act so independently. The official report on the demise of Barings suggests that the bank was negligent in failing to supervise Mr. Leeson more carefully, or to look into the enormous profits that were being run up in the Singapore accounts. That the bank itself was otherwise engaged in the somewhat dubious practice of front-running, trading on its own in advance of major activity for clients, might also have been a contributing factor.[3] This does not affect the observation that he could not have run up such huge losses without the access and range given him by the new techniques, or even attempted to do so before the creation of global markets in futures and derivative financial instruments.

Whatever his faults, Mr. Leeson was at worst a bad investor. In that he differs sharply from Joseph Jett of Kidder, Peabody, or Victor Gomez of Chemical Bank, who perpetrated direct fraud on their companies through access to their computers. And his mistakes were certainly less troublesome in the long term than those of Robert L. Citron, the treasurer of Orange County, whose speculation on derivative instruments tied to interest rates bankrupted it, threatening the stability of the entire American market in municipals and other interest-free securities.

Incidents such as these are neither new nor unique. As long as markets exist, there will be temptation; as long as information has value, there will be those who try exploit it; as long as some people are able to have direct access to company funds, and to the remote trading afforded by the computerization of financial markets, there will be those who seek to take advantage of it. And, particularly in the cases of Mr. Leeson and Mr. Gomez, as long as there are so many new opportunities for speculation and fraud afforded by direct access to internationalized secondary instruments and global financial markets, there will be those who try to make a quick killing, particularly if they do not have to bankroll their own gambles. Controlling such abuses has been one of the primary goals of market regulation. But neither national nor international governmental regulation has the means or the authority to gauge the honesty of another Jett, control the speculative activities of another Citron, or supervise the wide range of transborder activities that computers are now making possible.[4]

Self-regulation by the institutions themselves seems equally difficult, and perhaps equally improbable. The lack of oversight that character-ized so many of the cases mentioned previously was at least as remark-able as the cases themselves; senior managers (or, in the case of Mr. Citron, the county government) certainly bear some responsibility for having allowed such unsupervised discretion. But according to most reports, the advent of networked computer trading had much to do with it. With direct access to markets and accounts, trades are not "vet-ted" as they were in the days of traditional firms, where junior people could not exceed certain limits without approval. Banks and other financial firms are having a great deal of difficulty in controlling global, networked operations, particularly when faced with the time pressures of trading volatile instruments in computerized markets.[5] Moreover, as so clearly expressed by Saul Hansell in his story in *The New York Times*, "Another common problem is a financial generation gap. Often, the senior managers of a company who are supposed to be doing the mon-itoring do not really understand the complicated new instruments and take a laissez-faire attitude toward the younger financial traders who have grown up on this sort of financial Nintendo."[6]

In the long run, that may not matter. The human face of trading is vanishing. Morgan-Stanley has eliminated humans as much as possi-ble, with spectacular success. Most trading is becoming a "no-brainer," which could eliminate intermediary brokers and other middlemen. Even poor old Bertie in Belize, whose promotion was based on his care-fully acquired market intuition, will have difficulty holding his job against the latest generation of computer-knowledgeable whiz kids. And his demise may soon be followed by that of the institutions them-selves. With function and skill dispersed around the net, with a web of buyers and sellers working directly via computers, who needs Wall Street, or Chemical Bank at all, other than as a convenient location to cash in profits? And with full electronic banking and accounting, with transactions and accounts moving from paper into computers, who needs locations at all?

Trading in Cyberspace

In his 1984 novel *Neuromancer*, William Gibson, one of the founders of the "cyberpunk" genre of science fiction, coined the term "cyberspace" to describe an interactive electronic universe in which the accounts and data and information banks maintained by the world's economic and financial institutions were connected and interconnected by a vast and fully integrated electronic network.[7] The hero (or antihero), a futuristic extension of today's antisocial security cracker, is given the task of penetrating this electronic web in search of valuable information. He does so by "jacking in," plugging himself into an electronic device that projects his persona into an interactive space that is more a projection than a representation of the electronic instrumentalities and interactions. Data banks and sources of information appear as large physical structures, fiercely protected against intruders by electronic defense mechanisms known as "ice"—whose effects are not just virtual, but physical, propagated out through the electronic brain implants to which the jacking device is connected.

Today's electronic markets are not yet as interconnected, or as well defended, as those sketched out by Gibson a decade ago, but they are evolving much faster in that direction than anyone would have predicted. Cyberspace as metaphor, stripped of the more-than-virtual reality upon which Gibson's creation finally depends for much of its action, is becoming a common term to describe the network of rapid and tightly coupled interactions by which banks and other financial institutions are moving the symbols of financial value around the globe in unprecedented volume.

Because direct trading in commodities, securities, and financial instruments is still constrained to some degree by the physical reality of the commodity, or the firms and industries in whose name the original shares or instruments were issued, primary markets are not as much affected by electronic trading as are secondary ones (such as futures) or derivatives. The clearest example of what the future might bring is found in financial markets. Because they have long dealt solely with the exchange of symbols and tokens, contracts and promises, they were able to react more quickly than most to the increased capacity (as well as capability) provided by the new means of communication and interaction.

In the days when currencies were at least in principle redeemable for actual gold or silver, trading in money had definite limits. But the world monetary system, and, in particular, that part having to do with settlements and accounts, has long moved beyond representation to social construction. All that limits transactions is the need for reconciliation of the bookkeeping. Once institutional accounting was transferred almost entirely to computerized accounting systems and humans taken out of the transfer and exchange loop, the transfer of funds between one institution and another became limited in scope and velocity only by the size of the accounts involved and technical constraints on the transfer system.[8]

As improved means for interconnection increased capacity, the volume of traffic rose dramatically. The numbers involved are staggering. According to financial consultant Peter Schwartz, who helped London make its Big Bang transition in 1986, international foreign exchange transactions had already reached $87 *trillion* by 1986, more than 90 percent of it generated by electronic transactions.[9] By 1991, the daily flow of money in the United States was more than fifty times the amount held at the Federal Reserve for settlement of bank accounts; CHIPS, the Clearing House Interbank Payments System owned by eleven New York Banks, and the Federal Reserve were together moving more than $1.5 trillion over electronic networks each and every working day.[10]

How can the amounts be so large? Although reserves are finite, not only are electronic money transactions flows rather than stocks, they have become decoupled from the stock of underlying reserves. Transfers over the network are limited only by agreed upon rules and regulations. Before the electronic revolution, the minimum time required to move a dollar back and forth even between two banks in the same city was measured in hours. Now it is measured in fractions of a second, and the same symbolic dollar can move back and forth between continents many times in only a few minutes.

More rapid and frequent transactions in greater volume have essentially decoupled financial flows from movements in primary markets, or anything else connected with real-world economic activity.[11] Moreover, the size and complexity of the resulting flows, as well as their increasingly tenuous coupling to physical realities, has already led Schwartz and others to foresee the coming of "virtual reality" software that models the financial marketplace in three dimensions, perhaps representing each institution differently according to its reserves, the rate of activity, and the ease of doing business with it.[12] And of course, this virtual software would have to include even more robust defenses against attack by intruders and criminals than does the present system. Cyberspace indeed.

Vulnerability

As the financial world shifts over to an all-electronic system for transactions, the consequences of possible failures, whether of systems or of confidence, have become a matter of serious concern. Global markets in particular are now so dependent on electronic transactions that a single serious failure, or a case of fraud or theft that causes loss of confidence in the honesty or accuracy of transactions, would be extraordinarily costly. Indeed, there have already been some reports of electronic theft or fraud, some of it systematic, even if not (yet) at the scale of underground warfare glorified by the cyberpunk novelists.[13]

The temptation for intrusion into financial and other global markets is enormous, particularly since even the siphoning off of several million dollars would be noticed only in the final accounts; it would hardly be detectable given the volume of trading. As a result, financial and other institutions have made huge investments in secure encryption. Improvements in dual-key encryption, the most secure method, were on the verge of putting security almost theoretically beyond reach when the U.S. government stepped in, insisting on a method that would provide federal agencies with a passkey of their own. The resulting debate vividly illuminates the new range of issues appearing as indirect and secondary effects of the technological transformations that are accompanying the efforts to exploit the new technical capabilities of rapid, integrated, computer-based communications.[14]

The government's argument is that the availability of secured and encrypted networks for communication would provide to criminals a means of reliable coordination and interaction without fear that anyone was snooping or eavesdropping. Pornography, for example, could move freely over the net. Drug deals or terrorist planning could take place openly and without fear of eavesdropping. And large sums of money could be moved around rapidly and undetectably, either for the purposes of organized crime or to evade taxation. Encryption would interfere with snooping and reduce the opportunity for infiltration, two of the favored tools for penetrating such operations. The remedy was to propose restrictions on public codes of a specific degree of complexity (and therefore security) to those for which keys were available, and to further prohibit any unkeyed encryption beyond the government's capability to crack.

The results were about as would be expected. The initiative was opposed both by libertarians promoting web democracy and by businesses and other individuals seeking to ensure maximum security for communications and transactions. Meanwhile, those financial and other firms who could afford it began to move to private networks not subject to the government's restrictions, and therefore also not subject to any form of governmental regulation or control.

Few of these issues have been resolved as of this writing, and it is not certain how, or when, they might be. What is most interesting from the point of view of this book is how well they illustrate the ways in which the creation and expansion of new technical capabilities, even those as narrowly defined as better ways of moving bits of data between computers, may cause long-term and indirect effects that strongly alter the way in which people visualize and interpret their status and role in society, both with regard to relationships with governmental actors and with regard to other forms of social interaction.

Nor is the action of criminals the only concern where international markets and international networks are involved. The range of possible actions, legal, illegal, and of uncertain status, of legitimate traders seeking to exploit gray areas of behavior in the evolving electronic markets is as difficult to imagine and anticipate as that of presumptive criminal outsiders trying to attack them. Only constant monitoring would allow real-time control of, for example, traders seeking to manipulate markets to their own ends during off-hours or other slack periods.

Trading within formal rules has historically always had some regulation and control imposed upon it, even if that finally is no more than a moral code imposed to provide enough visible proof of fairness to encourage market outsiders to participate. But none of the regulatory strategies, formal or informal, that have historically been used to ensure market stability and fairness will likely be able to fully address the problems of safeguarding the increasingly complex, rapid, and automated electronic trading networks of the future. It is difficult at this point even to imagine what some of the possible modes of fraud and abuse might be. What we can learn from the history of human affairs in general, and markets in particular, is that this is one of those areas where human creativity exerts itself to the utmost.

Markets out of Control

The question of the stability and predictability of markets that have been fully converted to electronic trading is also still unresolved. The computers are playing a quick-response interactive game with open rules, incomplete information, and small but significant time delays. This can at times result in various modes of delayed feedback, positive and negative. Physical exchanges and human intervention provided a damping factor that usually prevented such mechanisms from running away.[15] The result could well be formal chaos; an interactive, aggregate system whose responses and fluctuations may be more a characteristic of the system itself than of any external factor.[16] If that is so, the market may rise, or fall, or crash, without warning.[17]

Considering the enormous concern that surrounded the loss of communications, or access to trading computers, in the wake of the market crash of 1987, or any other event that interrupted the normal flow of activity in computerized markets, it is remarkable that their vulnerability to a severe disruption, or to sudden loss of any of the major players, has never been carefully examined. Nor is it clear how effective are the measures that firms have taken to ensure their own continuity and records. Distributed computing has penetrated organizations so quickly that few have completely adapted to it.[18] Following the bombing of the World Trade Center, data recovery experts had many harsh words about the backup and recovery status of LANs and file servers. The loss of data after major disasters, or from servers and networks that are globally rather than locally linked, would be far more serious.

In a tightly networked system, particularly one such as global finance where electronic records are becoming primary, any incident that disrupts one of the major actors or major trading sites disrupts all. Manifest disarray, or uncertainty over the status of records and transactions, could have an aggregate ripple effect (e.g., through temporary withdrawal resulting from loss of confidence in the accuracy of trading) that far exceeds the direct costs to the organization or center involved, or, through the kind of feedback seen in 1987, drags markets down because potential buyers cannot gain access.

What is not known is the extent to which networked global markets are sufficiently robust, or sufficiently resilient, to absorb negative incidents ranging from a hacker attack to a bombing, or, if they are, what will happen if they are tested beyond the expected limits. In traditional, localized, nonautomated market systems, the human actors, and their written records, were the ultimate repository of information. They knew that if all else failed (and there was little else to fail), the market could be restored and the data recovered, even if they had to go back to trading by hand, or in closed rooms.

Those who transfer funds, securities, bonds, or derivative instruments over the face of the globe, along electronic networks whose details and structure they do not understand, between computers and computerized databases they do not fathom and cannot program or query without professional help, do not have that comfort. In that respect, they are similar to air traffic controllers deprived of their paper routing slips, or pilots flying aircraft with no manual controls. The difference is that the pilots, and the controllers, are very aware indeed of what the costs of loss of control would be. It is not at all clear that the same is true of those who are striving for further electronic sophistication in market systems in search of competitive advantage.

Global Markets

There are two competing visions of the emerging electronic markets. One, based on market experience, tradition, and the conventional social myths of the markets' meaning and purposes, asserts that the risks are minor, manageable, evolutionary, and constrained by objective reality.[19] The other, based on a less optimistic and less politically conservative view of the dynamics of technology and society, fears that the market will become deconstructed and fragmented—increasingly abstracted from historical and objective context, and increasingly separated from experience and tradition.[20]

Such fragmented markets, stripped of context, manipulating arcane symbols and eluding the understanding not only of regulators but also of the elites who create and operate them, seem to fulfill the nightmare visions of postmodern economics.[21] Wall Street was salvaged following the October 1987, crash by those who retained a vested interest in its well-being. But they were operating on a single, national market, with an electronic and communications network of limited scope, and limited trading capabilities, and within the known time boundaries of traditional trading hours.

The outlines of the future system are at best only dimly visible. Global trading is still in its infancy. Most twenty-four-hour trading at present is in foreign exchange, and many traders with formal twenty-four-hour profiles appear to maintain these more for the sake of presence and status than for the trading itself.[22] Global stock indexes and information systems have arrived, but despite all the hype that surrounded it in the late 1980s, round-the-clock, round-the-globe trading still has not.[23]

Some critics, such as Stoll, argue that it will not, using as an example the failure of Reuter's Globex system to create electronic trading on commodity exchanges.[24] After several years of operation, trading still takes place mainly on the floor on the Chicago exchange, as it does on London's Financial Futures Exchange. Stoll argues that the reluctance to move, despite demonstrable gains to be made in efficiency, is based partly on conservatism and inertia, and partially on the costs of running and participating in a twenty-four-hour market. More important, in his view, is the recognition by experienced traders that their expertise will be seriously devalued if the nature and structure of trading is significantly altered.

But most analysts believe that such an evolution is inevitable, driven by competition if nothing else, that global markets will grow in scale and volume and become accessible around the clock by integrated analytic and communications networks larger in scope and effect than any of the individual markets they affect, operating by rules even more arcane and abstracted from historical myths than the markets themselves. There is every reason to be concerned that the Crash of

1987 could be replicated on a larger scale, over a wider range of econo-mies, and without the pliability to remedial action that saved the NYSE.[25]

The remedies that were suggested following the 1987 crash seem modest in the extreme.[26] Even so, many were rejected by the financial community as excessive. Halting trading altogether in a crisis would be as likely to exacerbate as calm a panic; meanwhile, increased access to other markets via global trading systems would spread the effects around the world. What have been implemented are specific restric-tions on program trading, stricter controls on futures markets, and other "circuit-breaker" mechanisms that call for a temporary halt to program trading when the index moves more than a certain range.[27]

These are likely to be increasingly ineffective as trading becomes global, and far too slow for rapid response systems such as futures or currency. Volatility is making governments increasingly nervous, while the push for efficiency is exerting a constant pressure to move toward more powerful computerized trading that can only increase volatility. Moreover, the costs of retrieving the Crash of 1987 and a later minicrash in 1989 have caused many to become more cautious about intervention.

Even if intervention is attempted at a national level, it may still fail because of the dynamic that results from trying to reconcile cross-national markets, methods, and objectives. Some nations are bound to continue to heavily favor the free-market approach, arguing that regulatory costs are inefficient and drive participants to less regulated competitors. Given the new structure of the electronic net, firms and individuals would simply shift their base of operations to the least reg-ulated locations. This could lead to what OTA has characterized as "regulatory arbitrage," in which regulatory supervision of all markets is steadily driven downward to match the level of that in the least reg-ulated.[28] Over time, regulation would cycle down to the vanishing point.

The result would be a world where the demise of existing regulatory structures would not lag far beyond that of fixed markets and the large, internally differentiated and vertically integrated financial insti-tutions that grew up around them, leaving behind a truly dispersed net of aggressively independent, unregulated, highly competitive firms, each seeking competitive advantage by any means available.

Such postmodern anarchy would more closely resemble the classic Hobbesian world of each against all others than the visions of virtual community and cooperative enterprise put forward by the technical optimists.

Backing into the Future

Even in its infancy, global, computerized trading already poses challenges for regulators and governments, which is why Congress asked the Office of Technology Assessment to add to its extensive review some prognostications about the future. Charged with looking across the broad range of technical, structural, and regulatory possibilities, OTA put forward three dominant scenarios: gradual evolution from present arrangements, radical change from severe market disruption, and the initiation by markets and institutions of an entirely new set of rules and procedures.

The first scenario leads progressively toward global cooperation. Bilateral agreements slowly expand to regional and then to global scale. Outstanding differences over technical, structural, and regulatory matters are resolved one by one into a stable, overall framework. Or, in a more extreme variant, a period of weak economic growth and poor market performance leads institutions and markets to convince governments that radical movements toward integration are required. The result is much like the above, but less gradual. This vision is gentle, optimistic, and emphasizes cooperation, much like idealist views of the future of international politics.

The second and third scenarios are less optimistic. In the second, some event (e.g., a Tokyo earthquake, a major scandal in London or New York) triggers a crisis in markets already stressed by weak economic performance or structural or technical deficiencies. The major disruption that follows creates the political will to establish an international regulatory regime around a new international financial institution of even greater scope and authority than the World Bank or the International Monetary Fund. This agency then becomes the engine for global integration.

The third scenario is much like the second, but triggered by an endogenous event, such as a crisis of investor confidence. Bear markets and economic downturns slow market growth, and efforts at further international cooperation fade under national regulatory and protectionist pressures. Once again, a central institution is created on a global scale. But this institution is more like a central police force than a financial parliament, and would have to be given an effective arm with which to impose punitive damages if unheeded.

On the surface, these three scenarios differ widely. On second look, what is more notable is that all three cases lead to outcomes in which the historical concentration of power will persist, or even increase. This seems very much out of step with the conclusions being reached by other analysts, and with the evolutionary course pointed out in this chapter and the previous one. Why have OTA and so many other political actors spent so much time and effort on constructing in great detail scenarios that increasingly diverge from visible trends? One possible answer is that OTA is also a governmental entity, and believes in the vision of governments as the indispensable agents of legitimation and control.

Complementary to the OTA view is that of analysts from the traditional financial community, which is framed by the assumption that an integrated, worldwide electronic marketing network will contain no surprises because it is the creation of their will.[29] The political community simply reverses that causality, and, in the face of considerable contrary evidence, asserts that governments can always choose whether or not to control the effects of technical development, that it is a matter of will, and of politics, and not of technology.

Neither is willing, nor able, to abandon their traditional beliefs, to challenge the basis or relevance of their historical behavior, or to admit that they are losing control of processes they themselves had nurtured. The financial old guard seems not to have considered the extent to which both its legitimating myths and the social and historical contexts in which they were created are being rapidly deconstructed by the technological forces they so eagerly embraced. In that, they are probably acting no differently than other firms, in other sectors of industrial economies, for whom the evidence is less clear and the effects more subtle. James Q. Wilson once used as a metaphor for the description of mechanistic regulation the notion of a "dead hand" on the throttle, taken from the lore and language of railroad engineering.[30] It seems equally apt here, and perhaps more consequential.

Market or Matrix?

Primary markets trade in notional pieces of paper that are said to represent the actual business or company in which one invests. Secondary markets such as those in futures or interest rates instead represent bets (or, more politely, educated guesses) on primary market movements. The new electronic markets make possible a definitive move into a state of higher abstraction where the movement of movements can become the center of activity, creating derivative markets increasingly decoupled from the value of the industries and firms in whose name the original paper (if there was paper at all) was issued.

The paradoxes of risk and opportunity are clear. Extensive program trading requires constant monitoring and intervention via computers and computerized networks, but the growing volume of computer trading can marginalize or displace market experience. Market volumes and profits have increased greatly, but program trading tends to drive out small investors, and has been blamed for increased volatility and destabilization. Global trading via telecommunication and information networks opens world markets even to individual investors, but raises the prospect of rapid and destabilizing movements of capital across national boundaries. Integration of computers and information systems makes rapid decisions possible, but the rapidity with which actions can take place and the increasingly tight coupling between and among them may prove to be destabilizing.

Thus far, the benefits have been clear and the risks problematic, and the push for change therefore continues unabated. As the coupling among exchanges, and between exchanges and trading computers, becomes more important than the coupling to the real word of economics and finance, the electronic networks that the markets created will gradually supplant them not only as the focus but also the locus of major financial activity. And if present trends continue, electronic trading and computerized, programmed responses will increasingly replace estimates of the "value" of corporate stocks, or currencies, with prices negotiated automatically by computerized programs that deal purely in symbols.

As with so much of science fiction, the visions of the future offered by Gibson appear in retrospect to have been prescient. As trading moves from exchange floors to electronic networks, the computerized databases are becoming the "real" repositories both of the assets and of the rules, models, and calculations that underlie their trade. The links between them are creating a network of cross-market and cross-national trading that has been characterized as anywhere from confusing to bewildering to simply beyond understanding.[31]

The regulation and perhaps even control of global, computerized trading is not, in principle, an impossible task, but for a variety of reasons, social and political as well as technical and regulatory, it is likely to be a difficult one. As Passell has noted:

> What all the experts fear is what they do not know. Could the technology of funds transfer outrace the mechanisms of control, as it may have done in the early days of CHIPS? Could Wall Street, in its relentless quest for new products to peddle, invent one that unwittingly destabilizes the payments system? Could a competing payments network offshore, operating under other rules in other time zones, generate some perverse synergy that fatally damages [it]?
>
> Almost anything is possible, suggests James Grant, "in a world in which the electronic leverage—the ratio of newfangled photons to old-fashioned banking dollars—is enormous."[32]

Conclusion

Because financial markets trade mostly in symbols, and have always sought faster and more complete information, they are not only the most willing but also the best adapted of the large, complex institutions of modern societies to accept and incorporate computer-based, integrated systems as fundamental and constitutive elements of operation and communications. It is doubtful that any other large technical system would or could move as quickly, or as dynamically, particularly those that deal in products and other tangible artifacts. Even within the domain of markets, those that trade in futures or finance have moved more quickly and irreversibly than those trading in commodities or other instruments more closely coupled to physical reality.

If global markets continue to grow and integrate, they will become important because of the long-term social and cultural effects that the

loss of general and public control over such an extensive, major seg-
ment of economic activity would have on individuals' perceptions of
their role and status in society and the degree of control that they personally can exercise, alone or in combination, over large institutional
actors.

It is, of course, possible that the current wave of computerization of
markets will go not much further, or may even contract, that the futur-
ist vision of global electronic trading around the clock will prove to be
just that, a vision, and that traditional players with traditional interests
will reassert control over markets and mechanisms, if for no other reason than to defend the value of their carefully nurtured expertise
against computer-trading whiz kids. If that is so, they will set an interesting precedent, for the displacement of expertise is a more general
phenomenon that is taking place as the result of extensive computerization, with consequences that will be discussed in detail in the next
chapter.

Epilogue

Some events in the world move faster than one can write about them.
When I submitted the prospectus of this book in 1990, the volume of
trading in derivative financial instruments worldwide was about $4
trillion, and the instruments were considered to be interesting opportunities with some risk. By 1994, when the first draft was completed,
the volume had risen to $10 trillion and was growing rapidly, and
leading economists such as Henry Kaufman and Alan Greenspan were
already expressing their concern, both over the volume of the trading
and the nature of the traders. In early 1995, the collapse of Barings
P.L.C., and the impending bankruptcy of Orange County, triggered
another wave of even more serious concern.

On July 21, 1995, the weekly WNET financial show, "Adam Smith,"
analyzed the role of derivatives in the Barings collapse, and, the following week, ran a special show on the derivative traders in which
they were compared to "rocket scientists," operating highly sophisticated equipment and working through remote sensors on the basis of
elaborate and perhaps untested mathematical models.[33] The traders
were shown in their electronic control centers; surrounded by video

screens and computers, they did indeed look like a cross between mission control in Houston and the set of "Star Trek."

The show went on to make a series of further points: that the traders were generally young, technically skilled, and willing to take risks; that the older and more cautious members of the firms they traded for often had at best a very poor understanding of what derivatives were, let alone the nature of the market; that by their nature and the nature of their trading, derivative markets were not only more volatile than traditional ones, but capable of moving very much faster; that the computer models and computerized trading programs they worked with had never been tested in a crunch, let alone a real crisis; and that such traditional notions as market equilibrium had no real meaning for a fully computerized, high-speed global market trading in instruments that were based entirely on calculations and prognostications of what other markets might or might not do.

With businesses now trading around the clock as well as around the world, global trading in derivatives was originally intended to create a series of hedges for business against worldwide movements in exchange rates, commodity prices, or other factors not under their control or even the direct or regulatory control of their home governments. What it seems to have created instead was described in the show as something between a space shuttle launch and a video game, played in a not-yet-virtual space where only the new generation of traders feels entirely comfortable.

The show was full of wonderful images used to graphically illuminate the arguments: Frankenstein's monster, nuclear explosions, Cape Canaveral, video games such as "Mortal Kombat." But the most telling image, and the most lasting, was the explosion of the space shuttle *Challenger*. Point made.

7.

Expert Operators and Critical Tasks

> In the airliner of the future, the cockpit will be
> staffed by a crew of two—a pilot and a dog. The
> pilot will be there to feed the dog. The dog will
> be there to bite the pilot if he tries to touch any-
> thing.
>
> (*Commercial airline pilot*)

> I've never been so busy in my life, and someday
> this [highly automated cockpit] stuff is going to
> bite me.
>
> (*Another commercial pilot*)

Having the Bubble

Over the past few years, my colleagues and I have studied the operation of aircraft carrier flight operations, nuclear power plants, air
traffic control centers, and other complex, potentially hazardous advanced technologies, using interviews and field observations to find
out what it is that makes some operations reliable and others not.[1] Out
of this research has emerged the beginning of a better language for
understanding the difference between these complex, critical, and reliability-demanding operations and more mundane and ordinary ones
with which most of us have direct experience.

Every group of operators we interviewed has developed a specialized language that sets them apart. Although every group expressed clearly their very special response to the demands for integration and interpretation placed on them, only in the Navy did we find a compact term for expressing it. Those who man the combat operations centers of U.S. Navy ships use the term "having the bubble" to indicate that they have been able to construct and maintain the cognitive map that allows them to integrate such diverse inputs as combat status, information flows from sensors and remote observation, and the real-time status and performance of the various weapons and systems into a single picture of the ship's overall situation and operational status.[2]

For the casual visitor to the operations center, the multitude of charts and radar displays, the continuous flow of information from console operators and remote sources of surveillance and intelligence, the various displays that indicate weapons systems status, what aircraft are aloft, and who is in them, the inputs from ship and senior staff, are overwhelming. What surprised us at first was that even experienced officers did not attempt to make overall status assessments on the basis of a casual visit. Only when you have the bubble do these pieces begin to fall into place as parts of a large, coherent picture.

Given the large amount of information, and the critical nature of the task, creating and maintaining the required state of representational mapping, situational awareness, and cognitive and task integration is a considerable strain. On many ships, operations officer shifts are held to no more than two hours. "Losing the bubble" is a serious and ever-present threat; it has become incorporated into the general conversation of operators as representing a state of incomprehension or misunderstanding even in an ambiance of good information.[3] In principle, the process could be carried through by logical, deductive chains of reasoning even if the bubble were lost, but even the most experienced of tactical officers would rather relinquish operational control if he loses the bubble than try to press on without it.[4]

When we mentioned this terminology in air traffic control centers and other operations exhibiting similar behavior, it was met with an immediate and positive acknowledgment. Because it expressed in compact form what they often have difficulty in explaining to outsiders, it has even become widely adopted.[5] It was as much of a surprise to them as it was to us to find out just how much behavior and culture was held in common by operators performing complex and safety-critical tasks in a variety of seemingly disparate industries and work environments. Subsequently, we have been able to identify behavior that we would describe as functionally and operationally equivalent in other studies, performed by other field workers who did not have the convenient label to attach to it.[6]

Operators also shared a number of concerns about the consequences of the lack of understanding of the nature and special character of their work, particularly by the engineering and management divisions of their own organizations.[7] The operational divisions consider themselves to be the reservoir of expert knowledge of how the plant or system actually works, in contrast to engineering divisions and other technical professionals (including consultants), who tend to think of it more in formal terms, such as design, drawing, specifications, rules, and procedures. Although operators respect the status and expertise of engineers and other professionals, they are very wary of interference from those who have almost no hands-on experience or other practical knowledge.

This is particularly apparent when professional consultants are called in to improve performance or reliability at the human-machine interface through technical or human factor improvements to plant or operational controls. As nuclear plant operators put it, the "beards" come in here, look around for an hour or two, and then go back and write up all these changes to the controls. Because it will cost the company a fortune, the decisions are going to be made upstairs (i.e., by managers and professional engineers). We'll have to argue for hours and hours about changes that will interfere with the way we work. And sometimes they make them anyway.[8]

We have heard similar comments from others who operate in such diverse working environments as air traffic control centers, electric utility grid management centers, and military combat command centers. The autonomy of design mentioned in chapter 2 clearly extends even into systems for which the consequences of error or poor user adaptation can be serious. In an observational study of commercial aviation similar in design to our field work, Gras and colleagues found that 75 percent of the pilots felt that engineers did not take the needs of users into account when designing an airplane, and almost 90 percent believed that the logic of designers differed substantively from that of pilots and other users.[9]

To those who study the history of technology, or of industrialization, these comments may seem typical of those made by industrial workers in the face of technical change. But it would be wrong to write off the comments of this particular group of operators as reflecting no more than preservation of status, maintenance of traditional prerogatives, or reflexive reactionary protection of role and position in the workplace. The operators in the systems we studied differ greatly from the general run of office workers, tool operators, and even skilled plant and process operators. They are highly trained professionals in an already highly automated environment. They were selected for study because they perform extraordinarily complex tasks with demanding requirements and heavy responsibilities for human life and safety, and because they can perform them well only by always performing near the top of their intellectual and cognitive capacities.[10]

The introduction of advanced automation is not an issue because of any putative threat to jobs or skills. Extensive automation and computerized controls already play a major role in all of these operations. For the most part, these operators easily accept the new representations of work described by those who have studied similar transitions in other types of organizations. Most of them are comfortable with computers as intriguing technical artifacts as well as a means of operation and control, and have at least a passing interest in and knowledge of the technical details of the hardware and software they are using. Their objections arise not from unfamiliarity with what computers are, or what they can do, but from concern over what computers are not, and what they cannot do, or at least what they cannot do well.

Because the technologies they manage are complex and sophisticated, and the range of possible untoward events is not only large but in some sense unbounded, skilled operators have developed a repertoire of expert responses that go beyond simple mastery of the rules, regulations, controls, and process flow charts. Although this is identified in different ways by different operators in different settings, there is a common sense that the cognitive map that distinguishes the expert operator from the merely competent one is not well enough understood to be "improved" upon by outsiders, particularly those whose skills lie more with engineering and technical systems than with operations and human performance.

There is in the human factors research community a growing sense that the operators may have a point, that there is some danger in tinkering with the systems they operate without gaining a better understanding of how they become expert and what that means.[11] In particular, there is a recognition that the introduction of computerized methods into control rooms and controls may increase the chance of operational error by interfering not only with the processes by which experts "read" system inputs, but also those by which expert skills come to be developed in the first place. Since all of the systems we studied were safety-critical, and involved the active reduction of risk by human management of inherently hazardous operations, the consequences can be serious.[12] And nowhere has this been more apparent than in the ongoing debate about the automation of airline cockpits.[13]

Pilot Error

On February 24, 1989, United Airlines Flight 811 from Hawaii to New Zealand suffered major damage when a door blew off in a thunderstorm, taking with it a large chunk of fuselage.[14] In addition to severe structural and control damage, nine people were sucked out, and twenty-seven injured. Fortunately for those aboard the 747, Captain David Cronin was one of the older and more experienced pilots in the fleet (and only one month from mandatory retirement at age sixty). Relying primarily on his judgment and thirty-eight years of accumulated experience, he managed to retain control of the aircraft by "feel" and bring it safely back for a gentle landing, a feat that was regarded as near-miraculous by those who examined the airframe afterwards.

A few months later, United Airlines Flight 232 had a disk come apart in one of the engines; the fragments of the disintegrating engine severed all hydraulic lines and disabled all three of the hydraulic control systems.[15] For the next forty minutes, Captain Alfred C. Haynes, a thirty-three-year veteran pilot, and his flight crew "rewrote the book" on flying a DC-10, improvising ways to control it, and coming heartbreakingly close to making a nearly impossible landing at the Sioux City, Iowa airport.[16] According to investigators and other expert pilots, the ability of the pilot to keep his aircraft under control, at all, let alone try to land it, was almost beyond belief; nor could any flight computer system, however complicated, have taken over from him.[17] Although 111 died when the plane turned over at the last moment, 185 survived.

A similar performance with a better outcome was that of Captain Bob Pearson when Air Canada 767 ran out of fuel over Red Lake, Ontario, because of an error in calculating fuel load on the ground. Fortunately for all, Captain Pearson was not only an experienced pilot, but an experienced military glider pilot. He was able to remember the runway orientation at an auxiliary airport in Gimli well enough to bring his streamlined, 132-ton "glider" in for a successful dead-stick landing.[18] The investigating team noted that it was amazing he was able not only to fly his sophisticated airliner without power, but to bring it to a safe landing.

Mechanical heavier-than-air flight is an inherently unnatural act. Only if machines and operators perform correctly, according to rather specific rules, can it be maintained. The consequences (hazard) of an uncontrolled air-to-ground impact, from any altitude, cannot be avoided or mitigated. The twin goals of air safety are therefore to reduce the risk through reducing the probability of error or failure, whether from equipment or design or through flawed human action. As aircraft grow more complex, the number of possible mechanical failure modes increases. As their operation grows more complex, the number of things a pilot can do wrong also tends to increase. Automation may reduce some types of erroneous actions, or technical mistakes, but it also creates new categories and types of error.[19] Every effort has been made to engineer greater safety into each generation of new aircraft, but there are always technical or economic limits. A modern jet airliner is a tightly coupled technical system with a great deal of complexity and comparatively little tolerance for poor performance in equipment, maintenance, or operation.

In the early days of passenger flying, it was assumed that passengers were knowingly accepting the risk involved, not only from major events such as outright mechanical failure or vicious weather but from other types of mechanical or human failure that were uncertain and difficult to anticipate—perhaps unknowable in advance of actual circumstances. Pilots were not just operators, but "experts," expected to

provide not just flying skills, but the ability to cope with the unanticipated and unexpected. That is exactly what happened in the cases
mentioned previously; experienced pilots and crews saved many lives
by appealing to ad hoc flying experience, procedures based largely on
the accumulation of experiential knowledge and familiarity with their
aircraft.[20]

Of course, not every story about airline accidents has the same diagnosis or outcome. Although some are caused by mechanical failures,
or errors in maintenance or design, pilots, being human, will err,
sometimes seriously, and flight crew performance problems continue
to dominate the accident statistics.[21] If the implicit assumption is that
all pilots are hired specifically to be experts in the cockpit, anything
short of a gross physical or environmental disaster so direct and so
unambiguous that no action could possibly have saved the aircraft
from accident can almost always be blamed post hoc on what the pilot
did, or failed to do.[22] But what if the situation is presented in the cockpit in such a way that the correct choice is obscured, masked with ambiguity, or does not give the pilot time for interpretation and response?
Consider, for example, the following cases, all of which were eventually ruled to be examples of pilot error by the relevant boards.

In January 1989, a British Midland 737 crashed just short of the East
Midlands airport in England, killing forty-four of the 126 passengers
aboard. The left engine had failed; while trying to reach the airport, the
pilot mistakenly shut down the functioning right engine as well.[23] In
September, another 737 plunged into the water at La Guardia airport
when a young, inexperienced copilot hit the wrong controls on takeoff.
On February 14, 1990, an Indian Airlines Airbus 320 simply flew into
the ground near Bangalore when its crew was distracted and did not
notice the loss of flight energy because the automatic controls kept the
plane steady.[24] On January 20, 1992, another A-320 crashed in mountainous terrain near Strasbourg, apparently because the crew set up
the wrong mode on one of their computerized instruments.[25]

Although there is a certain air of familiarity about these events, the
question of the ultimate source or origin of the human action ruled to
be in error requires a little more thought. In each case, the proximate
cause could be found to be the negligence or error of the flight crew.
But in all four there is some question as to whether the information
presented for pilot choice was as clear, or as unambiguous, as it should

have been. It may be true that more experienced pilots than the ones involved might have noticed that something was wrong more quickly, and recovered the situation (indeed, the pilot of the British Midland flight kept control even without working engines, saving many lives). But, of course, not every aircraft can be flown by experienced and expert pilots in every circumstance, nor is a pilot likely to become expert without making some mistakes.

The assignment of blame to pilot error assumes that people given sufficient information and a working mechanism will not fail unless they err—either by doing something they should not (commission) or by failing to do something they should (omission). All four of these incidents seem instead to fall into a third category of "representational failures," similar to what Karl Weick has called mistakes of "rendition."[26] Automation, advanced instrumentation, and other electronic aids that have created what pilots call the "glass cockpit" (because of the replacement of dials and gauges with computerized panel displays) may have reduced the probability of direct pilot errors, but it may well have increased the incidence and importance of indirect, renditional, or interpretive ones.[27]

The Glass Cockpit

Every new airliner has had shake-out periods, not infrequently accompanied by crashes resulting from design flaws or other mechanical difficulties. But the Airbus 320 was a source of concern even before it was commercially flown. Because it was the first commercial aircraft with a fully automated cockpit, it was an aircraft "apart" to its pilots as well as to the general public.[28] The pilots actuated the control computers rather than the controls, and the control computers were able to impose limits on what the pilots could demand of the airframe. The multitude of lights, dials, gauges, and other direct readouts, each with its own unique function and physical location, were replaced with a few large, multifunction, flat panel displays, capable of presenting a variety of data and information that have been analyzed and integrated by onboard computers to an unprecedented degree. Pilots were not just in a new cockpit, but in an entirely new flying environment.

Because this was the first commercial aircraft for which there was no

manual backup or override for the flight controls, much of the attention at first centered on the question of the reliability of the electronic
flight controls and their computers. Without manual backups, there
was always the prospect that an electrical failure or error in programming or installation could cause an accident beyond pilot intervention.[29] Only over time was attention paid to the more indirect and
long-term concerns of the pilots about the potential for systemic, operational failures caused by loss of direct involvement with the aircraft
rather than by technical malfunction.

Some of the major concerns expressed by pilots to human factors
consultants and other researchers interviewing them about glass cockpits have been:[30]

- Too much workload associated with reprogramming flight manage-
  ment systems
- Too much heads-down time in the cockpit attending to the systems
- Deterioration of flying skills because of over-reliance on automation
- Increasing complacency, lack of vigilance, and boredom
- Lack of situational awareness when automated systems fail, making it
  difficult to identify and correct problems
- Reluctance to take over from automated systems even in the face of
  compelling evidence that something is wrong

The first three of these relate directly to concern that pilots were becoming equipment operators and data managers instead of flyers. But
the last three lead to something more subtle.

It was analysis of the first few A-320 accidents that first raised the
question in the aviation community of whether control and display
automation had created new categories and possibilities for errors or
mistakes. In the Indian Airlines crash, the pilots seemed absolutely certain that the automatic control system would not allow their mistakes
to become fatal; they were both overconfident and inattentive.[31] As a
result, all Indian Airlines A-320s were grounded until the aircrews
could be retrained. The Strasbourg crash raised the further question of
whether human factors engineering, which had resolved so many of
the problems of preventing pilot misapprehensions in the increasingly
complex cockpits of precomputerized aircraft, had really understood
how much the new cockpit environment could interfere with situational awareness.[32]

The other major thread running through the pilots' concerns was the question of what it means to be a "pilot" at all in a modern, fully automated aircraft. As with the case of the automation of the industrial and business workplace, insertion of a computer into the operating loop moved the pilot one step further from direct involvement with flight. In the new cockpit, the pilot is a flight-system manager, an operator of the control system computers instead of one who flies the aircraft, or adjusts its controlling machinery, directly.[33]

More often than not, errors and failures in the cockpit are made by younger pilots; only for a few "unlucky" ones has the error been so serious that they were unable to learn from it. For most, the accumulated experience of small (or even medium) errors has been the basis for becoming an expert pilot. But how would learning take place at all once pilots became the controllers or managers of their aircraft instead of flying it? Would younger pilots, trained to fly with automated control and navigation systems that provide little intellectual or tactile feedback, and almost no discretion, still be able to invoke their experience or "feel" some ten or twenty years hence?[34]

Even as late as the 1930s, aircraft carried few instruments other than airspeed and fuel indicators, oil pressure and temperature (when appropriate), some navigational equipment, and perhaps a simple turn-and-bank indicator. Although instrumentation was greatly boosted during the Second World War, only with the coming of jet aircraft and improved avionics were cockpits stuffed with the multitude of dials and gauges with which we are now familiar. By the 1970s, military pilots also had to master operation of a wide range of complex and sophisticated avionics instrumentation, much of it for the sake of electronic warfare.[35] Learning to fly such an aircraft also meant mastering a considerable amount of formal knowledge and technical competence, but there can never be enough sophistication for someone whose primary goal is surviving multiple electronic threats.

The move toward computerized, fly-by-wire control was at first also driven by military requirements. As was rediscovered in Vietnam, and institutionalized in the military's Top Gun school, human performance is still a primary requirement even for the modern military pilot, who still becomes expert by mastering the art of flying, more or less directly.[36] But many military aircraft are physically capable of maneuvers the pilot could never execute, or, in some cases, survive.[37] Some are even designed with inherently unstable flight dynamics through portions of the flight envelope, either to increase maneuverability or for the sake of low radar profiles ("stealth"). In these regimes, they can *only* be flown by means of a flight computer.

Military pilots are encouraged to fly to the limits of their aircraft, and the aircraft, and the control systems, are designed to take them to the limits of what can be achieved. In contrast, the premium in commercial flight is on efficiency, on smoothness in flight, and on avoiding the risk of making even small errors. All of these are vastly improved in the glass cockpit. But at what cost? According to one reporter, "Pilots who fly the glass cockpit aircraft say they have never been busier, even though automated cockpits are supposed to relieve workload."[38] But busy doing what? Programming and making data entry, primarily, and reading and interpreting all of the visual displays.

Commercial pilots have become much better data monitors than before: but are they as good at monitoring the physical situation required to detect the onset of problems or fly out of unanticipated difficulty? According to recent human factors studies, the answer is still ambiguous.[39] It apparently takes even longer to get familiar with a glass cockpit aircraft than a traditional one, and it is not entirely clear whether simulators or other artificial aids are as useful for physical orientation as they are for learning the electronics suite.[40]

Because of the high salience of aviation safety, and the ability of pilots and other flying associations to make their voices heard, these concerns have finally been given serious attention.[41] Even in the avionics industry there is growing criticism—based at least partially on the grounds of experiential learning—of those who design control systems that require placing arbitrary limitations on what the pilot can or cannot make the aircraft do.[42] Aviation magazines ran special issues or sets of articles on the subject,[43] and the phenomenon spawned a specific name—the "glass cockpit syndrome"—which has since been generalized to describe other cases where human operators are removed from tactile and direct modes of operation and put into automated control rooms where computerized displays are their only sensory inputs.[44] As a result, both the airlines and the electronics industry have recently taken a more subdued, indirect, and cautious approach to cockpit automation. Pilots are being encouraged to let discretion decide their use of automatic systems, and airline companies and designers are backing off enough to keep the pilot in the control loop as a flyer as much as a manager.[45]

Circumstances roughly paralleling those that have arisen over glass cockpits have been described by other operators, ranging from air traffic controllers and nuclear power operators to others operating similarly complex systems that are less hazardous and therefore attract less attention.[46] In each case, there is a construct that expresses the integration of technical, process, and situational complexity into a single, spatio-temporal image that organizes and orders the flow of information and allows decisions to be made on the basis of overall, systemic situations and requirements. And in each case, there has been similar concern over the long-term effects of the introduction of advanced, computerized operational controls and process displays. But the outcome in other industries, where operators have neither the status nor the authority of commercial pilots, is far less clear.

Air Traffic Control

Related to ongoing controversy over the long-term effects of cockpit automation is the continuing discussion over the future automation of air traffic control, which presents a greater challenge for cognitive coherence. The pilot has only one aircraft to manage. Air traffic controllers have to manage a system of aircraft operated by individual pilots, moving in three dimensions in different directions at different altitudes and with different destinations, without losing track of any, keeping them on course and on time, and not letting any of them collide, or even violate the several very strict rules on altitude and distance separation.[47]

Although there has never been a midair collision between two aircraft under positive control, the rapid growth in airline traffic over the past few years is already stretching the capabilities of existing centers to the limits of what can be achieved using present technology.[48] This has prompted the Federal Aviation Administration (FAA) to turn to computer technology as the only way to increase traffic without compromising safety. The FAA was not content to limit itself to marginal upgrades when modernizing its antiquated equipment. A few years ago, it began a process for the design and installation of an automatic control suite to replace the old consoles. But a series of delays for a variety of technical and financial reasons provided time for the controllers, and their human factors consultants, to intervene strongly in the process.

The debate was similar to that over cockpit automation, but at a different level.[49] What air traffic controllers do is cognitively more complex and abstract than what pilots do, and the environment they manage is more extended and complexly linked socially, even if technically simpler. The kind of mental map that controllers build is not easily describable, even by the controllers; it has been described as "holistic knowing," a fully accessible interpretive model of the airspace they are managing based on intimate involvement in and experience with every detail of the process.[50]

If you visit any one of the present en route air traffic control centers, you will see a large, open room filled with an orderly array of desk-sized grey consoles dominated by large, circular display screens.[51] Each console has before it an operator, staring intently at the display and talking into a headset. Each is managing a "sector"—a geographical subset of the air space assigned to the center—which may have several dozen aircraft in it. The display screen at each console is two-dimensional and indicative rather than representative. Although it provides a flat map of the sector, and other important landmarks, there is no visual display of the type, altitude, or airspeed of the individual aircraft. Instead, each is represented by a box on the screen carrying some limited information (such as the flight number), and a small track indicating heading. Lining the screen on both sides are racks containing small slips of paper, the flight progress strips (FPSs) with aircraft identification and salient characteristics written upon them.

The novice observer is totally incapable of forming any visual map of the reality that is represented. That is a very special and highly developed skill possessed only by trained operators. To them, the real airspace is being managed through mental images that reconstruct the three-dimensional sector airspace and all of its aircraft. The consoles are there to update and feed information to the operator, to keep the mental image fresh and accurate; they neither create nor directly represent it. The displays and display programs are more primitive than any personal computer they, or their children, might have at home.

Nor is there anything remarkable about the computers that control the consoles. Even in those centers where the computers have been recently upgraded, the most polite term for their implementation is "old-fashioned." And the FPSs with their scribbled annotations look like a holdover from another century.

At the present time, en route air traffic control relies primarily on three tools: the radar information provided on the console; radio and telephone communication; and the FPSs sitting in the racks next to the visual displays.[52] Controllers have long insisted that the FPSs, continuously rearranged and marked up by hand even while computerized systems are fully operational, are an important, perhaps essential element of their ability to maintain cognitive integration, particularly during heavy traffic periods. Given that automation would impede the present system of managing the strips, and advanced automation might replace them altogether, the argument over whether or not they actually serve a central communicative or cognitive purpose has been the subject of continuing debate.[53]

The general conclusion has been that there is some risk in replacing them with an automated equivalent—even a display that replicates them.[54] It is not just a matter of whether manual operation should be encouraged, or how much is appropriate, but whether and to what degree the reallocation of functions that accompanies automation, the degree to which the "operator" actually controls the aircraft as opposed to being the operator of a system that does the controlling, will affect the performance of the operator when he or she has to step in to retake control.[55] Moreover, a great deal of the observed teamwork in air traffic control centers that has been deemed essential for maintaining the culture of safety has been based on the "silent" practices of mutual monitoring and tacit task allocation, and it is not yet clear how new modes of automation will interact with or affect them.[56]

A second and very pressing concern, even if the manual systems continue to be supported and nurtured, is that the introduction of automation will provide both a means and an excuse for increasing both the density of air traffic and the number of aircraft for which a single control set will be responsible. At most of the present centers, operators are still capable of managing the system "by hand" if the computers go down, using the paper slips at the sides of the consoles to maintain the mental images, and reconfiguring the distribution of aircraft in the airspace to a configuration that can be managed without visual tracking. At the increasing workloads that would accompany further automation, breakdowns or failures would present a double problem. Even at present loads, interference with cognitive integration, or the inability to form a cognitive map quickly enough, whether because of lack of manual aids or a loss of operator skills and practice, could cause a collapse of control that would at best cause the entire air traffic system to shut down until automation could be restored.

At increased load, an electronics failure could well leave operators with a traffic pattern too dense, too complex, or too tightly coupled to be managed by human beings at all, whatever their level of skill or experience. Getting it disentangled safely would be as much a matter of luck as of skill. Yet, the economic goal of increasing traffic density remains at least as important in justifying the system as modernizing and updating the increasingly obsolete electronics.

It has been pointed out by many that those who operate commercial aircraft or air traffic control centers have unique access to decision makers, not only because of the public visibility and salience of what they do, but because those in power are among the greatest consumers of their output. Although controllers had neither the status nor the political clout of pilots, they, too, were eventually able to convince the FAA and its engineers that the present record of safety depends greatly on their ability to form and maintain the "bubble," and that automation that is insensitive to operators and their understanding of their own task environments could pose serious dangers. If all goes well, the new automation system that does finally come online will reduce controller workload without disturbing representation or situational awareness, and will provide a means for accommodating manual aids such as the paper strips.[57]

The optimistic view is that the new approach represents formal recognition that many of those charged with operating complex technical systems safely do so through a remarkable process of cognitive integration, and that there might be a direct correlation between disrupting their representations and controlling public risk. A more pessimistic view is that commercial aviation is a very special case and not a generalizable one, that there are many other socio-technical systems of comparable risk where elites are less directly threatened, operators less empowered, and the locus of performance and reliability more diffuse.

Industrial and Other Operations

There are in modern industrialized societies many other industrial and technical systems that depend on operators for achieving a safe balance between performance and efficiency. In many cases, what has evolved over time is a technical array of equipment and controls that is totally bewildering to the outsider, and difficult to learn and master even for their operators. In nuclear power plants, for example, walking the plant to observe almost every job and piece of machinery is an integral part of operator training; gaining this level of familiarity with the machinery is the foundation on which integrated mental maps are built.[58]

Plant operation traditionally has been a form of integrated parallel processing. Operators integrate the disparate elements of the board conceptually, scanning instruments in known patterns and monitoring for pattern as well as individual discrepancies; when an alarm goes off, or there is some other indication of a problem, they scan rapidly across their varied instruments, seeking known correlations that will help diagnose the severity and cause of the event. There is increasing concern among the new generation of human factors analysts and human performance psychologists that automation, particularly if poorly done, will undermine this ability, reducing the ability of the operators to respond quickly in complex situations.

It has also been suggested that automation could actually increase workload in a crisis. Computer-displayed serial presentation of fast-moving events rather than the present essentially parallel system of more primitive displays may inhibit operators from keeping pace with events or quickly finding the most critical one.[59] Individual consoles improve data access, but also tend to block communication and otherwise interfere with collective interaction. This matters not only in emergencies, where rapid and coordinated response may be vital, but even in the course of ordinary task performance, where shared communication, especially regarding errors, is critical to the robustness and reliability of the task.[60]

Even when task integration is done at the individual rather than the team level, it is not an isolated activity, but part of a collective effort involving all members of the team, crew, or shift. Moreover, the processes of communication are not always verbal or visible. Because all controls and displays in a traditional control room have fixed, known locations, operators are able to maintain a situational awareness of each others' actions and make inferences about their intentions by observing their location and movement at the control panels. The use of CRT (cathode ray tube) displays and diagnostic aids such as expert systems linearizes and divides the process, organizing both data and presentations hierarchically and categorically according to engineering principles.[61]

The issues facing nuclear plant operators, chemical plant and refinery operators, and many others in the face of automation of plant control are therefore very similar to those facing pilots, or air traffic controllers.[62] But plant operators lack the status and public visibility to mount a similar challenge. Their concern is clear: that the new, computerized systems will remove them not only from control of the machinery or other operation, but from real knowledge about it. Although differently expressed, they also fear that expertise will be lost through evolution, that those who eventually supplant them will be trained primarily on computers and management systems, that no one with a deep and instinctive anticipatory sense for trouble will be at the controls, that taking away the easy part of an operator's tasks will make the hard ones more difficult.[63]

This was brought home to me quite sharply when I was interviewing in a nuclear power plant control room, and heard an operator say that he "did not like the way that pump sounded" when it started up. Although the instrumentation showed no malfunction, the pump was stripped down on the operator's recommendation, at which point it was found that one of the bearings was near failure. My research notes (and those of others doing similar work) contain dozens of similar stories, ranging from detection of the onset of mechanical failures to air traffic control operators intervening in an apparently calm situation because they did not like the way the "pattern" of traffic was developing.

"Smart" computerized systems for diagnostics and control will radically alter the situational and representational familiarity that fosters that level of expertise. As summarized by Hollnagel and colleagues, in their report of a recent workshop on air traffic and aviation automation, "Understanding an automatism is, however, often difficult because their 'principle of functioning' is different and often unknown.

Automatisms may be more reliable, but they are also more difficult to understand. In highly automated cockpits the basis for acting may therefore be deficient."[64] Chemical plant operators interviewed by Zuboff expressed similar concerns, in almost identical language:

> The new people are not going to understand, see, or feel as well as the old guys. Something is wrong with this fan, for example. You may not know what; you just feel it in your feet. The sound, the tone, the volume, the vibrations . . . the computer will control it, but you will have lost something, too. It's a trade-off. The computer can't feel what's going on out there. The new operators will need to have more written down, because they will not know it in their guts. I can't understand how new people coming in are ever going to learn . . . They will not know what is going on. They will only learn what the computers tell them.[65]

The Computer in the Loop

Computer-aided process control can serve as a useful aid to human judgment, in the cockpit as well as on the assembly line. Computer-aided diagnostics may aid pilots in diagnosing engine problems, nuclear power plant engineers in wading through the complexity of design books and blueprints, managers in establishing flow diagrams and sequences, and administrative and finance officers in evaluating how individual actions will ripple through a large and complex organization. And computerized displays and data management can analyze almost instantly a diverse and complex series of inputs and provide to the operator a variety of models and representations of the current situation.

But humans are human, and human error remains. The temptation is to try to reduce risk further by removing even the potential for human error, by inserting computers directly into the action loop to ensure that tasks, and in particular small tasks, are executed correctly. This is what was done to the Airbus to limit the maneuvers the pilot could order, and to military aircraft to prevent the pilots from flying into an unstable or dangerous part of the flight envelope. It is being considered in air traffic control to maintain separation, and in control rooms to prevent certain actions from being taken under predefined combinations of circumstances, such as opening an outside vent when an inside valve is leaking slightly radioactive steam.

This is the area of most contention between operational approaches, with their emphasis on crew and team performance, whole system overviews, integrative pictures, and near-holistic cognitive maps, and engineering approaches that seek to reduce the prospects for risk one element (and often one person) at a time. On the one hand, most errors are made during routine tasks; if computers take these over, the probability of error should decrease. On the other hand, depriving the human operators of practice, and possibly even context, might increase the chance of error in more critical and discretionary situations.

Human learning takes place through action. Trial-and-error defines limits, but its complement, trial-and-success, is what builds judgment and confidence. To not be allowed to err is to not be allowed to learn; to not be allowed to try at all is to be deprived of the motivation to learn. This seems a poor way to train a human being who is expected to act intelligently and correctly when the automated system fails or breaks down—that is, in a situation that comes predefined as requiring experience, judgment, and confidence as a guide to action.[66]

Computerized control systems can remove from human operators the opportunities for learning that make for correct technical judgments. In so doing, they may also remove from plants and processes those operators for whom personal responsibility and action was the prime motivation for engaging in such difficult and often unrewarded tasks. Yet, the growing complexity of many modern technical systems and the growth of the demands for both performance and safety that are placed upon them clearly requires better operators as well as better control and display systems. In principle, sensitive and interactive processes of design and implementation could show progress on both fronts. In practice, that is usually not the case.

The implementation of computer control almost inevitably causes the organization to seek greater efficiency sooner or later.[67] Even when that is not a primary purpose, managers are almost always quick to realize that automation will allow supposedly accurate situation evaluation and response in times much shorter than that required if humans are involved. For many of the new automated systems, the consequence is to reduce the margin of time in which any human being could evaluate the situation and take an action, rendering supposed human oversight either moot or essentially useless. Those humans who are retained are increasingly put there as insurance that someone will be around to mop up the mess if and when it occurs—or to divert the blame for consequences from the designers and managers. The epigraph at the beginning of this chapter was completed for me by a pilot to whom I repeated it. His version continued with an airline executive explaining why high-salaried pilots were not just phased out entirely. "Because," said the executive, "accidents will always happen, and no one would believe us if we tried to blame the dog."

The engineering solution is often to provide for additional redundancy by providing multiple and overlapping systems to monitor or control critical activities. Three separate and separately programmed control computers may be required, or three independent inertial guidance systems. But safety in the expertly operated systems we have studied depends not only on technical redundancy against possible equipment failures and human redundancy to guard against single-judgment errors, but also on that wonderfully scarce resource of slack—that sometimes small but always important excess margin of unconsumed resources and time through which an operator can buy a little breathing room to think about the decision that needs to be made, and in which the mental map can be adjusted and trimmed.

In many of the newer automated systems, however, such human requirements as slack, excess capacity, trial-and-error, and shift overlaps are often assumed to be wasteful, an inefficient use of resources to be engineered away.[68] In the worst case, that can lead to a plant or process that has no extra resources and no backup, and can collapse much more quickly in the case of extensive failure.

Computer-aided decision making, whether in actual operations or in management, finance, or administration, can serve as a useful aid to human judgment, and a source of rapid access to a considerable body of knowledge otherwise not easily retrieved. Indeed, many of the most successful of the current attempts at deploying "expert systems" fall into this domain. Other, similar systems may aid pilots in diagnosing engine problems, nuclear power plant engineers in wading through the complexity of design books and blueprints, managers in establishing flow diagrams and sequences, and administrative and finance officers in evaluating how individual actions will ripple through a large and complex organization.

As with the implementation of "expert systems" in other domains, the claim being made is that what is being introduced is not an autonomous system, but one that intelligently supplies the correct information needed to make informed decisions in complex task environments. But as computers are given such mundane tasks as managing and presenting information, there is a constant risk of a gradual slide into automation, which, by removing task definition and control from operators, begins to coopt context and rendition, to define and bound both the task environment and the discretionary time or range for human action. If the system designers have thoroughly explored the possible boundaries, well and good. If not, the potential problems are limitless.

For the operator in an emergency, deprived of experience, unsure of context, and pressed into action only when something has already gone wrong, with an overabundance of information and no mechanism for interpreting it, avoiding a mistake may be as much a matter of good luck as good training. The presumption is often that the person in charge is by definition an expert, and is there solely for the purpose of taking correct action when it is needed.[69] If that does not happen, the air is filled with cries of error and blame, on the outrageous, but not untypical grounds that it is the job of the operator to make good judgments, evaluate situations quickly, and act correctly, whatever the circumstances, whatever the context, and however infrequently the opportunities to learn from experience.

Conclusion

What having the bubble expresses in compact form is the formation and maintenance of an integrated, expert, cognitive map of a complex and extended set of operations by human beings performing critical operations in an environment where information is always too plentiful and time always too short. As might be expected from the description, such representations cannot be acquired quickly or simply. They require prolonged and stable apprenticeships, tolerance for the errors and blind alleys of learning, and elaborate and overlapping networks of communications both for their establishment and for their maintenance and support. Aboard U.S. Navy ships, for example, procedures for transferring and communicating information during shift changes are extensive. Tactical operations shifts overlap by up to an hour to ensure smooth transfer to the succeeding tactical officer without a potentially dangerous break in routine or perception. Similar procedures are followed in air traffic control, and, depending upon circumstances, in many other less pressing systems, such as nuclear power plant operations.

The costs are not small. For some, such as air traffic controllers, who feel their responsibility for human lives directly and frequently, these costs are often manifest at the personal as well as the professional level. Even for the others, the stress of their work and the responsibility they bear are considerable. Yet, these operators have for the most part chosen their line of work, they were not forced into it. Stress and responsibility also mean continuous challenge, sometimes excitement, and a real pride in their skill and accomplishments that does not require much in the way of public acknowledgment.

For the most part, neither their equipment nor their task environments have been optimally, or even coherently, designed. But the operators are intimately familiar with both and have mastered them. However designed or laid out, the controls, dials, and other instruments of their working environment become part of the structuring of control room processes and procedures, dynamically interpreting and translating the technical environment into action and social process.[70]

Operators can, and do, adapt to changes, particularly those that can be demonstrated to promise increased situational awareness and better task integration. But adaptation takes time, and effort; it is not something that operators should be put through without good and sufficient reason. Unless the instrument or control in question can be demonstrated to be faulty, ambiguous, or misleading, the operators would rather live with what they have than submit to changes that will impose upon them an additional learning burden without providing provable benefits.

Engineers and other experts involved in the specification and design of new automation systems for aviation were at first relatively insensitive to operator concerns and operating procedures.[71] The concerns of pilots and controllers about the realities of operation in the real world (as opposed to the idealized one in which designers operate) were brought into the process only as the result of a major struggle, and only when the operators themselves found allies among political and business elites, as well as in the professional community of consultants and advisors. In less salient and more ordinary cases where a similar degree of automation of similarly complex, and similarly hazardous, technical operations is taking place, the very similar concerns of the operators are rarely given serious consideration, either by elites or by designers and managers. And that is, or should be, a major source of potential concern. Otherwise the traps being set by clumsy automation, poor definitions of human factors and human performance, and insensitive computerization may have consequences extending far outside the boundaries of the organization.

8.

Smart Weapons, Smart Soldiers

> It's my view that this society has decided that it
> will only use a certain fraction of its human effort
> in its own defense in peacetime. The imperative
> just isn't there . . . so consequently we have no
> other alternative but to turn to high technology.
> That's it.
>
> (*DARPA Director Richard Cooper*)

Introduction

In the early days of smart weapons, military officers were fond of saying that the new weapons were "designed by geniuses to be operated
by idiots." The argument, made by military officers as well as in the
Pentagon, was that there was a difference between a complex weapon
and a sophisticated one—if all you must do to make them work is
press a button, they are not complex, they are sophisticated.[1] This attitude was not created by the military; it simply mirrors in the military
realm the arguments made over automation, efficiency, and deskilling
in the workplace. Given that one facet of the modernization of officer
training was to send them to business schools, that is perhaps an un-
surprising outcome.

As in the civilian world, the push toward more complex and automated equipment was soon overtaken by the realization that although
use of the new technologies required fewer operators, they had to be

better educated and better trained. Moreover, the new equipment greatly alters the balance of "tooth-to-tail," the ratio of actual fighters to noncombatant support personnel. It no longer suffices to train troops, arm them, and send them into battle. For every sophisticated weapon at the front, a long and increasingly tightly coupled train of logistics and other support is required.

The transition to the electronic office, and the electronic factory, also brought with it an increased web of tight dependence on those with particular skills in computer software, interlinkage, supply, and maintenance that changed both the culture of the workplace and the balance of power.[2] As was discussed in the preceding chapters, the consequences have been serious enough for some organizations, particularly those performing demanding and safety-critical tasks. For the military, the consequent changes in structure have been external as well as internal. They have affected combat units, combat systems, and the structure of military command, as well as the risks, role, and purpose of the military in an era of smart (and therefore expensive) weapons and highly trained (and therefore increasingly valuable) personnel.

Industrial War

For more than four thousand years, military history was dominated by the search for better ways of organizing mass formations for massed fire. Historical studies of the use of technology in warfare have shown a consistent pattern of conservative behavior with regard to innovation and change.[3] Until recently, the military tended to adopt new technical devices and methods from the civilian sector rather than generating them internally or providing support for specialized technical development. Innovations in time of peace were incremental and relatively slow extensions of more general changes taking place in the broader civil and social environment. Even when experience in war forced rapid adoption, it was often only temporary; after the war the military often sought to restore the status quo ante.

Change began with the first modern industrial war, the American Civil War, fought not on open fields in colorful uniforms, but in trenches and from behind walls, trees, and fortifications, by soldiers dressed more or less uniformly in relatively colorless Union blue or

Confederate grey.[4] What had changed was the ability of mechanized, industrialized societies to engage their new technologies of production, transportation, and coordination in the military enterprise.[5] Mass production and interchangeable parts resulted in better clothed and armed armies than any before them.

But military attitudes toward technical innovation were still changing very slowly. Even at the height of the war, General James Ripley, the Union Army's Chief of Ordnance, blocked the introduction of repeating rifles and magazine carbines for more than two years.[6] The arguments he used were to become familiar over the ensuing decades: the repeating rifle would make men careless in their use of ammunition; it would spoil the tradition of aimed fire (which was the pride of eighteenth- and nineteenth-century warfare); it would ruin the discipline instilled by having to hold fire and aim. In short, the repeating rifle did not fit into the image of accurate massed fire the military had been nurturing since the doctrinal and tactical reforms of Marlborough and Frederick the Great.[7] It was culturally disruptive.

After the war, the U.S. Army chose to return to the single-shot rifle designed in its own Springfield armory.[8] For the next twenty years, it issued only a few of the famed Spencers, and adopted such other innovations as the Gatling (machine) gun and rifled artillery only for specialized purposes.[9] The doctrine of accurate aimed fire led to retention of heavy, long-barreled, bolt-action single-shot magazine rifles as the standard weapon of the U.S. infantry right through World War II.

The Gatling gun and other predecessors of the twentieth-century machine gun went through a similar historical cycle. Pushed into service in the Civil War, they were never effectively used by the infantry. In subsequent years, machine guns tended to be mounted on carriages and assigned to cavalry units rather than to the infantry.[10] The Army kept evaluating it as light artillery even as the weight of the gun went down and its mobility went up. Because it did not fit well into the tactical structure of the artillery either, it fell between organizational stools and was almost completely ignored by the military until the First World War.[11] Despite abundant evidence of the power of the gun against Dervishes, Africans, and even in Tibet, it seems to have been considered a weapon to be used primarily against mass attacks by primitives, not on the orderly field of battle on which Europeans fought each other.[12]

Even more remarkable was the resistance of navies to specific forms of technical change in the midst of the greatest reconstruction of naval weapons and doctrine in history. Driven by the British-German naval competition, the navies of the world were to move in less than twenty years from an era of sailing ships with smooth-bore cannon to huge, steel-hulled, steam-driven battleships with rifled guns. The range of both ships and guns was thereby increased, but accuracy on the rolling sea did not keep up with the new propensity to stage duels at comparatively long range. The laying of guns (timing the firing to compensate for the roll of the ship as well as the motion of the enemy) remained one of the premier forms of professional expertise, at times approaching an art form.

Near the turn of the century, individual entrepreneurs within and without the military combined to develop a set of means and mechanisms for continuous-aim naval gunnery, in which the gun is fitted with sensing and driving mechanisms that allow it to perform controlled movements to counter the rolling of the ship.[13] It is estimated that continuous-aim technology improved the accuracy of naval gunnery in the British and American fleets by nearly a factor of thirty in six years between the turn of the century and the launching of the famed HMS *Dreadnought*, the first huge, steel-hulled, heavily armored battleship with large, stabilized, remotely fired, rifled guns.[14] Yet, both the British and American navies at first strongly resisted the change, yielding only when the political pressures became too great and higher authorities intervened.

Despite these pockets of resistance, both the weapons and the structure of military forces were by and large transformed by the technological arms race of the early part of the twentieth century. But the general officers in charge at the outbreak of the First World War were still largely of the old school. For the most part, the technical innovations that had transformed the capabilities of warfare had not yet completed the systemic cycle of technological change; military organizations and military cultures had not fully adapted. Armies hastily outfitted with the latest in military technology, including accurate, rapid-fire artillery pieces, chemical weapons, and the machine gun, were trained and led into battle by generals whose model and conception of warfare was still based on well-drilled soldiers walking across a battlefield, firing careful shots until they got close enough for a bayonet attack.[15] What resulted was stalemate in the trenches and carnage when the armies left them.

It has been said that the greatest invention of the industrial revolution was the invention of the method of invention. For the military, that experience was not transferred until the First World War. Innovations such as chemical weapons, military aircraft, the tank, and the submarine made it clear to a few younger officers that the military advantage to be gained by seeking not just technical but technological change, by reconstructing force structure and doctrine rather than fitting new armaments into old ones, outweighed the arguments for stability and tradition.

The struggle between these cadres and the military traditionalists has been reviewed many times.[16] Those arguing for such changes as armored cavalry (tanks), strategic bombing, aircraft carriers, long-range submarines, and long-range fighter aircraft remained lone, and sometimes lonely voices, more often than not cut off from the career lines that would lead them to power. Militaries did continue to welcome a series of other innovations of apparently smaller scope and scale, particularly with regard to electronics and communications. Even so, it was only the growing threat of war that would move first Britain, and then the United States, toward the cycle of innovation in military technology that was to continue during the war and accelerate after.[17]

Techno-Industrial War

The Second World War was in retrospect three wars. One was fought in secret, in the realm of electronics, communication, radar, and cryptography.[18] Another, fought even more secretly on the mesas of New Mexico and along the Tennessee and Columbia rivers, was to provide the dramatic ending at Hiroshima and Nagasaki. But most of the resources were devoted to the other, more ordinary war, where military tradition and military influence were still dominant over the scientific and technical, and the desire to innovate had to be balanced against the need to keep feeding men and machines into the maw of battle.

The costs of command rigidity in the First World War remained vivid, and the concrete-bound traditionalists and technical reactionaries were usually weeded out once they were identified. But there were still many instances of traditionalism and resistance. The U.S. Navy was relatively quick to transfer its allegiance from the battleship to the aircraft carrier, but at first neglected its submarines, sending them to sea poorly supported, unevenly crewed, and with notably defective torpedoes. At Guadalcanal in November 1942, Admiral Callaghan, steaming into the night waters of "Iron-Bottom Sound" with the first screen-display naval radars, refused to open fire without visual sighting of the enemy, and suffered terrible losses at close and bloody range in the melee that followed. The antitank bazooka issued to American soldiers lacked the known technology of the armor-penetrating shaped charge. The U.S. Air Force suffered huge bomber losses during deep daylight air strikes in the fall of 1943 before developing long-range fighter escorts. Coordination between ground and air forces during the rush across Europe in 1944–1945 was ad hoc and technically improvised, and air cover could not be supplied at all during bad weather.

To some extent, the resistance to innovation and change in conventional weapons systems was a conscious decision made in Washington, based on the recognition that the greatest asset the United States had was the productive power of its industrial base and its ability to sustain large combat losses. The Second World War was fought and won as a war of attrition, as were the First World War and the Civil War before it.[19] It was easy for postwar critics, particularly from the academic, scientific, and technical communities, to once again raise the accusation that militaries, and in particular military staffs, were technically backwards—if not positively reactionary.

The record of technical advancement and innovation in transforming conventional military operations in the Second World War is nevertheless impressive.[20] Among other things, the war produced Blitzkrieg, massive tank warfare, maneuver warfare using tactical air power for close support, extended submarine warfare, the air wars in the Pacific and in Europe, strategic bombing, air defense and air-to-air radar, the V-1 and V-2 missiles (predecessors of later generations of cruise and ballistic missiles), operations research, and the first jet aircraft. But in the long term none of these matched the long-range impacts of the other two wars, those waged by scientists and engineers outside the historical military sector to develop the atomic bomb and modern electronics.

The Postwar Transition

Nuclear weapons had the most visible and immediate impact on military organization. Later analysis of U.S. and British strategic bombing showed that the effects of conventional bombing on morale and industrial structure had been greatly exaggerated (as they were to be again in Korea and Vietnam). But the bombs that hit Hiroshima and Nagasaki were beyond exaggeration. No future war could be fought without dominance in the air. Indeed, it might reasonably be argued that in a nuclear-armed world no future war could be fought at all, and survived. Bernard Brodie, working for the newly created RAND think tank, put it best in his typical clear and precise style: "Thus far, the chief purpose of our military establishment has been to win wars. From now on, its chief purpose must be to avert them. It can have almost no other useful purpose."[21]

This was the ultimate challenge to traditional military organization and culture. But Brodie and his colleagues lived in a somewhat simpler time, when central war with the Soviet Union was seen as the single driving purpose for the U.S. military. As nuclear weapons became more powerful, and more threatening, and the United States and the Soviet Union settled into a pattern of mutual deterrence, fighting the "big war" seemed less and less likely. There were other modes of warfare and arenas of possible conflict to deal with for which nuclear weapons were unsuitable.

The most lasting and long-term effect of the involvement of academic and research scientists and engineers in the war was their continuing involvement in military affairs afterward, and their increasing influence over weapons and policy. As the military-industrial complex built up during the war expanded into a military-industrial-scientific-academic complex, technical radicals and strategic revisionists in the military found new allies in their long-standing fight against conservatism and tradition. The military intellectuals and service-funded technocrats argued that military advantage was now to be gained primarily through exploiting the discoveries of science and technology. Policy shifted from entrepreneurial and armory-driven adaptation and innovation to the systematic, government-funded search for new weapons and new military technologies that we now take for granted.

As might be expected, the course of technical innovation was not free from the sharp and frequently bitter interservice rivalries that had plagued the military during the peaceful interwar years.[22] What was most remarkable given military history and tradition was that most of these struggles were over the shape and control of the military technology of the future. Much of this had to do with computers. Four of the five key innovations arose during the generative period 1940–1960: as an embedded means of fire control for artillery and anti-aircraft guns;[23] as solvers of long, complex technical and engineering problems; as elements of advanced command and control; and as the basic tool for strategic analysis and war gaming.[24] A fifth, only to come later with advances in miniaturization, was as embedded and programmed controllers for self-guided weapons.

The lesson that the new strategic advisors and military technocrats derived from their studies of military history and technology was that traditional attitudes and culture created officers who were inflexible and slow to learn and change, who defended tradition even at the price of capability. In the future, they argued, the emphasis would have to be shifted to encourage them to adapt rather than to resist. The military was to become actively involved in the processes of innovation, invention, and analysis. As a consequence, technology became a career path for a new cadre of ambitious and aspiring young military officers.

The newly formed U.S. Air Force, separated at last from the Army, set the tone. As a new service, it had no tradition, and no core of traditional backers in Congress or industry. Realizing from the outset that its future lay with advanced technology and continuous innovation, the Air Force set about institutionalizing the processes of scientific and technical advice, supporting research and creating its own think tank, RAND, in 1946. It was one of the prime promoters of numerically controlled machine technology during the 1950s, and of the progress in computers necessary to program them.

The U.S. Army and Navy were also to maintain connections with the intellectual community through hired consultants and other think tanks. The Office of Naval Research became a prime basic research contractor; the Army Signal Corps provided most of the funding for the early development of the transistor; the newly created ARPA was the prime supporter of basic computer research. As Eisenhower was to note, the military-industrial-complex (or, more properly, the military-technical-university-industrial-complex) had become a permanent feature of modern industrial societies.

The argument about the technological backwardness of military staffs could no longer be made. In his book on the development of the ICBM, Edmund Beard states:

> The disposition to innovate [is no longer] generally inhibited by a technically illiterate and conservative military leadership. Having witnessed the decisive impact of novel weapons on the battlefield in World War II, and having been entrusted with the responsibility for maintaining a continuing deterrence, generals and admirals have been transformed "from being the most traditional element in any national society—hanging on to their horses, or their sailing ships, for as long as possible—into the boldest innovators."[25]

At first, most of this process was devoted to the development of nuclear weapons, nuclear delivery systems, and nuclear strategy. But the Korean War, fought more or less with the weapons and tactics of 1945, made it abundantly clear that not all conflicts would be nuclear (and perhaps that none would). Given its newly accepted role as an interventionist world power, the United States would also have to develop suitable weapons and tactics for its "general-purpose" forces.

Between 1964 and 1972, the military, down among the weeds in Vietnam, was still in a period of transition, and it showed. The cumbersome and complex weapons, systems, and tactics developed for the purpose of fighting a postulated, if unlikely, central war with the Soviet Union in the relatively flat and unencumbered landscape of Europe proved inappropriate, and at times counterproductive, when fighting insurgents and infiltrators in the jungles of Southeast Asia. Supersonic jet aircraft and fast, heavily armored tanks were sledgehammers swung at mosquitos. Strategic bombing could destroy the North's cities, but not its fighting capabilities. Perhaps most damaging of all, command and communications technologies had far outstripped other aspects of military technology, not only enabling but fostering the constant intervention of remote commanders into even the smallest details of battles on the ground.[26]

Technical innovation proved very uneven. There were such now-famous excesses as the attempt to wire the Ho Chi Minh trail with electronic sensors, or build an electronic fence along the border, or to fit helicopters with a "sniffer" that would detect Viet Cong by picking up the traces of ammonia from their urine. Such excesses eventually earned a name of their own from the hard-pressed grunts on the ground: "blip krieg."[27]

There were, however, also some signal successes that were to prefigure subsequent developments in weapons and systems. The most notable among these was the "smart bomb," the first of what were eventually to become known collectively as precision guided munitions (PGM). In 1972, toward the very end of the war, a single flight of Phantom aircraft armed with laser-guided Paveway bombs destroyed a bridge at Thanh Hoa that had survived eight hundred previous sorties with iron bombs.[28] The advent of PGMs seemed to provide a technical alternative to risking American lives, provided that targets worthy of their cost could be found.[29]

Quantity versus Quality

Vietnam was a turning point for the United States in more ways than one. The military came out of that war determined not to fight again unless it could win; the public acquired a greatly decreased tolerance for human loss of life, particularly in overseas policing operations; the politicians came away looking to satisfy both constituencies. What all seemed to have settled upon, despite evidence to the contrary, was the notion that a new generation of high-technology weapons was needed.[30]

This was not a new idea. With Eisenhower's "New Look" in the aftermath of the Korean War, the United States shifted to a policy of massive retaliation, to a dependence upon nuclear weapons as a cost-effective alternative to building up large conventional forces. Now that it was widely accepted that there was no natural link between nuclear weapons and the need for conventional forces, the new emphasis on PGMs allowed a partial return to the earlier strategy, but this time with an emphasis on smart conventional weapons.

The 1970s were a time of turbulence and transition as a series of struggles took place over a whole generation of emerging new weapons.[31] Controversy over such weapons systems as the TFX fighter (later to emerge as the FB-111 bomber), heavy versus light ICBMs, air defense systems, and the next generation of fighter aircraft were to some extent the result of the usual processes of bureaucratic infighting and interservice rivalry, now augmented by political scrapping over the distribution of increasingly scarce procurement funding.[32] But they also reflected some real dilemmas as to the choice of military strategies and military postures, both of which were now seen as intimately connected with the outcome of technical choices as to weapons and weapons systems.

The use of computers was clearly to be central, but there remained two quite distinct, and often conflicting, paths. The first emphasized the creation of more complex and sophisticated man-operated integrated systems, such as the F-111, the B-1 bomber, and the M-1 Abrams tank. With their array of powerful computer-aided equipment, these were far more capable and lethal than anything that had preceded them. But they were also far more expensive than the systems they replaced, which meant that far fewer could be afforded.

The other trend was away from manned systems and toward advanced self-controlled or pre-programmed PGMs such as the Tomahawk cruise missile, launched from a distance by existing platforms or from specially designed, less expensive "stand-off" launching vehicles. Self-contained, computer-guided, and unmanned, the combination of PGMs and dedicated, relatively low-performance platforms was estimated to be far cheaper than attempting to deliver the same ordnance via a manned system, particularly when probable combat losses were taken into account. But they did entail complete reliance on an electronics package rather working a human being into the final control loop.

The debate that followed mirrored a continuing split over the nature of combat in the computer age. It also mirrored the contemporary debate in the business world between networked offices built around central computer systems and decentralized ones based on individual desktop computers. Although almost all in the military were now technology promoters, there were several camps, each with a different vision of the relation between soldiers and weapons, and between weapons and military doctrine and posture. Was the primary role of the soldier to be a directly engaged, armed fighting man, or the remote operator of a technology for fighting at a distance? Were remotely controlled or automatic weapons more or less reliable than humans in uncertain battle and electronic environments?

Cost also became an issue. With large sections of the military now convinced that only state-of-the art technology could offset Soviet numerical superiority, new systems were developed and old ones modified at an unprecedented pace, which in turn led to exponentially rising costs for such items as fighter planes, helicopters, missiles, and tanks.[33] This in turn caused a back reaction against what critics saw as a military being driven by technology for its own sake, regardless of mission or combat requirements.

The ensuing debate saw a historical role reversal, with those in power arguing for sophisticated and complex "high-tech" weapons even at the cost of being able to buy very few ("quality"), and a highly professionalized military to operate them. The reform movement argued instead for much larger quantities of cheaper, possibly unmanned weapons with less complexity and a different kind of technical sophistication ("quantity"), on the grounds that numerical superiority and mass production should continue to be the U.S. strong suit in a major conflict.[34]

The proponents of advanced high-technology systems perfectly expressed the post-Vietnam attitudes of the United States to armed conflict. The key words were "force multipliers," rapid victory, a smaller and more professional military, reduced casualties, and the immorality of sending U.S. troops to battle in any but the very finest equipment money could buy. Those on the side of quantity replied that one man's force multiplier is another's high-value target, that failure to obtain a rapid victory would deplete both weapons and personnel much faster than they could be replaced, and that war without casualties was a dangerous illusion. Although the reformers clearly stood closer to the historical U.S. tradition, the growing perception that mass armies, attrition warfare, and the traditional acceptance of casualties in search of victory were no longer publicly acceptable under any reasonable scenario for military action prevailed.[35]

The reformers were not alone in arguing that the military had gone too far in seeking to introduce businesslike methods to justify the new systems. The valuative criteria and strategies of civilian organizations may not be applicable to militaries, who are not fighting each other for profit or market share. Civilian organizations seek to maximize both efficiency and effectiveness. This may suit military organizations in peacetime, but in time of war efficiency and effectiveness (military success) not only differ, they may work at cross-purposes.[36]

The ideal of concentrating on a very few, very sophisticated weapons, increasing standardization within and between the services, and still avoiding the potential vulnerabilities entailed is no simple task.[37] As was increasingly true in the world of business and industry, the new powers of the general-purpose computer were appealed to as showing the path to the future.

Flexible, programmable computers and computerized systems could adapt to circumstances and learn from error, so that standardized systems could be built to adapt and learn even in the midst of conflict. The use of computers in manned systems was to make them far more effective in offense, and far less vulnerable in defense. The use of computers in smart weapons would allow militaries to buy far fewer to accomplish the same ends, since these weapons would have such a high success rate that there would be no need to buy the huge stores required in the days of artillery barrages or mass bombing. And the use of computers to gather and distribute information and coordinate and integrate military efforts would make the whole system more efficient (and presumably more effective), reducing the need for stocks and reserves.

The next wave of computerization was to allow the independent development of weapons and platforms with state-of-the-art technology at both ends. There were to be numerous self-guided or remotely controlled munitions and vehicles whose cost would be brought down by economies of scale in production, while the number of very sophisticated and very costly platforms for bringing them to the battlefield could be greatly reduced. As will be discussed in chapter 11, this required a series of elaborate new systems for C³I (command, control, communications, and intelligence) to inform, guide, and control the whole. This added greater complexity to the rising costs of integration, but that was a task for which the computer was thought to be especially well suited.[38]

Although disputes lingered, the quantity-quality debate was essentially over by the early 1980s. The Reagan administration made a conscious choice for high-technology military systems, rejecting the "smaller is better" arguments while keeping and expanding upon the idea of computerized and sometimes self-guided precision weapons.[39] But it did so in the context of a broader decision to move the United States from a small professional core able to expand quickly as a conscript army to a fully professionalized military. Because human life could no longer be treated as a commodity, even in warfare, it was necessary to invest instead in high-technology systems, with high-technology, highly trained people to run them.[40]

As the new systems emerged, so did the open acknowledgment of the rationale for the longstanding support of American electronics and computer research.[41] As Richard D. DeLauer, then undersecretary of defense for research and engineering, so clearly put it in 1982: "Electronics is the most critical of all technologies for the maintenance of peace. The *raison d'être* of the U.S. Department of Defense is peace, and the unparalleled strength of U.S. defense capabilities depends upon electronics in one form or another."[42]

Trading Tooth for Tail

Some of the short-term consequences of the move to computerize various aspects of the military will be discussed in more detail in the next few chapters. But as with business and personal computing, there are also long-term and indirect consequences that may eventually become more significant, and more durable. Militaries are more than collections of people and technologies; their organizations are structured, interdependent, and highly complex, even by the standards of comparable industrial organizations.[43] Technical traditionalists were correct in their belief that major changes in the nature, and not just the quality, of weapons and weapons systems, communication systems, and control systems have long-term and transformational effects that are difficult to understand and, unlike business systems, are unlikely to be fully tested until irreversibly committed in the full-scale test of combat.

The following chapter will explore some of the effects as they played out with specific weapons systems under specific circumstances. There is also a discussion of some of the more long-term and permanent effects, including the redistribution of resources, that modern, computerized weapons and systems are bringing about. For every element in the fighting "tooth" of an army (or navy or air force), there is always a necessary train of logistics, support, information, and command-and-control that makes sure that the tooth can bite when called upon. Historically, that logistic "tail" was kept as small as possible to conserve resources for massing forces—which provided one motivation for standardization of weapons and low differentiation.

In a modern combined military force, there is not just one type of weapon at the front but many, each of which has distinct and often narrowly defined missions and tasks that must be monitored, evaluated, and integrated. The operational and support requirements of sophisticated, computerized weapons systems are far more demanding than for the simpler systems of the past. Fewer trained personnel are required at the front, but far more are needed behind it. The number of nominally noncombatant personnel necessary to make the new weapons effective has been growing in concert with their new capabilities. In addition, they must be maintained, supported, coordinated, and directed by a complex military support system whose personnel are far more differentiated and highly trained than in any military in history. The resulting military organization more closely resembles the classic definition of a vertically integrated complex bureaucracy than the rigidly hierarchical structure that has historically been considered the military model.

In the Second World War, about 65 percent of the Army's enlisted personnel were combat soldiers (which was considered by many a relatively poor ratio). By 1990, only 25 percent were listed in the "occupational category" of combat; of the rest, 20 percent were in very technical categories, 14 percent in technical, 31 percent in administrative, and 9 percent in semiskilled.[44] This may actually understate the effects of technology, since it is not clear how many of the administrative jobs were created to serve the technical cadres.

Moreover, the demands for education and skills even for simpler jobs, such as craftspeople or clerical workers, have risen, just as they have in the civilian work force. The number of military occupation specialties in a modern army runs into the hundreds, some twenty or thirty times as high as it had been in 1945. By 1985, 20 percent of all jobs in the U.S. Army, 28 percent in the U.S. Navy, and 20 percent in the U.S. Air Force were electronics-related.[45] Many are in computer-related categories that could not have existed even as recently as the late 1960s.

When the U.S. Army first moved to "black boxing" electronics in the

1970s, part of the reason was the need to isolate the very expensive equipment from the increasingly less-educated pool of draftees. The philosophy became known as "Smart Machine—Dumb Maintainer."[46] Maintenance at the front was to consist primarily of pulling faulty black boxes and replacing them, thereby reducing the training requirements for front-line maintainers. The costs turned out to be higher than expected. Front-line diagnosis required another layer of complexity: sophisticated front-line diagnostic testing equipment. And doing maintenance at the rear involved yet another trail of logistic and equipment support, not to mention management and control of inventories, loss of time and availability owing to false positive rates, and so on. This was exacerbated by the continuing problem of the vulnerability of the very few maintenance shops, which required that they be kept far to the rear and/or heavily defended.

In the 1990s, with a professionalized military, the new systems require a much higher level of training all around. The smart machine, as it turns out, requires smart people to operate it as well as to maintain and support it. And as the level of required training and experience increases, the cost to the unit (and its effectiveness) of losing a single individual grows proportionately larger. Those experts in the logistics, maintenance, and supply train who have special skills have a particularly high value.

The demanding knowledge and communications requirements of the new systems requires that a greater portion of what is nominally the support structure be moved closer to the arena of combat. Given the greater range of new weapons, more people will therefore be placed at risk. The incentive then grows to increase both longer-range striking power and the distance between enemy and friendly troops. As the distance between the forces grows larger, the military organization with supposedly superior technology will grow more confident of its ability to use technology rather than ground forces to minimize the risk of losses. Smart weapons are valuable and require smart people; smart people are valuable and require smart weapons to protect them.

In a superb essay on the nature of technology, Langdon Winner has pointed out that artifacts have politics.[47] Needless to say, politics also have artifacts. What the computer made possible in the aftermath of Vietnam was a military whose posture, doctrine, and weapons were based on reducing the traditional American reliance on numbers, mass, and endurance while increasing capacity for the rapid and precise application of very large amounts of force, albeit for a comparatively short time. And the complexity of operation and differentiation of skills also mean growing a larger and more complex organization to manage and coordinate it all.

The resulting logic also drives the system not only toward higher weapons costs, but also to much higher costs to compete for trained personnel. The military tooth may be sharper than it has ever been, but at the expense of an ever-growing and more expensive tail. Higher pay on fixed budgets means less people, which means the need for smarter weapons, and so on. At the same time, the increased status and training of personnel in the smaller and more professional army makes policy makers less willing to risk their lives, thereby initiating yet another cycle of sophisticated weapons design. All of the feedback loops are positive.

Conclusion

With each new generation of smart systems, computing power becomes more deeply embedded as an indispensable technical element of military systems. As the military shifts to ships built totally around their combat electronics and missile suites, to tanks, gun systems, and missiles that require electronics for control as well as for aim, and to aircraft that can neither fly nor fight effectively without relying on their sophisticated electronics, effectiveness and reliability come to depend upon an elaborate, tightly linked web of maintenance, logistics, and repair.

The social effects on the military have been profound. The change in warfare did more than increase the overall complexity of the military.[48] The reduction in the ratio of warriors to support personnel, and the attendant shift in emphasis from manning the weapons to designing and controlling them, reconstructed the balance and distribution of power within the military, diluting the importance of tradition, rank, seniority, and even leadership.[49] More than one analyst was heard to remark (usually in private) that the next set of training manuals might as well be titled: "War: The Video Game." Moreover, future military officers are very well aware that intellectual and computer skills are growing in importance compared to the physical and emotional ones that once dominated.

When the smart weapons revolution began, the leading objectives were to maintain stable deterrence in Europe without building a force that would have to resort immediately to nuclear weapons, and to "deter" the Russians from assisting or intervening in other theaters where the United States might be politically invested or militarily involved. The most probable scenarios, such as the United States having to fight a land war in the Persian Gulf, or possibly (again) in Asia were not something that could be sold to the public as a normative posture. Not every intervention would be a Grenada.

Attempts to remedy this dilemma with technology led to a series of military force postures of increasing complexity, both in the nature of the weapons systems and in their integration with command-and-control and intelligence networks. AirLand Battle, the doctrine underlying the U.S. Army's field manual *FM 100–5*, issued in the early 1980s, for example, stated flatly that the future combat would take place on an integrated battlefield, characterized by deep attacks against follow-on forces behind the front lines (popularly known as FOFA, for follow-on forces attack). As will be discussed in chapter 11, increased coordination would be required between ground and air operations, in an extended battlefield that encompassed a wide array of electronic sensors, communications, and mechanisms for integrated and coordinated fire control and command.[50]

The military of the future increasingly began to look like the corporation of the future, consisting of units that were formally dispersed but tightly coordinated through vertical chains of command, and complete with communications and information mechanisms that allowed for micromanagement at all levels. The implications of the transformation that would result are not widely appreciated, but they were well set out by James William Gibson in his review of vertical integration and micromanagement during the Vietnam War:

> The same "fetishism" of technological production systems found in foreign policy similarly occurs within the military. The *social relationships* within the military disappear and all that remain are technological-production systems and ways of managing them.... Combat leaders inspire troops to fight in dangerous battles; social relationships of loyalty

from top to bottom and bottom to top are crucial. Managers allocate resources. As two other military sociologists . . . say, "no one expects anyone to die for IBM or General Motors."[51]

For the U.S. military, this seemed to be the dominant, and perhaps
the only, option. With the United States unwilling either to give up its
role as the leading world power, to build and man large armies, or to
incur significant losses, technical innovation is seen not just as a pallia-
tive, but as the determinative answer. Although the growing demand
for low-intensity intervention and peace-keeping missions once again
made it clear that nothing can ever replace the physical presence of
combat troops as a decisive factor in warfare, it was also increasingly
clear that the United States was prepared to go to extraordinary technical lengths to ensure their safety before committing them to combat.
The era of attrition warfare was over.

This was to have consequences at every level of the U.S. military,
from the organization of infantry companies to the structure of command and control. The following chapter will examine how the new
systems affected the performance of some of the newer combat systems, including the advanced missile cruiser USS *Vincennes*. Fitted
with the extensive computerized battle displays, threat analysis, and
weapons control computers, the *Vincennes*, caught fighting a relatively
simple battle against relatively unsophisticated opponents, formed
and held to a false image of a sophisticated attacker—a situation much
closer to the one she had been designed and built for. As will be discussed in chapter 10, similar problems were also to emerge even in
operations Desert Shield and Desert Storm, which are held up as models for how much a highly technical military can accomplish with very
low casualties.

9.

Unfriendly Fire

Introduction

In 1868, the U.S. Navy launched the *Wampanoag*, the most advanced naval weapon of her time.[1] Steam-powered, propeller-driven, with a hull designed primarily for speed, she was heavily armed with ten 8-inch rifled guns, a 60-pounder, two 100-pounders, and four howitzers. During her trials she maintained speeds of over sixteen knots for over twenty-four hours in seas that were at times heavy. There was no warship afloat that could match her, and there would not be for nearly twenty years thereafter.

The *Wampanoag* demonstrated her seaworthiness and efficiency in a year of service, during which time her officers and crew could find no major faults at all. Nevertheless, a naval board inspecting her a year after her commissioning declared on the basis of their opinions, and in the face of the evidence, that she was a problematic and unseaworthy ship, "a sad and signal failure, and utterly unfit to be retained in the service."[2] However outrageous they now seem, the board's claims and findings were never successfully challenged. After being laid up for a year, she was transferred to noncombat duty for several years before ultimately being decommissioned and sold. It was not until the 1880s that the U.S. Navy was to move beyond sail to the first steam-powered and steel-hulled warships.

The story of the *Wampanoag* is often told as an example of bureaucratic resistance to change in the military. Traditional militaries were islands of stability in time of peace. A great premium was placed on compliance and routine, on keeping a low profile: "The Navy officer was an organization man. He spent his life both obeying and giving orders within an institutional context, moving up gradually through the ranks, preserving and identifying with the status quo, honoring tradition, defending the organization that provided him with security and recognition."[3]

The usual argument is that what the Navy sought was to maintain stability, to arrest change so rapid that it would dislocate both the military bureaucracy and the civil economy with which it interacted.[4] In this frame, the case of the *Wampanoag* is not substantively different from historical cases of resistance to naval radio, submarines, precision gunnery, and automatic weapons around the turn of the century, or to the tank, the submarine, and the bomber between the two world wars.[5]

On second look, however, the Navy's decision on the *Wampanoag* is more complex than simple resistance to change. According to Elting Morison, the concluding section of the Hearing Board's report reflects a real concern, and not just bureaucratic inertia or a desire to preserve tradition:

> Lounging through the watches of a steamer, or acting as firemen and coal heavers, will not produce in a seaman that combination of boldness, strength, and skill which characterized the American sailor of an earlier day; and the habitual exercise by an officer of a command, the execution of which is not under his own eye, is a poor substitute for the school of observation, promptness, and command found only on the deck of a sailing vessel.[6]

In the 1870s, at the threshold of the most rapid change in naval technology in history, the board feared the possibility that radically new weapons and systems would seriously disrupt patterns of social and organizational behavior in ways they could neither foresee nor control. Morison goes on to remark:

> What these officers were saying was that the *Wampanoag* was a destructive energy in their society. Setting the extraordinary force of her engines against the weight of their way of life, they had a sudden insight into the nature of machinery. They perceived that a machine, any machine, if left to itself, tends to establish its own conditions, to create its own environment and draw men into it. Since a machine, any machine, is designed to do only part of what a whole man can do, it tends to wear down those parts of a man that are not included in the design.[7]

In his repetition of the story, Deitchman points out that similar concerns persist in the modern age, where the power, complexity, extent, and rate of technical change are immeasurably greater than they were in the 1860s, or the 1930s. Although he makes the familiar argument that the current situation is exactly opposite to that surrounding the case of the *Wampanoag*, that our defense "now depends on high-technology industry that is built on the concept of continual change,"[8] he also notes that the systemic, technological changes that will ensue will not come easily or quickly, or without pain or the possibility of fundamental surprise.

Militaries share with civilian organizations that manage safety-critical technical systems a deep concern over the possibility of unanticipated side effects or unexpected consequences, particularly when they affect the performance of their troops. The old slogan "we train like we fight" expresses perfectly the purpose of military training—to make behavior reliable and reasonably predictable in combat.

Because the new, far more complex and sophisticated equipment now being put into place is much more demanding of the time, attention, and training of the people who man it, it is even more likely to create its own environment and draw its operators into it. The next two chapters will discuss the historical evolution both of automated and computerized military equipment and of the use of new information and communication techniques for advanced command and control. This chapter provides context by setting out in brief three examples where the consequence was not only surprise but tragedy. In all three cases, the electronic warfare systems designed to enhance warnings and facilitate engagement actually contributed to the errors in cognitive framing that occurred, both directly through changing the nature and balance of the process of decision and indirectly through the changes that electronic warfare has made in the combat environment.

A "Reasonable Choice of Disaster"[9]

On February 21, 1973, two jet fighters of the Israeli Air Force intercepted a Libyan airliner on its way to Cairo. For a number of reasons, the plane did not realize that it had wandered off track, on a day when a sandstorm over Egypt and the Sinai blocked direct visual verification of course. Instead, it was heading over disputed territory in the general direction of Beer Sheva and Redifim—an Israeli air base near Bir Gafgafa.

Unaware that they had wandered off track, and insensitive to the potential dangers of flying over neighboring Israeli territory, the Libyan crew consistently misread almost every signal they were given by Cairo or the Israeli fighters right up to the moment when they attempted their emergency landing. They did not realize they were lost, even when Cairo airport informed them that it had no idea where they were. They misidentified the Israeli Phantom jets as Egyptian Mirages; even when warning shots were fired, their response was to call Cairo and complain. They took none of the standard actions agreed upon for hostile intercepts (such as lowering the landing gear).

When the Libyan plane failed to respond in return, the Israelis flew close by, reporting that "all the window shades were down"—in itself an unusual and somewhat suspicious appearance. After the first warning shots, the Libyan crew did lower the gear and descend toward Redifim. Mistaking it for Cairo East, an Egyptian military base, they climbed out again seeking to fly westward to the more "correct" international airport at Cairo West.

Once the airliner re-ascended from its approach to Redifim, the Israelis concluded that it was trying to escape. The air force commander decided that it was a hostile flight, and that allowing it to escape would encourage another attempt. He therefore ordered the fighters to shoot at the base of the wings to force it down immediately.[10] The Israelis fired again, but the liner continued to fly westward. At this point, the Israelis fired once more, hitting the base of the wing. The airliner tried to land on the flat sand but failed. After a short run on the ground it crashed, killing all but six of the 116 people aboard.

The Libyan crew seemed somewhat confused (the captain and engineer were French, the copilot a Libyan who spoke little of it). The behavior of the Israelis was composed and consistent, even if it did not correspond to the "realities" that emerged after the cockpit tapes of the doomed airliner were reviewed. The Israeli pilots did identify the airliner as Libyan, which meant potentially hostile. Their aircraft were clearly marked with the Star of David, and did execute the maneuvers internationally agreed upon—signaling and rocking their wings.

Lanir points out that the sequence of events was highly improbable statistically, making the event something that could not have been anticipated or foreseen—as much of an "inconceivable occurrence" as having an Iranian airliner pass over the USS *Vincennes* in the middle of a surface fire fight, or a Korean airliner turn up over Kamchatka. Both sides acted rationally and correctly within the (erroneous) cognitive frames in which they were made.

Any cognitive framing is based on an initial set of assumptions and distinctions. Once the frame is set, these are difficult to challenge, particularly under stress, and most particularly when accompanied by pressure to act quickly. Lanir argues that the cognitive frame of the Israelis was largely predetermined by their own electronic command and control system. The fighters were not sent into the air to explore an uncertain and presumably unknown situation, but to carry out a mission.

The Israeli Defense Force is proud of having highly trained and independent fighting units capable of acting flexibly without central control. But the presumed discretion of the pilots to act on their own judgment and initiative turned out to be illusory. Instead, their actions and responses were framed by the causal logic of the early warning system. The unanticipated outcome of the electronically integrated system was to create a disaster out of otherwise "reasonable choices," rather than from the human errors the system was put in place to avoid.[11]

The USS *Stark*

The attack by an Iraqi Mirage jet on the USS *Stark* during the Iran-Iraq war is in many ways similar. On May 17, 1987, the *Stark* was on routine patrol in the Persian Gulf to protect neutral shipping. At about 8:00 A.M., a long-range U.S. electronic warning and control aircraft (AWACS) picked up an F-1 Mirage, positively identified it as an Iraqi aircraft, and passed the notification on to U.S. Naval units operating in the Gulf.[12] A little after 9:00 that morning, the aircraft was picked up as an unknown on the *Stark*'s radar, at a range of about seventy miles.

Under the Rules of Engagement then in force, the *Stark* was not compelled to wait out an attack. Three days earlier, an Iraqi aircraft had come within forty miles of the USS *Coontz*. The *Coontz* not only transmitted an interrogation, it turned broadside to the aircraft, unmasked its radars, armed its chaff dispensers, and mounted an anti-aircraft missile. The Mirage eventually closed to ten miles, but never turned toward the ship (it went on to attack a tanker).

Once the Mirage had closed to less than seventy miles, the Tactical Operations Officer (TAO) of the *Stark* was tracking it continuously. When the aircraft closed to thirteen miles, the *Stark* identified itself by radio, and requested identification from the aircraft. A second inquiry at a range of eleven miles also brought no response. At about 9:11, the operator of electronic intercept equipment aboard the *Stark* reported that it had been locked onto by the aircraft's fire control radar.

When the TAO discovered the lock-on by the Mirage's radar, he immediately started to bring the ship's Phalanx close-in gun system up. He also requested a lock by the ship's air defense radar. However, the attack was coming in over the port bow, and the primary radar was blocked by the superstructure. At 9:12, the TAO ordered a secondary radar brought up, but before it could be activated an Exocet missile hit the ship, severely damaging it and killing thirty-seven aboard. A second missile impacted shortly thereafter. It ignited a large fire in the aluminum superstructure that was not put out for some time. The ship had neither taken evasive maneuvers nor brought its defensive weapons systems to bear.

Subsequent to the U.S. Navy's own inquiry, the Staff Report of the Committee on Armed Services concluded that although the Rules of Engagement allowed for a more aggressive defensive posture, the real world was more difficult.[13] At that time, Iraq was considered a near-ally against Iran, and had never attacked a U.S. ship despite several opportunities.

In all probability, the incident had been caused by complementary errors of interpretation. The Iraqi attack was probably inadvertent, given that their cognitive frame was one of expected hostility. In the era of electronic warfare, the fear that he who hesitates is almost certainly lost leads to a policy of attacking immediately almost anything the radar engages. In contrast, the *Stark* suffered from being caught in a cognitive frame in which an attack was unexpected. They regarded the closing of the Mirage as a puzzle rather than a threat, and did not take action to unmask its defensive systems in time for them to engage.[14]

Was this, too, an avoidable incident from which useful lessons could be learned? Perhaps. However, the lessons that were thought to have been learned by the U.S. Navy were not about cognitive disjunctures, but about quick response. This was to be a contributing factor in framing an even more consequential event in the Gulf the following year.

Tragedy over the Persian Gulf

In July 1988, the USS *Vincennes* was patrolling the restricted waters of the Persian Gulf, as she had been for several weeks as part of the fleet enforcing the U.S. embargo of Iran.[15] Also in the vicinity were two U.S. frigates, the USS *Elmer Montgomery* (FF 1082) and the USS *Sides* (FFG 14). Like many of the U.S. ships involved in the Gulf patrol, all three were designed and built to be blue-water fighters, part of the U.S. global maritime strategy. Bottled up in the Straits of Hormuz, these billion-dollar bundles of sophisticated and advanced technology were mostly worried about low-technology attacks from mines and Iranian speedboats.

Like other *Ticonderoga*-class Aegis cruisers, the *Vincennes* is a fast, lightly armored ship built on a long, narrow destroyer hull. Although armed with various surface-to-surface guns and a variety of systems for close-in air defense, she was optimized for providing blue-water air defense to an aircraft carrier battle group. Her real "main battery" of standard SM-2 anti-aircraft missiles stored deep in her magazines are controlled by the advanced Aegis electronic fire-control system around which she was built.

Aegis was designed to be capable of processing, interpreting, and displaying the data from a complex air battle extending over many hundred square miles, and displaying it on an enormous visual display in the Command Information Center (CIC). In order to perform effectively, the electronic suite must be able to track and distinguish friendly and potentially hostile aircraft at ranges of tens of miles while engaging a variety of potential targets ranging from high-flying reconnaissance aircraft to high-speed cruise missiles. The resulting array of computers, modern displays, and other data gathering and command posts being too large for the narrow hull, it is located up in the superstructure behind the phalanx of huge phased-array radars.

Surface Attack

With the memory of the attack on the USS *Stark* the previous year still fresh in every sailor's mind, all weapons and warning systems on the

Vincennes were up and fully manned. On July 2, several armed small boats of the Iranian Revolutionary Guard Corps (IRGC) had positioned themselves at the western approach to the Straits, and were challenging merchant vessels. Late that day, the *Montgomery* had come close enough to a ship attack in progress to fire warning shots at several of the IRGC boats.

Earlier on the morning of July 3, the *Montgomery*, at the northern end of the Straits, reported another attack by seven small IRGC boats armed with machine guns and rockets. Shortly thereafter, another wave of thirteen such boats was reported, in three groups, one of which took a position of the *Montgomery*'s port quarter. At 7:42 A.M. local time, the *Vincennes* was dispatched to the area to investigate the situation. At about 9:45 A.M., one of her helicopters sent out to monitor the situation having been fired upon, the *Vincennes* went to General Quarters and took tactical command of the *Montgomery*.

As they approached the position of the boats, several were observed to turn toward the U.S. ships and close in a threatening manner. Taking this as *prima facie* evidence of hostile intent, Middle East Joint Task Force Command gave permission to engage, and the *Vincennes* opened fire at 10:13 A.M., starting a surface meleé that was to continue throughout the incident. The IRGC boats, fully aware of the advantage conferred by their small size and maneuverability, did not flee, but turned to engage, hoping thereby to inflict some damage on the far more expensive and valuable U.S. ships.

Four minutes after she opened fire, a bad round fouled the *Vincennes*'s forward 5″ mount. Because she was armed with only one gun fore and one aft, the TAO was forced to maneuver the ship radically— using 30 degrees of rudder at a ship's speed of 30 knots—to bring the after 5″ mount to bear on the most threatening of the small boats. This caused the ship to heel dramatically, sending loose equipment flying. Because the CIC, which contains not only the Aegis displays but all other displays and consoles from which the ship is fought, is high above the water line, the effect was particularly dramatic. Books, publications, and loose equipment went flying off desks. Desk and file drawers flew open. Many of those on duty had to grab for the nearest support to avoid being thrown to the deck.

The surface engagement ended inconclusively at 10:33, the *Vincennes* having expended seventy-two rounds of 5″ ammunition and the

Montgomery 47. The IRGC boats were then in retreat, one of them having been sunk by U.S. gunfire. But in this relatively short period of time, the *Vincennes* had detected, identified, and shot down an Iranian airliner that had the bad luck, or bad judgement, to overfly the scene of battle.

Iran Air Flight 655

That same morning, the captain and crew of Iran Air Flight 655 were at Bandar Abbas airfield in southern Iran, preparing for a routine 150-mile flight over the Gulf to Abu Dhabi. It was one of the many ironies of the half-war then being fought in the Gulf that such commerce proceeded almost routinely, in, around, and through what amounted to open combat zones. Even the status of Bandar Abbas itself was ambiguous. Several Iranian F-14 fighters had arrived only a day or two earlier, and their purpose and mission on what was primarily a civil airfield was never made entirely clear.

Like most modern aircraft, the Iranian airliner was equipped with an aircraft identification transponder, a modern form of the old "identification, friend or foe" (IFF) system of World War II. When interrogated by a radar signal from a potential adversary, the transponder "squawks" (gives off a specific response signal) in a prespecified, fixed mode. The Iranian F-14s at Bandar Abbas are presumed to have been set to squawk in "Mode II," a mode that would identify to the U.S. ships that the aircraft in question were military, and Iranian. Being a commercial flight, Iran Air 655 was instructed to squawk in Mode III, a signal that identifies civilian traffic. A unique transmission code number, 6760 in this case, was assigned to distinguish this particular flight from others.

Scheduled departure time was 9:59 A.M. local time. The usual mixed load of businesspeople and relatives was making the quick hop to the comparative peace and luxury of the eastern Gulf. The flight was assigned routinely to commercial air corridor Amber 59, a twenty-mile-wide lane on a direct line to Dhubai airport. Owing to the short distance, the flight pattern would be a simple trajectory—climbing out to an altitude of 14,000 feet, cruising for a short time, then descending gradually into Dhubai.

The matter of life or death for those aboard seems to have been settled by a still unexplained (but not uncommon) eighteen-minute delay in departure. After taking off from runway 21, Flight 655 was directed by the Bandar Abbas tower to turn on its transponder and proceed over the Gulf. Because of the delay in takeoff, it appeared on the *Vincennes*'s radar at 10:17, just after the duel with the IRGC patrol boats had begun. At 10:19, the *Vincennes* began to issue warnings on the Military Air Distress frequency, and at 10:20 began warnings on the International (civil) Air Distress frequency as well. It was just at this moment that the TAO ordered the sharp turn that created havoc aboard.

During the next three minutes, with the ship in a radical heel, the CIC in confusion and disorder, and while continuing to engage the IRGC boats, the *Vincennes* issued a number of warnings on both military and civil distress frequencies, it (mistakenly) identified the Airbus 320 as a possible Iranian F-14, it (mistakenly) reported hearing IFF squawks in Mode II, and it (mistakenly) reported the aircraft as descending toward the ship when it was in fact still climbing according to its usual flight plan.[16]

Having informed Joint Task Force Command that a potentially hostile aircraft was rapidly closing to within potential missile attack range, the *Vincennes* received permission to engage. Captain Rogers, the Commanding Officer (CO), held out for a minute or two more, by which time the still unidentified aircraft had closed to fifteen miles and was still being reported as descending toward his ship. At about 10:24 A.M., seven minutes into the Iranian Airbus's flight, and eight minutes into *Vincennes*'s fire fight, the CO fired two SM-2 standard missiles at the unknown target.

A few seconds later, with the Airbus still on its assigned climbout, and slightly to one side of, but well within air corridor Amber 59, it was intercepted by one or both of the missiles at a range of eight nautical miles and an altitude of 13,500 feet. Flight 655, with some 290 people from six nations aboard, tumbled in flames into the Persian Gulf. The whole flight had taken less than seven minutes. There were no survivors.

By noon that day, Iranian helicopters and boats began to search the area and recover the bodies. It was not until later in the day that the officers and men of the *Vincennes* would learn that what they had shot down was not an Iranian F-14, but a commercial, civil flight.

Command, Confusion, and Cognitive Locking

Since the "black box" flight recorder on board the Iranian Airbus has been irrecoverably lost in the waters of the Persian Gulf, we shall never know exactly what her flight profile was, whether the crew ignored the American challenges or simply did not hear them, or whether they were aware of the fight going on beneath them or the impending attack.

However, the *Vincennes* had a black box of its own. The SPY-1A, Command and Decision, and Weapons Control System computers were all equipped with magnetic tape equipment that tracked and recorded all of the signals received and processed by these key pieces of electronic equipment.[17] Because of this, we have been able not only to verify the timing and nature of all of her actions, but also to obtain a remarkable, perhaps unique, cross-check of the way that scenario preconceptions can distort both perceptions and memory.

The situation aboard the *Vincennes* that day was one of confusion and disorder. This harsh judgment is borne out by the transcript of the Navy's official investigation report and, in retrospect, by the divergence between the memories and oral testimony of the officers present and the actual, recorded sequence of events.[18]

The story told by the data tapes is straightforward. Iran Air Flight 655 took off from Bandar Abbas at 10:17 A.M. on the morning of July 3, on a heading of 210 (runway 21). Squawking Mode III, Code 6760 continuously, it kept on a more or less constant heading of 210, climbing steadily to its cruising altitude while gradually gaining speed. Data and testimony from the USS *Sides* corroborate the flight path and the Mode III IFF squawk. Indeed, the *Sides* was to identify the unknown aircraft as nonhostile and turn its attention elsewhere only seconds before the *Vincennes* launched its missiles.[19]

The story told by those inside the CIC aboard the *Vincennes* is quite different. From the first alerted contact, various personnel began to report a "Mode II" squawk on a code associated with Iranian F-14s. Although none of the data recorders reported any IFF response other than Mode III, Code 6760, those aboard the *Vincennes* continued to consistently misreport the signal.

As the range closed, the *Vincennes* began to broadcast increasingly urgent warning messages to the unknown aircraft; at first, these were general challenges on both military and international civil distress nets. But as the notion that the aircraft was indeed an F-14 became fixed in the minds of the key operators, the challenges were made more specific and were addressed only to an unidentified "Iranian F-14." A quick thumb-through of a listing of commercial flights missed the clear listing for Flight 655, although it was on course and nearly on time.

A warning of possible "COMAIR" (commercial aircraft) issued a minute or two later was acknowledged by the CO, but essentially ignored. At this point, the ship was still engaging the Iranian surface boats. Moreover, the ship was heeling sharply with loose books and equipment flying about the CIC. With the TAO concentrating on the surface battle and his attention divided, and the Anti-Air Warfare Commander (AAWC) new to his post (and generally regarded as inexperienced and a weak leader), de facto leadership fell upon the more junior Tactical Information Coordinator (TIC), who by that time was almost literally shouting about the immediacy and seriousness of the threat.

To give Captain Rogers credit, he did allow the unknown aircraft to close to well within its possible missile firing range before asking for and receiving permission to intercept, and he did so only after repeating the challenge several more times. Only then, convinced that the threat to his ship was too serious to ignore, and under pressure to act quickly to avoid the earlier fate of the USS *Stark*, did he authorize the firing.

Was he justified in his perception of a real threat to his ship (which was the Navy's claim)? Were the Iranians reckless for flying over a fire-fight in progress (which they may have been—*if* those at Bandar Abbas were aware of the exact position of the fight)? Was the whole incident a regrettable, but unavoidable, accident of war (which is precisely what the resulting U.S. attitude was, in the Pentagon, in Congress, and in the press)? Possibly all three of these U.S. assertions are true. But are they relevant?

The first question to be asked is: Was an error made on the U.S. side at all? The U.S. Navy finally claimed that Captain Rogers of the *Vincennes* acted correctly in appraising the threat, and ultimately awarded him a medal for his performance in the Gulf that day.[20] Others in the

United States asserted that such blame as there was attached solely to Iran.[21] Iran, on the other hand, went so far as to claim that the United States had shot the Airbus down in full knowledge that it was a civil aircraft, which of course would have been an evil deed rather than an error.

It would be better to follow Lanir's example and ask whether there was an error made at all. Complex military-technological systems such as those aboard the *Vincennes*, designed to reduce the incidence of human errors, also provide mechanisms for producing new ones. The question, then, is not whether any individual could have acted correctly in theory, but how and why the socio-technical command-and-control system contributed to the consequential failure that occurred.

The Investigations

The large-scale technical military system operating in the Persian Gulf that day, of which the *Vincennes* was the central feature, was not waging total war, but rather a highly selective engagement in an arena known to be filled with civil traffic on air and sea. This very sophisticated piece of equipment had been placed in a situation for which it had never been designed precisely because it was thought to be most capable of making the kinds of quick and accurate judgments that would be necessary. It failed.

Of course, the *Vincennes* itself is a piece of machinery, and only human beings can make "errors." Once they had ascertained that the equipment had operated properly, the only question for the investigators was whether the source was at the personal level (i.e., the performance of the CO or the TAO) or the group level (i.e., collective failure in the CIC). It was this general approach that framed the subsequent investigations.[22]

Navy hearing boards such as the one convened to review the events of July 3, 1988, are unique in focusing on the CO, owing to historical naval tradition that it is the CO, and only the CO, who is responsible for anything and everything that happens on or to his ship. As often as not, judgment calls are made on the simple basis of what the hearing officers would have done in the same situation, given the same information.

This tradition worked against the possibility of a comprehensive, systemic investigation into the circumstances preceding the missile firing.[23] For the question should not have been whether the CO was justified in taking the actions he did given the situation and the information he had, but *how* the situation had developed so badly and *why* the information being provided was so skewed from reality. These matters were in fact addressed by the investigation, but by no means to the degree or depth that would have been required to develop an adequate set of answers.

The investigation board was convened by Rear Admiral William M. Fogarty at Bahrain beginning on July 6, while the events were still fresh in the minds of the participants. Formal hearings began a week later, and the entire procedure was completed and the report delivered to the Navy on July 28.[24] Even in the cleansed form provided to the public, the report is rich in personal and technical detail. Perhaps the most striking feature is the degree to which the recollections of the participants as to the nature and assessment of the presumptive threat differ, and the variance between what was reported by the SPY-1A computers and what its human interpreters were reporting.

The record shows that the decision to fire was taken more or less calmly and deliberately on the basis of personal advice passed from junior officers to the senior AAWC, and from the AAWC to the CO—in the face of a stream of contrary evidence from the electronics aboard. Confronted with the problem of reconciling the manifest mistakes made in interpretation of technical evidence, the board concluded that "stress, task-fixation, and unconscious distortion of data may have played a major role in this incident."[25] The report then went on to attribute the distortion to the relatively junior TIC and Identification Supervisor (IDS), who became convinced that the track of Iran Air 655 was an F-14 after an IDS report of a momentary Mode II squawk.

The Fogarty report states: "After this report of the Mode II, TIC appears to have distorted data flow in an unconscious attempt to make available evidence fit a preconceived scenario ('scenario fulfillment')." This fulfillment including continuing to read the Iran Air flight as descending toward the *Vincennes*, even though the information being presented by the electronic suite was contradictory. In such circumstances, it may indeed be remarkable that the CO, deprived of any direct source of information or data, was able to delay his decision so long.

Whether or not he would have been justified to shoot if the evidence were simply ambiguous or the uncertainties known is not the center of our concern here. Rather, the focus of my analysis is the manifest failure of the decision-making system on the *Vincennes* to interpret the evidence correctly. The system "failed" in that a false hypothesis was constructed and maintained, serving as the basis for all subsequent actions. This would have been as serious a matter even if Captain Rogers had decided *not* to fire, although it is most likely that we would never have learned about it. Among the conclusions of the Fogarty report is a general recommendation:

> Since it appears that combat-induced stress on personnel may have played a significant role in this incident, it is recommended the CNO (Chief of Naval Operations) direct further study be undertaken into the stress factors impacting on personnel in modern warships with highly sophisticated command, control, communications, and intelligence systems, such as AEGIS. This study should also address the possibility of establishing a psychological profile for personnel who must function in this environment.

Stripped of its deliberately restrained prose, this is a quite remarkable admission that the very sophistication of the system may in itself have been a contributory factor. This is the only statement in the official report to acknowledge that it might be wise to differentiate between questions of personnel performance and training at the individual and/or group/ship level and more systemic factors.

Nevertheless, and following U.S. Navy tradition, the entire review process was treated as a search for "culpability." Having absolved the individuals of blame, the Navy, as well as the press and Congress, then moved rapidly to the highest possible level of political analysis; if there was no personal malfeasance, and the Aegis system had worked perfectly, the result could only be attributed to the misfortunes of war.

On October 6, 1988, a panel of five psychologists chosen through the American Psychological Association testified at a hearing of the House Armed Services Committee.[26] As the Fogarty report had done, the expert panel pointed out that in an era of increasing technical complexification, it will no longer do to continue to point only to "operator error" as the source of malfunctions and disasters.[27] Rather, what happened aboard the *Vincennes* on July 3 could be seen as part of what one psychologist characterized as the "glass cockpit" syndrome discussed in chapter 7, the result of humans operating large-scale, highly sophisticated technical systems under conditions of high stress, high consequence, and high visibility.[28]

Regrettably, the congressional hearing panel was more interested in the question of the functioning of the *Vincennes* electronic hardware (and software) than in its human interface. Much attention was paid to whether the very expensive and highly sophisticated Aegis radar system did work, *as* a technical system. In fact, it did work—in the sense of identifying and correctly tracking Flight 655 almost from the moment of its takeoff—although it did not, and could not, given its technical limitations, identify the type of aircraft, or even its size. The rest of the electronics suite also worked well. As with Lanir's case, the "surprise" was the degree to which the system lent itself to misinterpretation and mindset by its operators.

The *Vincennes* failed as an operating organization, however perfectly its equipment was operating.[29] Yet, the emphasis in the official investigation, and in the reports of the five APA psychologists, was on the role played by stress. "Scenario fixation," in which the Iran Air flight became embedded in the collective consciousness of those in the CIC as a hostile Iranian F-14, was derived from and attributed to the degree of stress present rather than to the human-machine interface.

The testimony was almost unanimous in stating that stress in CIC was very high, although there is no way retroactively to determine just how high it was, or whether the sense of near-panic so clearly evinced by the TIC was spreading. But what are the expectations of a combat system such as the *Vincennes*, or of the CIC as a war-fighting center? That stress would be low? That battle conditions would be other than confusing? That the ship could be attacked on the surface, or from the air, but not both simultaneously—not to mention possible subsurface attacks in other circumstances? If these are or were the assumptions under which the Aegis cruisers were designed, than the *Vincennes* should never have been deployed into the Gulf.

Stress was clearly a contributing factor, but its presence is in no way explanatory, and by no means exculpatory. Stress is, or should be, a central assumption of battle, along with confusion, uncertainty, and

risk. To design military systems otherwise would be folly.[30] Looking back over naval history, there is no evidence that the *Vincennes*
was under a degree of stress greater than one would expect for a ship
in combat, in strange waters. If the ship as a system is incapable of
operating correctly under such circumstances, she is a failure as a
weapons system, however well her machinery, electronics, and missiles perform.[31]

The Navy sought to excuse the *Vincennes*'s performance on the
grounds that the technology worked as designed, but the imperfect
human beings did not. But these are empty excuses. Any real-world
technology must be designed around the fundamental premise that
humans are imperfect. Neither the unanticipated combat situation, nor
the degree of stress that was manifest, nor the resulting confusion that
occurred aboard the *Vincennes* can excuse her poor performance. Military systems that cannot function under stress, or amid confusion, or
while under multithreat attack, are useless in the real world.[32]

Conclusion

Taken as isolated events, these three cases may seem to be no more
than another tragedy of armed conflict. In a tense situation in a combat
zone, an unfortunate mistake caused the deaths of several scores or
hundreds of people. It has happened in every war, and will happen
again in the next. There appears to have been little interest in it as a
case of malfunctioning technology. As a purely political story, it was of
continuing interest for a while because of the subsequent attempts by
both countries to assign culpability, and perhaps deliberate malfeasance to the other.[33]

When similar errors occur in the fog and confusion of real war, it
is often difficult to disentangle the circumstances. But these three incidents occurred in relative isolation, and under relatively clear and
uncomplicated circumstances. What they have in common is that each
represents a case where the system failed even though the equipment
worked perfectly. In each case, the ultimate cause was more than just
cognitive failure or undue stress. It was a failure of representation
based primarily on the difficulty of forming an independent interpretation of the situation in the environment created by the new
equipment.

The Israeli aircraft had no interest in shooting down an unarmed airliner, but the command-and-control system had shaped a decision that it was a hostile aircraft. The attack on the *Stark* was probably not deliberate, but rather the consequence of quick-response high-tech warfare, and the *Stark* itself was vulnerable because its automated quick-response defenses were considered potentially threatening to other aircraft in a presumably moderate threat environment. The very sophisticated, high-technology Aegis aircraft detection and track identification system that is the heart of the *Vincennes*, designed to discriminate between U.S. and hostile aircraft at high speed in the heat of combat, provided a frame in which quick response was the dominant concern, providing neither space nor time for reflection on the nature of the putative threat.

Because the United States has been heavily investing in the kind of sophisticated, computer-aided and controlled technological military systems these examples represent, and will be relying even more heavily on them in the future, it is doubly unfortunate that the official investigations left so many avenues unexplored. But that has been the usual situation in almost every similar circumstance, civilian or military, despite a growing body of literature on systemic failure in complex, high-technology organizations.[34] The most durable pocket of military tradition is the belief that human beings are ultimately responsible and ultimately in control, until and unless their equipment fails them.

In her extensive study of the effects of automation and computerized equipment in a variety of civilian work settings, Zuboff has noted that the transition to a more computerized workplace is also accompanied by a transfer of emphasis from oral-culture oriented, action-centered skills to reflective, intellective ones. In contrasting an older and still traditional plant (Piney Wood) to a newer and highly automated one, one worker summed up the difference in reaction to problems and difficulties this way: "When there is a problem at Piney Wood, someone goes out and kicks something; when there is a problem at Cedar Bluff, the operators have a meeting."[35] Clearly, when the human in the loop is not fully a part of it, what is most desperately wanted is some reflective and digestive time. This raises serious questions about the wisdom, or effectiveness, of inserting highly automated equipment into an environment that is by tradition very much human-oriented and action-centered.[36]

That the overall effect of the new technologies might be a situation where people acting as expected with equipment that is functioning perfectly will fail to arrive at the objectively correct interpretation is rarely, if ever, considered. The Navy hearing boards never considered the possibility that the failure lay in the theory of design, that a highly automated, rapid-response battle system that depends for its function on real-time interactions between complex computerized systems and human operators may have an inherently high probability of error in any crisis situation that has not been anticipated, planned, and rehearsed.

Because fundamental surprise has long been identified as the essence of warfare, the prognosis for the future is frightening. But as will be discussed in the following chapters, this has not stopped the military from moving ever more rapidly to extend computer control and automation onto every aspect of the battlefield, from missile defense in outer space to fire control for the grunt in the foxhole.

10.

The Logistics of Techno-War

> [The Gulf War] was the first space war . . . it was
> the first war of the space age.
>
> *(General Merrill McPeak)*

Introduction

Despite its hyperbole, the preceding statement by General McPeak, then chief of staff of the U.S. Air Force, represented the dominant politico-military view of the U.S. performance in the 1991 Gulf War that drove the Iraqi military out of Kuwait.[1] The minority view that it was logistics and preparation rather than technology that was responsible for the quick victory was perhaps best expressed at the time by Lawrence Korb: "If you've got enough time, American logistics will always overwhelm you. . . . You would not be writing the same story if the war had come in August or September."[2]

This pair of quotes beautifully represents the two ideal positions in the longstanding argument about quality versus quantity in military weapons systems, exposing in the process the generational differences that underlie the two positions.[3] Korb speaks from the conservative historical tradition, in which wars are won on logistics and organization, on fundamentals and mass, providing both robustness and resilience against the expected surprises of armed conflict. McPeak belongs to the new generation of technicians, whose military thinking is based on the introduction of high technology and computers everywhere possible, in "smart" weapons and smart systems, under computerized command and control, with complete computer-mediated connectivity and integration both horizontally across the battlefield and vertically from the smallest fighting unit to central command.

The defeat of the traditionalists was probably inevitable even in the case of the U.S. Army, long dominated by conservatism and tradition. Military officers, particularly senior ones, have careers that are intertwined with the civilian economy, and, in particular, with those sectors most closely connected with the military. The shift in the civilian economy from mass-production industry to high-tech industry, with its focus on technology and change as the basis for competitiveness and success, caused a marked shift in the balance of power in the military from warriors to technocrats.[4]

The traditional warriors might nevertheless have won more often in the political struggle if it were not for the persistent social and political denial in U.S. history and politics of the difference between U.S. conduct in warfare and its stated politico-military doctrine. From the Civil War through Vietnam, the United States has always emphasized the quality and performance of the individual, and, by extension, the quality and superiority of his weapons. But when war has come, be it the Civil War, the two world wars, the Korean War, or Vietnam, the United States relied for victory far more on quantity then quality, depending more on its huge industrial base and manpower pool than on technology or training to wear down its opponents.[5]

The "U.S." side (i.e., the Union) in the Civil War was infamous for pouring men into slaughterhouse battlefields to overwhelm the Confederates by sheer numbers.[6] The United States behaved no differently from any of the Western powers in the equally horrible trench battles of the First World War. And victory in the Second World War was clearly based more on logistics and industrial might then on technical innovation.[7] Victories in both wars resulted from the ability and willingness of the United States (and its allies) to maximize effectiveness even at the expense of quality, to absorb losses in attrition warfare with a view to wearing the enemy down rather than outfighting him.[8]

Unable to make use of nuclear weapons, or to fully exploit its slim margin of superiority in radar or other electronics, the U.S. experience in Korea was little different. Only the long and painful experience of fighting a nontraditional conflict in Vietnam was to expose the cost of the traditional American way of war, and lead to increasing pressure to substitute money, equipment, or technical sophistication for the loss of American lives.

The United States was not the first great power to be faced with the dilemma of seeking to preserve hegemonic control in the face of political protest against the costs, nor will be the last.[9] During Britain's long reign, it vacillated between exporting the costs (e.g., by using colonial troops) and mobilizing public opinion (e.g., the War of Jenkin's Ear).[10] But in the U.S. case, there was already a putative resolution on the table. The long-term investments made by ARPA and other government agencies in computer technology were just beginning to turn into real products,[11] and the resulting transformation of American society and industry was already under way. Advanced technology, and, in particular, advanced computer technology, in which Americans held an enormous and unchallenged lead, was to allow the United States to continue to project power overseas without at the same time putting American lives unduly at risk.

As was discussed in chapter 8, the high-technology approach that had thus far been restricted to space programs, satellites, nuclear submarines, advanced aircraft, and other areas where technical superiority was primary began to spill over into more traditional areas of the military. On the ground as in the air, on the sea as under it, the United States was to shift away from a historical dependence on mass production and mass attacks, from a draft army outfitted with weapons of middling quality to an all-volunteer force equipped with the latest and most sophisticated technologies.

The first real test of the newly designed, newly integrated military was to come not on the battlefields of central Europe for which the expenditures had been justified, nor in the jungles of Asia, which remain the most problematic arena for technological warfare, but in the flat sands of the Middle East, on a ground more closely resembling American weapons test ranges than even the most optimistic of the new weaponeers could have hoped for.

The Gulf War

When Iraqi forces invaded Kuwait in August 1990, they did so at least partially under the delusion that the United States would have neither the will nor the capability to fight the supposedly experienced Iraqi forces in the desert.[12] Following the amazing success of the United States and its coalition allies in the hundred-hour ground war in February 1991, neither the will nor the capability of the United States and its coalition allies could be questioned. And neither, apparently, could the decision to modernize and computerize American and NATO military forces.

The verdict in the quality-quantity debate seemed clear.[13] Promoters of the high-technology strategy proclaimed that the new weapons systems were the key to victory, that their performance discredited critics of high-technology military postures, and that the war further demonstrated the ability of "smart" weapons and other sophisticated technical systems to fight effectively while minimizing U.S. casualties.[14] Building on globally televised images of smart bombs flying down air shafts, Tomahawk missiles cruising the skies of Baghdad looking for their targets, and Patriot missiles rushing skyward in a great plume of fire and smoke to hunt incoming Scuds, promoters of sophisticated military technologies boldly announced that technological innovation was now proven to be the best and most reliable guide to the future of American military forces.[15]

The official Department of Defense assessment of the Gulf War therefore took a more sober and balanced approach than that of the technology promoters inside and outside the military.[16] The war demonstrated dramatically the possibilities of the still-ongoing technological revolution in weapons and warfare. Many of the platforms, weapons, and systems were used in combat for the first time, and most performed superbly. Coordinated air power in particular was used with extraordinary effectiveness. But this technological euphoria overlooked the special conditions under which the war was fought, including not only the availability of a neighboring country as a base and lack of Iraqi opposition during the buildup, but also the desert climate, the clear weather, the political isolation of Iraq, and the lack of any other disturbance abroad to divide our attention and assets.[17] The war also exposed serious vulnerabilities in the network of intelligence, logistics, communications, and other infrastructure required to support the sophisticated and complex military technologies.

The high costs of the advanced weapons had been justified as necessary to counter a sudden Soviet attack in Europe, to offset NATO's numerical inferiority and choice of defensive posture. Instead, they were deployed in the Gulf with abundant time and adequate buildup, and launched in a time and place of our own choosing, against an enemy with numerical inferiority and poor morale, in combat that turned out to be of no more than moderate intensity. Moreover, the decline of the Soviet threat allowed the United States to divert resources, manpower, and equipment from all over the world. Weapons and systems that had been developed to fight a high-technology war on the central front in Europe while coping with a second, regional conflict were brought to the Gulf to forge and sustain General Schwartzkopf's buildup in Saudi Arabia.

Despite minimal Iraqi opposition, and six long months to prepare and position forces without significant interference, the logistics chain was stretched to the utmost. By the time the ground war started in February, the United States alone had transported more than 500,000 troops, 3,500 aircraft, 4,200 armored vehicles, and seven million tons of cargo to the Gulf—a buildup that gave Desert Storm more ground and support forces to dispose of than had been available at the peak of the war in Vietnam. The U.S. Air Force deployed to the Gulf almost half of its total available combat force, including more than 90 percent of all aircraft capable of designating targets for precision-guided weapons, two-thirds of its total stock of laser-guided bombs, more than half of its electronic warfare and command-and-control aircraft, and 90 percent of all of its mobile fueling equipment.[18] Almost all its airlift capacity was pressed into use on an overtime basis, just to meet the demand for operations-critical items. The U.S. Army moved 60 percent of its total inventory of modern M1 Abrams tanks and M2 and M3 Bradley fighting vehicles to Saudi Arabian bases, along with almost three-quarters of its truck companies (and 100 percent of its heavy trucks), to support only one-quarter of its combat divisions. And although the U.S. Navy deployed almost all of its own combat logistics force, inadequate capacity let to extensive chartering of commercial carriers—over half of which flew a foreign flag.[19]

It was known even before hostilities began that there would be little capacity to surge production of major weapons or systems—one of the known problems with advanced, high-technology, low-production rate goods, whether military or not. The need for manufactured goods was greatest for secondary parts for maintenance and repair, such as transmissions and engines. But production capacity was marginal even for peacetime attrition rates, which could have had serious consequences had the ground war begun earlier, lasted longer, or been more costly. The estimated surge time was six to nine months minimum, even for such low-technology items as barbed wire.[20] By some estimates, there was not even enough ammunition for the Army and Marines to have fought for another week, and no capacity to surge production to make up the shortfall.[21]

Fortunately for the coalition, the attrition rate during the air war was much lower than expected, and the ground war swift and relatively low cost in equipment as well as personnel losses. Given the other factors, such as Iraqi incapabilities in electronic warfare and poor morale, it is by now generally agreed that neither the air war nor the actual ground fighting provided a real test of U.S. military strength or overall performance.

Caring Enough to Send the Very Best

The ambiguity in the use of the term "high technology" in both military and popular reporting of the war also tended to confuse the issues. It was rarely clear in any instance whether the term was being applied to individual pieces of hardware, integrated technical fighting components, technical infrastructure, or the integration of the force by the web of communication, surveillance, intelligence, and command-and-control required. Equally praised for their performance, for example, were: laser-guided bombs (ordnance); the F-117A stealth aircraft (platform); the Tomahawk cruise missile (weapons system); satellite photography and communications (infrastructure); "AirLand Battle" (doctrine); JSTARS, the experimental Joint Surveillance Target Attack Radar System (combat intelligence); and the actual management of the complex, multinational force (integration).

In the absence of reliable battle damage assessment (BDA), early reporting from the front tended to exaggerate the effectiveness of some of the weapons used.[22] The most glaring example was the performance of the Patriot missile. Hardly a week went by without some dramatic footage of a Patriot blazing off into the sky to intercept a Scud heading for our bases in Saudi Arabia, or for Israel. Even before realistic assessments could be made, the performance of the Patriot was being used to justify further expenditures on ballistic missile defenses and other advanced, highly computerized, high-tech "Star Wars" systems. Later assessments were more sober.[23] Many reported Patriot intercepts were hits on discarded missile bodies or other parts as the Iraqi-modified Scuds broke up in flight. The warheads were usually not destroyed; they were just very inaccurate. Indeed, many in Israel now believe that more damage was done with Patriot in place than would have occurred without it.[24]

There was hardly any system that did not experience some operational surprise. F-16s, for example, had problems with their electronic countermeasure pods because their onboard computers were so packed with information that they could not accommodate the programming to update them for new weapons systems.[25] When friendly-fire incidents started to occur, an emergency order was put through for special infrared emitting attachments to provide better identification.[26] Perhaps more relevant to the future of electronics in warfare, the many laptop and desktop computers shipped out to the Gulf began to collapse under the heat, sand, and strain of operations in the theater—to the point where the United States was seriously considering treating them as disposable items.[27] Ruggedized models were eventually shipped out as replacements, but that took time. Even the invulnerability of the F-117 has been called into question: "It is also debatable whether the F-117s emerged unscathed because of superior stealth technology, the effectiveness of allied air defense suppression aircraft, the incompetence of Iraqi air defense operators, or some combination of all three."[28]

The tactical problems of sending high-tech systems against low-tech armies were prominent in the "traditionalist" position in the quality-quantity debate. The disruption of large, complex, tightly integrated, highly specialized, high-technology militaries can at times be accomplished even with relatively simple weapons. The classic examples come from the Vietnam and Afghanistan wars, in which relatively primitive opponents were able to bring down expensive, highly capable helicopters with small arms and man-carried surface-to-air missiles because low-level attacks were necessary to find the enemy amidst the ground cover.

Small-arms fire and other portable small weapons were still a very real threat to the expensive, high-technology aircraft providing close air support in Iraq. Fighter and helicopter pilots had to be retrained to fly their attack missions at higher altitudes, or to loiter behind sand dunes and "pop up" for attack to avoid anti-aircraft fire; the long-standing assumption in European war-gaming had been a requirement for low-level attack to avoid the presumably more serious threat from Soviet high-altitude air defenses.[29] Had there been a real air war more evenly matched in electronic as well as airframe capabilities, even one not involving continual or heavy combat, the struggle for air superiority would not have allowed such free choice of gaining height or loitering whenever desired.

Even without serious enemy challenge, deadly surprises and close calls occurred. Tactical aircraft and tanks working in daylight hours produced an unprecedentedly high rate of casualties from "friendly fire."[30] Satellites passing overhead mistakenly identified a flight of B-52 bombers as a barrage of Scud missiles. Airborne Warning and Control Systems aircraft (AWACS) had to intervene to prevent allied fighters from attacking their own returning bombers.[31] And, in the few cases when tanks did become entangled in more traditional battles, close air support often had to be foregone to avoid indiscriminate attacks on friend and foe alike.

The success of military technology is measured by the performance of those systems for which electronics, and in particular computerized electronics, is central to performance as well as missions: intelligence and surveillance; navigation; air-to-air and air-to-surface missiles; and, above all, the ability to create, supply, inform, coordinate, and integrate the forces in the field. Although these capabilities were tested in the Gulf War, the inability of Iraq to interfere or intervene, particularly with electronic countermeasures, made it more of a field exercise than a real combat situation.

But separate assessments of individual weapons or systems are not really to the point. Because modern militaries are increasingly designed to operate in a computer-integrated environment when the level and intensity of conflict is high, an *overall* assessment of system performance is required. Given the nature and duration of the battle in Iraq, all that has been proven is that the forces we have are very successful given open skies, a preponderance of force, and minimal effective opposition.

Iraq had no meaningful capability at all in the critical area of electronic warfare, enabling coalition forces to move freely while keeping close tabs on Iraqi forces, particularly at night. Furthermore, the conditions of desert warfare—flat and open land free of the dense jungle cover of Vietnam or the mountainous and craggy terrain of Afghanistan—also provided little or no natural interference with surveillance, intelligence, and communications, and no place for Iraq to hide, disperse, or mask their combat forces effectively.

The Logistics of Cyberspace

With six months to establish the command-and-control network and accumulate supplies without interference, combat experience provided few surprises. In contrast, the more general lessons about the organization, management, and integration of forces were numerous, and potentially disturbing. The organization behind the weapons did work, but only at tremendous cost, even under uniquely favorable conditions. The United States was able to mobilize, on its own schedule, whatever pieces were required out of a force structure intended to fight one and a half wars simultaneously, and then to use it to fight a half-war under maximally favorable conditions, at the cost of almost totally stripping Europe and the United States of systems, spares, and maintenance.[32]

Up and down the line of logistics and supply, the United States and its allies had time to train, to tighten up, to identify problems, and to reflect upon the battle terrain in ways that would not otherwise have been possible. There is every reason to question whether the coalition would have been able to act as well, and with such small losses, if it had been denied the time to mobilize and prepare its forces, the logistics to bring them to the battle and keep them resupplied, and the freedom to use its advanced intelligence and communication technologies without hindrance. Although U.S. forces arrived in Saudi Arabia quickly after the first Iraqi move in to Kuwait in August 1990, there was a lengthy period thereafter when the coalition could not have defended its bases or its position from a follow-on Iraqi invasion.[33]

Considerable resources had to be diverted even in the relatively one-sided conditions. High-technology weapons systems using black boxes operated smoothly, but only at enormous expense, and at the cost of moving almost all of the U.S. reserve repair capacity into sprawling Saudi bases that would have been quite vulnerable to a seri-

ous Iraqi attack. As many as eight scarce and expensive electronic warfare aircraft were used to cover a dozen F-16s on a raid; the high ratio
of support to combat aircraft was not untypical for air operations, and
in some cases was a limiting factor. Satellites intended to cover the
Soviet Union and other areas of the world had to be moved into position to provide surveillance and intelligence. Command-and-control
resources intended to fight a major, global war were diverted to the
Gulf to manage the intricacies of the battle.

The high level of redundancy in resources and ample preparation
time made possible by the six-month buildup preceding hostilities
were not as apparent to the press, or as widely publicized, as fancy
weapons; but they were unquestionably the most important factors in
the smoothness and effectiveness of military operations, particularly in
the four-day ground war. That time was needed to test, adjust, maintain, and make fully operational a large number of the high-tech platforms and systems. It was also needed to collect data and develop intelligence and information. At the beginning of the buildup there were
almost no up-to-date photos of the combat area. In fact, it took almost
all of the six months to acquire, analyze, digitize, and program the key
terrain and target information needed for programming the Tomahawk cruise missile's guidance computers.[34]

As materiél and logistical support accumulated in the theater by
stripping units in Germany and the United States, maintenance bases
in Saudi Arabia had virtually unprecedented access to parts and to
diagnostic and other critical skills in a U.S. military establishment designed and sized to fight not one, but two global wars. National guard
and other reserve units were mined for resources. Missing personnel
for critical slots, always in short supply even in peacetime, were
sought out and brought to the theater. Even active duty personnel
for whom there was no immediate use were nevertheless alerted and
retained.[35]

Military skills were further augmented by an extraordinary amount
of on-site contractor expertise, in the form of special teams of civilian
experts who helped diagnose problems and supplied needed parts.[36]
In many cases, this involved direct communications with or transport
to and from the United States. Computerized electronic warfare
aboard aircraft, for example, needed to be updated constantly to adjust
to changing evaluation of threats. At first, this involved the awkward

and time-consuming shuttling of tapes between the U.S. and the Saudi bases. Given the time to adjust, the United States was able to establish direct, secure communications links, allowing the direct updating and reprogramming from the United States of aircraft computer systems located in the Gulf.[37] And many of the black box electronic packages aboard tanks and naval vessels as well as aircraft were shuttled back and forth for maintenance, updating, and servicing.

The amount of expert support needed to achieve high levels of availability was never given much prominence in military or press accounts, even though they foreshadow the demands new weapons systems will impose upon even a smaller high-technology military. Many support roles have been transferred to civilian employees or contractors to conserve military manpower; many more are being so designated because the specialized skills are not and will not be available. As the DoD report concludes: "It seems clear that future contingencies also will require the presence and involvement of civilians in active theaters of operations."[38] But "active theaters" generally mean within zones of combat. Given that civilians are, after all, civilians, and receive no hazard pay and few awards for being in a combat zone, it is an open question whether maintenance bases will be able to draw as easily on civilian personnel if U.S. forces are required to construct and use their forward bases under the threat of serious enemy attack.

Some of the war's success stories become more problematic when examined in this light. Although such adaptations are normal for battlefield conditions, these conditions eliminate many of the supposed advantages of advanced over-the-horizon and fire-and-forget weapons. Rather than adding flexibility, these advanced systems must be closely constrained in their application by integrated command networks that guarantee that they are allocated efficiently, and that the right targets are being destroyed. The resulting military organization needs relatively predictable conditions to assure that these networks perform successfully, and is less likely to be effective in a disruptive, hard-fought conflict.

This vivid demonstration of the depth and breadth of support necessary to support a large, complex military organization equipped with advanced, complex, and often fragile technologies and machines is perhaps the single greatest lesson of the war in the Gulf, however long it took to sink in. It is not clear if even six months would have been adequate if Iraq had been willing (or able) to actively disrupt organizational growth, training, and integration.

The Electronic Web

The DoD noted that: "The services put more electronics communications connectivity into the Gulf in 90 days than we put in Europe in 40 years."[39] The largest complete C³I (command, control, communications, and intelligence) system ever assembled was put into place to connect not only the U.S. forces in the Gulf, but to sustain bases in the United States, the national command authority in Washington, and other coalition forces. The achievement was so stunning that the mere existence and reliable functioning of the network was one of the great successes of the war. But later analysis has also shown that the performance of the electronic warfare and command-and-control systems left much to be desired.

Shortfalls in operations caused by lack of equipment hampered many operations, particularly of the more advanced weapons and systems. "The greatest limitation on the U.S. ability to apply combat power . . . was our own lack of systems to support combat aircraft in theater. At any given time we were only able to use 25 percent of the combat air assets we had in theater simply because it took . . . 100 percent of the electronic war assets to support that limited effort."[40] Aircraft IFF equipment reliability and maintenance was a constant problem, both at the individual aircraft level and to the airborne war-fighting command posts. This was further exacerbated by the lack of interoperability or standardization among the several coalition air forces. Some analysts even suggested that the United States would be better off investing in more electronic warfare equipment instead of buying more combat aircraft.

The demand for intelligence data, particularly satellite and reconnaissance imagery, for targeting precision-guided munitions, was insatiable, and simply could not be met even by the commitment of as many U.S. resources as could be made available.[41] Nor were the services able to organize, process, and coordinate it efficiently. The volume of data simply swamped the tactical intelligence system, and came near to paralyzing other systems for electronic integration and command-and-control.[42] And it is likely to continue to do so in the future, no matter what steps are taken, since data-gathering technology tends to stay ahead of data processing capabilities, and perhaps always will.

Maintaining the volume of communications also turned out to be an incredible problem even in the absence of effective Iraqi capabilities for jamming or other counter-communications measures expected in a major combat theater. At the peak, 286 separate communications centers were interacting with each other, and with out-of-theater command centers. A hybrid telephone system made up of several generations of different communications equipment from different services, and from different countries, handled more than 700,000 telephone calls and 150,000 important messages a day. Daily management and monitoring of more than 35,000 frequencies was required to assure that channels were clear and free of interference.[43]

Communications links included SHF military satellite channels, UHF tactical channels, the military's automatic digital network (AUTODIN) and worldwide military command-and-control system, and even channels made available over more secure defense satellite systems intended for other purposes. Even that was not enough. The Navy's UHF satellite communications links were so overtaxed that at one point in late November, Naval Space Command announced that no more coverage was available. Commercial terminals and leased commercial channels were used to augment the capacity, including INTELSAT and even the Saudi national telephone service. Some commercial equipment was even installed on Navy ships.[44] The serious weakness of the resulting system, its vulnerability to both electronic and physical interference, was never exposed because Iraq never put it to the test.

Other command-and-control problems were worked out during the six months of buildup to the point where little friction occurred during the operational ground war phase. This was no small task considering the number of allied as well as U.S. units that had to be integrated into a single, coordinated structure, and the breadth and complexity of the frontal attack that had to be synchronized. Even so, the postwar evaluation was that combined forces command and control is still rudimentary, and might have proved inflexible and unwieldy if there had been any setback or surprises during execution of planned joint maneuvers. As it was, technological improvisation was called into play many times to develop innovations or other workarounds. Once again, the amount of time available to test systems and practice using them proved crucial.

The greatest success of C^{3}I was in the critical task of integrating and coordinating the air war, both before the ground attack and during it. When data and targeting information were available, mission planning was frequently accomplished in hours, rather than the days that had characterized combat in Vietnam. Also highly praised was the NAVSTAR Global Positioning System (GPS), a network of satellites whose transmitted data allow accurate determination of the receiver's position to within a few meters. Indeed, some units used comparison of GPS position readings as a method of IFF verification during the ground war. In addition to terrestrial navigation, GPS was also used to improve aircraft navigation accuracy and provide midcourse guidance for cruise missiles.

On the other hand, there was often some confusion and delay in getting ground targets identified and targeted, owing to the long and complex chain of command involved. The shortage of military GPS receivers also forced mass purchases of commercial units, which in turn meant that the United States had to disable the security provisions of GPS that normally deny such accurate positioning to non-security–cleared receivers.[45]

Fortunately for the coalition, the rapid Iraqi collapse eased the strain as the war went on instead of increasing it. Such rudimentary electronic warfare capabilities as Iraq had were targeted early on and quickly rendered inoperable or unusable, and other, more devious strategies for interfering with the web of coalition communications and information nets were apparently not tried. But at no time did the Gulf War test whether the required electronic infrastructure was really robust or resilient against a systematic, capable, and determined effort to disrupt it at either the tactical or command level.

Redefining Effectiveness

Military technologies, like civil ones, are subject to the familiar drive of the "product displacement cycle."[46] The United States can attempt to maintain dominance by continuing to generate ever more advanced and complex weapons systems, even as the last generation is sold to or co-produced by our allies. If the historical cycle holds, European powers will then buy or co-develop the equivalent of today's high-tech systems, while the United States continues its search for newer, more advanced, and far more expensive ones. In turn, the Europeans will seek to keep their costs down by marketing their technology, or their skills, to the richer of the developing countries. This, at least, would replicate the history of the arms race in the Middle East.

Under such circumstances, the future U.S. force would still be capable of inflicting greater and greater damage, but at ever increasing costs and risks. It could be used with assured success only against opponents who lack the countering technical capabilities. Given the vigor of the arms markets, especially after the Gulf War, the number of such convenient countries will continue to decline. The United States would then be unable credibly to protect its interests, or project force, against less accommodating opponents who are too large or too technically knowledgeable for the intricately integrated U.S. systems to defeat with the required minimal casualties.

Until recently, U.S. armed forces justified their "inefficiently" duplicative resources in terms of slack—unused reserves to be drawn upon and orchestrated when these inevitable disruptions occur. The move to greater efficiency by reducing organizational slack, to cut personnel and compensate with computers and electronic networks, to substitute "just-in-time" resupply for stockpiles, is familiar enough to students of modern industrial policies. But civilian firms that rely on electronic systems, and, in particular, on computerized equipment, for integration, coordination, and control generally do not face the same consequences if systems fail, and are almost never expected to perform under armed attack.

Able to purchase fewer and fewer of the new systems in times of budgetary restraint, the U.S. might increasingly shift to forces shaped primarily for high-tech intervention without a full appreciation for the risks that might be entailed. Claiming to have learned the double lesson of high-technology and low-cost intervention from its success in the Gulf, the military might well move toward a high-technology "surgical" force directed primarily at smaller and less capable powers. But to do so without providing a proportionately larger support system will produce a military that lacks robustness and resilience against errors, against surprises, and against clever, if unsophisticated, countermeasures.

The modern U.S. military is increasingly becoming a complex, highly interconnected, integrated socio-technical system with high interdependence between and among units.[47] As such, it requires intensive, timely logistics and information support. The high-technology weapons were effective because their support systems were allowed to train and operate without hindrance, and almost without time or resource constraint. Because the conflict did not test the combat robustness of U.S. forces adequately, there is reason for caution about potential vulnerabilities if the United States is pressured by time or circumstance to deploy against a similar opponent at less than full strength, or against a more powerful opponent even if its full strength can be brought to bear.

The Gulf War victory crystallized the emerging redefinition of military effectiveness through advanced technology as a substitute for American lives discussed at the beginning of this chapter. This emphasis may be more sensible in peacetime than in war. Peacetime militaries are not threatened with a sudden loss of staff as a matter of daily routine. They do not face a malicious enemy trying to physically cause as much trouble as possible to critical communication or information links.

The underlying arguments of the quantity-quality debate concerning robustness, reliability, and the ability to cope with fundamental surprise have not been resolved. What is more, the subsequent political and bureaucratic reinforcement of those who have based their careers and their futures on advanced, computerized military technologies almost certainly guarantees that they will hardly be addressed.

Computers and the Transformation of War

Because of the many special conditions, the coalition's invasion of Iraq bore more resemblance to an elaborate simulation, or perhaps video game, than the hyper-complex, high-attrition, electronic scramble that is usually envisioned when analysts talk about the coming technological transition in warfare. This goes beyond the question of what success the United States would have had if the Iraqis had fought back effectively. Given the positions, the isolation of Iraq, and the military asymmetries, the coalition would have won regardless. But the costs might have been far, far higher.

The most lasting lessons of the Gulf War were the indirect ones learned by the troops in their day-to-day operations; the real transition that is taking place is more a transition in the perception of combat than in the nature and structure of warfare. In the future, survival in combat may come to depend almost entirely on getting off the first accurate shot.

Even without a major war, the battlefield environment has been transformed by technical innovation in the past fifty years. It is a long way from the desperate and closely fought tank meleés of the Ukraine or North Africa to an M1A1 commander blowing up Iraqi tanks with precise single shots while moving across rough terrain. Fighter pilots operating under the control of AWACS with an umbrella of electronic warfare support, firing missiles at signals seen only on their radar, are even farther technically from the Battle of Britain. And the pilot of an F-117, flying to Baghdad in a cloak of stealth with television-guided precision weapons, may not even have been born when James Michener immortalized the dangers of flying into the teeth of air defenses in Korea to attack the bridges at Toko-ri.[48]

When the rain of arrows fell on the French knights at Agincourt, the archers knew that they were no longer fodder to be fed into the periphery of battles between armored nobles, even if the kings and princes were slow to catch up. The U.S. Marines cheering the Gatling guns at San Juan Hill, the British Maxim gunners mowing down rank after rank of Dervishes at Omdurman and Zulus at Mome Gorge, and even the Tibetans, Furani, or Ashanti who simply dropped their weapons and walked away once they realized what was happening, knew that the day of infantry advancing in formation across open ground was over, even if the generals refused to listen.[49] At some future date, the single-shot kills of the M1A1 tanks in Iraq may rank with these as a turning point in the understanding by soldiers of the nature and risks of a new battlefield.

Warfare is being transformed by the combination of computerized systems: high-technology weapons; communications; command-and-control. The Gulf War demonstrated clearly how much military analysts believe that it has already transformed military operations.[50] Massive attacks, front lines, indeed the whole apparatus of attrition warfare are now claimed to be obsolete. Instead, it is argued, the new mode of war will be "nonlinear"; an assemblage of small units, moving quickly and independently, striking at will and at night, coordinating with each other flexibly as the situation demands.[51] This new "maneuver warfare" would seem very postmodern indeed, were it not for the massive requirements for central control and coordination built in to AirLand Battle and the other new force structure designs and doctrines.[52]

Having overcome what they regarded as the traditionalist school of linear, attrition warfare, the new cadre of senior officers is now trying to lead rather than follow, to promote rather than resist. The smart-weapon, smart-system revolution has penetrated the military establishment from top to bottom, from the grunt on the ground confirming his squad's position with GPS or using satellite communications to call in a precision air or artillery strike to the general or admiral monitoring or being briefed on the progress of the fighting almost in real time. At every level, and in every service, the introduction of weapons based on or incorporating computers and the rapid and elaborate communications and data processing they make possible has transformed not only the nature and definition of combat, but the linkage among and between commanders and soldiers, the front line of battle and the zones behind it where the smart weapons are mustered, launched, and directed.

It is this complex web of interactions and relationships and the degree of control they make possible that makes the new weapons systems usable and effective. It is force structure and doctrine that determines their role. Yet, arguments about the modernization of military forces almost always focus on the cost and performance of the weapons, neglecting both the costs and the vulnerabilities of the increasingly complex organization needed to support them. This inevitably leads to the conclusion that small numbers of new systems with greater individual capabilities should replace larger numbers of older, "dumber" ones, reinforcing and building on the judgments and evaluations of the personnel who use them.

But wars are won in the large, not in the small; cost-effectiveness is properly measured in terms of the goals of war and not the protection of individual lives. What is not generally realized is how the cost and scarcity of the new systems lock them into networks of mutual dependency, reducing unit autonomy by forcing integration into large-scale tactics and doctrines. Units now fight more effectively, but far less independently. These tendencies were most apparent in the coordination of air power; however, the tendencies were already apparent in other, more traditional areas such as artillery coordination and tank movements.

Unwilling, and perhaps unable, to fight another high-loss war of attrition, the United States and other NATO powers claim that the new high-technology weapons increase both the power and the autonomy of smaller units. But as is discussed in the following chapter, the future battlefield is being designed as an electronic "battlespace," and the need to maintain tightly integrated command-and-control will overwhelm the presumptive discretion given to individual soldiers or units with supposedly smart weapons, even if those weapons are independently targetable and programmable.

11.

C³I in Cyberspace

> No commander is less fortunate than he who
> operates with a telegraph wire stuck in his back.
> *(Field Marshall Helmuth von Moltke)*

Introduction

From Agamemnon before the walls of Troy to General Schwarzkopf at the border of Iraq, military commanders have had to deal not only with leadership, authority, strategy, morale, and tactics, but the more down-to-earth details of information, communication, physical movement, and supply. Although particular attention is always paid to the unique qualities of leadership and inspiration that make great commanders, social historians are always careful to emphasize as well those qualities needed to organize, supply, and direct an army in the particular social and economic environment of the times.[1]

Because military organizations bear many similarities to civil ones in the differentiation of task and equipment and the growing scope and scale of their operations, the other functions of "command" in modern military organizations are very similar to those performed by "management" in the more familiar world of business and economics.[2] Because they both share the problem of integrating, coordinating, and maintaining control in the face of growing complexity of the organization itself, the environment in which it operates, and the means by which information and other forms of intelligence are gathered and managed, both have a growing demand for improvements in C³I—command, control, communications, and intelligence.

The traditional factory of the nineteenth century was a relatively simple operation to manage. No matter how large, it essentially consisted of many people doing more or less the same thing, using more or less the same kind of machine or tool. A solid block of men moving and fighting together is also relatively simple to command.[3] Subdivision into units with different missions, increases the problems of coordination, which continue to grow as the number of units, the differentiation of their weapons and missions, and the space over which they must operate increases. What is often characterized as growing sophistication and professionalism in military as well as civilian organizations can therefore also be described as an increase in formal complexity.[4]

Given the growth of technical experts and expertise in both domains, it is not surprising that civil and military responses to an increasingly complex operational environment have been similar, and technical. Rather than accepting the necessity to cope with the irreducible increase in uncertainty brought about by complexity, military bureaucracies and organizations, like their civil counterparts, have turned to computers and information systems as a panacea, hoping through the use of elaborate models and networks of integrated communications to defeat uncertainty through various methods and modes of positive control.

Many of these new technocrats treat command-and-control as if it were a single and indivisible term, or even confuse the one with the other.[5] This is in part because of the general tendency of the managerial and business literature to treat control as something of a portmanteau, covering almost any intention or means for seeking the prior determination of outcomes.[6] But control properly defined is not the same as management, or command.[7] Control involves feedback, learning, and the cumulation of knowledge, for the specific purpose of framing an action in deterministic certainty. Command (like management) is more of a one-way process in the face of irreducible uncertainty, sometimes based on experience, sometimes on heuristics, and sometimes just on "right feeling."

Martin Landau has described the modern organization's search for control as a search for knowledge—empirically verified observations, theories based on them, and predictive models not only of organizational behavior, but of the organization's environment. The key word is "predictive." With a predictive model, and a verified theory, an organization can exercise "control"; it can make precise corrections by comparing feedback from its actions with the predictions of the model. If the organization's knowledge is sufficiently comprehensive, there will be very few unanticipated events around which it has to improvise.

The more complex the organization and its environment, however, the less likely that it will ever be able to behave like a social thermostat. What is needed to cope are people who have the ability to make decisions on the basis of partial knowledge and partial information, openly recognizing the inadequacy of available models and heuristics, and to correct on the fly via a process of trial and error. Instead, many organizations saw in such new management tools as game theory, decision analysis, operations research, and econometric model building a way to substitute predictable formal and analytic skills for managerial (and command) ones that could never be perfectly known, or predicted, in advance.

As noted in chapter 4, the advent of the small, affordable digital computer furthered this trend by allowing the construction of more complex and elaborate models, by vastly increasing the amount of data that could be stored and manipulated, and by running the whole increasingly elaborated and complex process more and more rapidly. In a social and business environment where quantitative analysis and esoteric computer skills were becoming increasingly valued, this tended to have positive feedback, further transferring power within the organization from the traditional managers with their tacit and difficult-to-quantify skills to the new cadre of data and model manipulators.

Modern military officers, trained in and familiar with the techniques and trends of modern schools of business and management, have not behaved much differently. One result for the U.S. military, as for others, was the rise in power and importance of those who sought deterministic models and methods for fighting wars.[8] As business and management schools became more familiar with what computers could do, and management theory moved away from determinism and toward "flexible" and "adaptive" control fostered by the ability of those in control to gather and process directly information even from the smallest unit, rather than through middle management, so also did the military. Dreams of being able to cut through the fog of war and intervene directly in the course of battle were evident even before the introduction of computers and the information and data systems they made possible, but they were once held by only a small group of techno-visionaries. Now they have become the dominant vision.

Because of the historically unprecedented rapidity with which the technical systems progressed and developed, the ongoing and potentially productive arguments about how, when, and where the new capabilities might be used were cut short. The United States is now on the verge of being fully committed to a military that is fully interconnected horizontally and vertically, without any real sense of what the increased dependence on information management, data flows, real-time battle management, and other manifestations of the computer transition will do either to organizational structure and behavior or to performance in combat.[9]

The Ways and Means of Modern Warfare

Since the beginning of military history, those seeking to increase their fighting power by increasing the size of their armies have been confounded by the difficulty of coping with the attendant increase in the scope of battle. Without adequate and sufficiently rapid communications, commanders were unable to manage and coordinate large and dispersed forces, let alone to control their actions in battle. The dominant strategies were to plan carefully in advance, depending on order and discipline among the troops, and then to gather what information one could and exercise whatever control was possible through a system of couriers.[10] That may have sufficed for armies that still moved slowly and on foot, but was historically inadequate for combat at sea.[11]

Nor was there any way to coordinate the growth and dispersion of the logistic "tail" needed to supply large armies, which increasingly became independent units foraging on their own. The Romans of the late empire were able to manage and feed their geographically dispersed forces through strict discipline and an elaborate and very sophisticated network of camps and roads, which effectively kept the armies in Roman territory even when out in the field, but that in turn limited their exploits to expansion and defense only along the borders of the empire. In medieval and early modern Europe, as in antiquity, armies tended to be small and highly mobile; logistics away from home (and sometimes even when not away) more often than not consisted of foraging in the countryside, especially when on the move.

Massed Fire

The modern problems of logistics, as well as of command-and-control, properly start with the reforms of Frederick the Great in the seventeenth century. Faced with the dual technical and social problems of seeking to make better use of the potential firepower at a time when warfare was growing in scope and scale, he not only introduced standardized uniforms, but standardized methods of training, including formal drill and massed fire. This in turn involved formal separation of function and differentiation of mission, greatly increasing the problems of battle management.

Open order drill and separation of function required intelligence and training of troops and professional military staffs; modern artillery required technical training; the larger armies required conscription, which called for formal standardization. The commander of the army was now also its chief bureaucrat.[12] But the preindustrial mass army remained fundamentally uncoordinated until the time of Napoleon and the huge, democratic armies of revolutionary France. Improvements in roads, in communications, and, perhaps most important, in agriculture allowed the larger armies to remain mobile without assigning large parts for supply or foraging.[13] Solving the problem of command-and-control, however, was not so simple.

In the time of Napoleon, each component of the *Grand Armeé* (infantry, cavalry, artillery) was composed of many identical small units such as artillery batteries; formations could continue to fight, at some level, even after sustaining enormous losses. Moreover, their tasks were predesigned, as communication during battle was at best imperfect; they were not only able, but also expected to fight on their own even if communication with commanders was delayed or severed.[14]

In the language of organization theory, Napoleonic armies, like most of those before them, were formally decomposable. Interdependence between large formations, or between infantry and artillery, may have at times been high, reflecting the need to try to coordinate the battle in an integrated way, but given the poor state of battlefield communications, units at the same level had to be ready to pursue their objectives without coordinating too closely with others.[15] Napoleon himself was reluctant to delegate, and centralized command even though he could exercise only the most limited control of a battle once under way. His genius lay with planning, and with the traditional qualities of intuition, insight and, particularly in the earlier years, charismatic leadership. When these ebbed, he was defeated tactically as well as strategically.

The Napoleonic era also saw the birth of total war; in France, the army, the government, and the people had been merged to a single force. But neither Napoleon nor his opponents grasped the organizational or technical implications of the growing industrialization of Europe. Nor, finally, did Clausewitz, who focused almost entirely on the social and political dimensions and remained somewhat indifferent to the effects of technical and economic ones. Nevertheless, it was Clausewitz, writing in an era of growing devotion to rational analysis, who first pointed to the importance of "friction," to the human elements of uncertainty and chance, the "fog of war" that undermines all attempts to carry out rational plans laid in advance.[16] The task of the commander was to accept that uncertainty, and to be prepared to master it.

Industrial War

The American Civil War is generally regarded as the first modern "industrial" war, harnessing the newly available productive and technical capabilities of the industrial revolution to the purpose of waging total war. Nearly complete economic and technical as well as social and political mobilization was achieved. The use of the railroad and the telegraph was central, both for logistics and for communications. But the results were mixed. The command-and-control structure of individual battles was not that different from those of the Napoleonic Wars, which had been assiduously and carefully studied by Union and Confederate generals alike. Sherman's march to the sea was the first modern expression of the Clausewitzian notion of total and absolute war, waged against the social and economic structure as well as the troops in the field, but Sherman's army moved autonomously and not under central control.

The real innovator was the often-maligned Ulysses S. Grant. Leaving the charisma of command and the romance of dramatic victories to the Confederacy, Grant adopted from Napoleon and Clausewitz the precept of total war—that the key to victory was annihilation of the enemy and not simply defeat. Rather than seeking decisive battles, or even decisive outcomes in battle, Grant consciously adopted the strategy of using the greater Union resources to wear the Confederacy down.[17] Abandoning the notion of trying to exercise direct control, Grant was content to coordinate and plan overall strategy, letting each battle unfold as it would.

European militaries were also undergoing a transition to the modern era of "technological" warfare. Although not so dramatic as the Civil War, the triumph of Field Marshall Helmuth von Moltke and the Prussian campaign of 1866 that ended with the defeat of the Austrians and Saxons at Königgrätz (Sadowa in Bohemian) created a new model of the European army. Of the two new innovations, the German general staff and the telegraph, more credit is due to the former than the latter.[18] The battle itself was too wide-ranging and diffuse to be controlled by any technology using fixed infrastructure. But it was the first European war of the modern industrial age, using weapons and technical tools derived from the power of steam, the new techniques for producing steel, and the first signs of the coming transformation in communications and information-gathering capabilities.

Better use was made of both telegraph and railroad during the Franco-Prussian war of 1870. The very existence of the telegraph had already changed the representation of battle for the commander, who now felt more closely coupled to the battlefield, and it was widely believed that the Prussians used telegraphy extensively for integration of the battlefield. But Moltke himself recorded in his memoirs that once battle was joined there was little that he, or the general staff, could do to affect the outcome.[19] Furthermore, he had considerable respect for Clausewitz's "fog of war," and exerted strict controls over the flow of information in order to maintain a strong sense of independence and balance among his forces rather than trying to overcontrol them.[20]

By the time of the First World War, the telegraph was more mature, and in wider use, but the lessons from attempts at integrating communications to couple commanders to the battle front were at best ambivalent. The contribution of the telegraph to the rapidity of the early movement of the German armies through Belgium, or of the independent, motorized taxi fleet that saved France at the Marne, were almost forgotten in the ensuing four years of trench warfare, as immobile technically as it was physically.

The most famous, and disastrous, case of command rigidity was the battle of the Somme in 1916. The British part of the campaign was planned in advance in such detail, and with so little discretionary power given to subordinates, that General Haig and the others at headquarters did not even know for days that it had failed—although the troops on the field knew that within a few hours. Moreover, even if opportunities and breakthroughs did fortuitously occur, they could not have been exploited, because the technical requirements of the artillery had rendered the plan linear and inflexible.[21]

More of a premium was put on retaining control to assure that the battle went according to the prescheduled timetable than to managing the actual advance toward the German lines. But there was still very little reliable wireless communication; what the armies had available consisted mostly of hard-wired communications that required the time-consuming (and dangerous) laying of copper lines. The requirement to keep in constant touch with headquarters therefore tied the field officers down to their original positions instead of having them advance with the troops. What the British had done was to incorporate modern techniques into a battle plan that was wholly mechanistic, with no means for error detection, let alone error correction, and no flexibility. As van Creveld notes:

> The characteristics of the British command system at the Somme are worth summing up, however, since they represent, in as extreme a form as can be found, a school of thought that has adherents from Plato onward. Under this system, carefully laid plans rigorously and undeviatingly carried out are regarded as the one way to overcome the inevitable confusion of the battlefield.[22]

The plans of the Fourth Army at the Somme were as minutely detailed as they were rigorous. At Waterloo, Wellington did not even have a written battle plan. A century later at the Somme, the British XIII corps alone had thirty-one pages of plans; Queen Victoria's Rifles, with only 1,000 men, had twenty numbered paragraphs. In the words of John Keegan: "It is a spirit not of providing for eventualities, but rather of attempting to preordain the future; a spirit borne out by the language of the orders: 'infantry and machine guns will be pushed forward at once . . . the siege and heavy artillery will be advanced.' "[23]

This the British did, and costly it was. The British troops advanced when they were supposed to, and paused when they were supposed to, moving behind an artillery "barrage" that was simply not accomplishing what the plan had said it would. Moreover, each formation moved straight ahead in its slice of the sector, walking steadily with bayonets fixed, with no communication with units on either side. The lack of ability to lay telegraph wires as the British troops advanced allowed the artillery barrage to keep moving even when the infantry lagged, removing their protective cover and allowing the Germans to rise back up out of their trenches behind it. It was a prescription for disaster, and the disaster was historical. There were 60,000 casualties the first day alone.

That this was a cognitive and not a technical failure is shown by the performance of the German Army in 1918, when it was finally given the discretion to act flexibly and adaptively in a major battle. Using the same basic technical means for signals and communications, the Germans demonstrated a completely different and far more flexible command system in their final offensive, perhaps the most successful on the Western Front during the whole war.[24] Planning was to be as detailed as possible, but not to rob front line units of discretion. There were planned "lines" to be attained, but the army was explicitly told these were primarily for the sake of orderly planning and was "encouraged" to do more if they could (and they knew the risk that entailed if it exposed their flanks or supply lines). Commanders were to follow their units and lay communications lines. Observers were to be placed wherever possible. But most important, the outcome of the attack was held to be inherently uncertain, so that the staff prepared to exploit opportunities as they arose, as best they could, and put a heavy emphasis on independent action by subordinate commanders and even by individual soldiers.[25]

In an era of social and industrial rationalism, the generals on both sides had fallen into the Taylorist trap of believing that reality could be coerced to fit predetermined models, and that what was needed in the face of failure was better and more thorough planning. Military commanders of the First World War were fixed on the notion that the new military techniques provided a means of total control, that better information, better communication, and a better grasp of scientific principles had transformed the uncertain environment of combat into one that could be made formally controllable, even if not totally predictable. The human cost of that rigid and unadaptable belief was the most remembered lesson of that war.

Techno-Industrial War

The period between the First and Second World Wars was one of great innovation and technical advancement in a number of militarily relevant fields, such as metallurgy, wireless, and aviation. When the race to re-arm began in the 1930s, militaries drew as much as possible on the interwar developments to build modernized, integrated forces. After the first exploratory years, nearly instantaneous wireless information and communication were used to develop new modes of integration unprecedented in warfare. Submarines at sea and the task forces that hunted them; naval battle groups with integrated air support; the entire air war in Europe and the Far East; the Battle of Britain and the Normandy landings; the rapid, mobile tank battles on the Russian plains and in North Africa all became centrally dependent upon one innovation or another in electronics. Radio communications, command-and-control, and aerial intelligence revolutionized even the ground war, always the last to be subject to innovation.

By the end of the war, the U.S. advance across Europe integrated armor, infantry, and tactical airpower into an enormous combined force of unprecedented power and efficiency. But demands placed on logistics and communications networks were unprecedented, and individual units were growing less capable of fighting independently if logistics or coordination failed. Patton had to stop the advance across France when he outran his supply train; U.S. troops caught in the Battle of the Bulge had to await clear weather for the air-dropped supplies they required.

During and after the war, much emphasis was placed at home on the quality of U.S. equipment and its advanced capabilities, as well as on the quality and morale of its soldiers. In reality, U.S. conduct in the war was primarily a technically augmented extension of the tactics and strategy of Ulysses S. Grant.

> [I]t would appear that the U.S. Army, backed by a gigantic productive
> engine and possibly looking across its shoulder at the organization of an
> automobile factory, chose to regard war not so much as a struggle be-
> tween opposing troops, but rather as one whose outcome would be de-
> cided largely by machines. Rather than concentrating on fighting power,
> therefore, it aimed at confronting the enemy with the greatest possible
> firepower. Not attention to the needs of the soldier, but scientific man-
> agement and optimum distribution of resources became the name of the
> game.[26]

The role of scientific and technical innovation, particularly in the
"wizard war" of cryptography, radar, communications, and operations research, was far from negligible,[27] but the central war, in
Europe, was finally won on the ground, through attrition and industrial dominance. And so was the war in the Pacific. Even the atomic
bomb was as much a product of American economic and industrial
capability as of Allied scientific and technical ingenuity.[28] Both efforts,
however, had the effect of moving scientists and engineers into positions of authority, and sometimes power, in military matters that completely and irreversibly changed the relationship between militaries
and innovation.[29]

Postwar Integration

During the course of the Second World War, increased logistical demand and specialization of function moved the armed forces of the
several great powers further from decomposability toward integration. The pooled interdependence that had characterized earlier militaries allowed individual units to fight on their own for long periods.
At the beginning, only loose coordination of units was required for
effective performance. Toward the end, the U.S. military was already
moving toward more demanding sequential interdependence, in
which individual units could not perform their functions until some
other unit—whether fighting or logistic—had performed a prior one
assigned to it. The demands placed on the coordinating and integrating functions of the command-and-control system were thereby
greatly increased, but there was still some flexibility in scheduling.

The more technically advanced forces built up after the war gradually began to move to a third kind of interdependence—reciprocal—in which separate units no longer have self-contained tasks that can be autonomously pursued.[30] Instead, they must negotiate with each other in "real time" for any of them to perform as designed. But the limits on integrative and analytic power were still not enough to cut through the fog of war. As demonstrated in Korea, units were still "loosely coupled" to each other in organizational terms. If commanders tried to use their new communications power to exercise too much control, if they did not allow room for adjustment and discretion, the outcome was still likely to be disastrous.

The information pathologies produced by centralization in the face of the complexity of unconventional warfare in Vietnam created a kind of informational inertia that infected the entire system. General Heiser of the First Logistic Command wrote that it would be necessary to resort to a less centralized system in the future and to restore service units to their parent outfits, thus doing away with much of the requirement for information even though at the expense of creating some slack resources. In the First World War, the generals had tried to manage uncertainty through planning instead of a working system of command; in Vietnam, they tried with communication and data processing. Once again, van Creveld has the last word: "To study command as it operated in Vietnam is, indeed, almost enough to make one despair of human reason; we have seen the future, and it does *not* work."[31]

Moving toward Cyberspace

In the late 1970s, the U.S. Army, faced with the double problem of seeking to remedy the shortcomings demonstrated so clearly in Vietnam and attempting to maintain conventional deterrence in Europe, was charged with rethinking its doctrine. The first attempt, the 1976 revision of the Army's primary training document, *Field Manual (FM) 100-5, Operations* turned out to be yet another restatement of the traditional doctrine of attrition warfare.[32] Critiques by various elements of the military reform movement led to a second revision in 1982, which many felt to be the most extensive change in the fundamentals of U.S. military doctrine since the Civil War.

The initiative that led to the revision had begun even before the advent of the small, powerful digital computer. In July 1970, General William Westmoreland told a congressional committee:

> On the battlefield of the future, enemy forces will be located, tracked, and targeted almost instantaneously through the use of data links, computer-assisted intelligence evaluation, and automated fire control. . . . I am confident [that] the American people expect this country to take full advantage of its technology—to welcome and applaud the developments that will replace wherever possible the man with the machine.[33]

At the time, there were as yet no technical means to carry out this ambitious agenda. By the 1980s, they were at hand.

The 1982 revision of *FM 100-5* rejected attrition in favor of maneuver warfare, introducing not only the concept of fully integrated AirLand Battle, but also the idea of deep interdiction, of striking enemy reserves far behind the front.[34] Carrying out such a strategy required the further development of computerized smart weapons and tightly integrated command-and-control networks. But this first attempt at designing a tightly integrated battlefield ran into considerable social and political opposition, here and in Europe, because it was seen as encouraging the early use of nuclear or chemical weapons.

By the early 1980s, the computer revolution was well under way, and the nascent military computing program had evolved into the Strategic Computing Initiative, with ambitious overall goals and three specific program areas: autonomous vehicles, a "smart" pilot's assistant, and battle management.[35] The goals of the latter were specifically directed toward information and data processing, as spelled out to Congress in 1983 by DARPA director Robert S. Cooper: ". . . with increasingly massive amounts of valuable data collected, no commander can possibly keep up and make full use of the information, making an accurate picture even less likely . . . revolutionary improvements in computer technology are required."[36] This was, of course, the driving purpose behind ARPA's longstanding support of the computer industry.

During the 1970s, the scientific-academic debate over grand strategy, automated systems, and C^3I focused almost entirely on nuclear weapons. By the late 1980s, this had extended to conventional forces and conventional weapons systems, including, inter alia, mathematical equations for combat effectiveness, real-time surveillance and data gathering, computerized control systems, and battlefield integration. In retrospect, these controversies, and the growing interest of the technical and analytic communities in their outcome, were a sign of the rapidity with which the technological transformation was taking place.

Building upon the new research program, *FM 100-5* was revised again in 1986 to play down the offensive nature of AirLand Battle and reduce dependence on tightly coupled battlefield integration. Nevertheless, the dependence on computers—for planning, information processing, communication, and battle management—not only remained, but was given greater emphasis. As the U.S. forces scaled down and professionalized, integration, firepower, and efficiency were to compensate for the mass and endurance that could only come from large, conscript armies.

For the military reformers, now cast in the role of traditionalists, there was a remarkable contradiction between the degree of integration and control embedded in *FM 100-5* and the U.S. Army's claim to have evaluated, learned from, and adopted the tradition of *Auftragstaktik*, the spirit of independent fighting and discretion that characterized the German Army since the time of Moltke.[37] Within NATO there were complaints that the increased electronic management of battle would greatly reduce the tradition of discretion and freedom of action that was still a basis of officer training in the Bundeswehr. The U.S. response was logical, if disquieting: In the new age of smart weapons and smarter electronics, of integrated battles and combined force operations, a small force trying to fight on its own would not long survive.

Modern integrated combat systems, such as naval battle groups, armored divisions, or tactical air wings, require not only an enormous amount of direct support to keep supplies and spare parts flowing in, and to actually perform repair, but also place increasing demands on information and communications to keep the flows ordered and arranged. Moreover, as the individual weapons become more expensive, and therefore increasingly scarce and valuable, it has become important to control individual decisions. The chain of command exists but often may be superseded by an information and command net capable of reaching past intervening commanders to individual pilots or small unit team leaders. What were once relatively simple military hierar-

chies that could communicate and coordinate flexibly, fighting together or separately according to the flow of battle, were transformed
in the 1980s into a set of rigidly integrated hierarchies connected by
electronics. Now they have evolved further into networks of specialized forces whose coherence and integrity must be preserved at all
costs to maintain control of the fighting in order to fight at all, let alone
to fight effectively.[38]

For many military systems, increased specialization and consequent
functional separation has been accompanied by a set of mutual dependencies that encourage the use of the vastly increased ability of
communications equipment to increasingly network and centralize
command-and-control. Electronic jamming must take place at the correct moment, and not just in the correct place; artillery and tactical air
strikes have to be laid on just at the edge of the battle, and just before
ground forces engage. Critical supplies and maintenance must be
available just when and where they are needed if the very expensive
weapons platforms are not to be useless or immobile. The linkages are
now both reciprocal, and "tightly coupled."[39]

The military reformers of the 1980s were at heart combat line
officers, firmly grounded in their belief that "no plan survives contact
with the enemy"; they saw their Pentagon counterparts and civil managers as striving not just for innovation, but for deterministic planning
and centralized control.[40] In the 1990s, even their reforms were absorbed by the promoters of battlefield computer technologies. What is
now under way, according to many reports, is a military revolution,
based largely on the ability to gather and control the flow of information and use it to integrate and control all aspects of the battle.[41] The
next war will be a struggle for dominance and control of an information battlespace whose dimensions are measured in wavelengths as
well as kilometers, and whose logistics extend to digital data as well as
fuel and ammunition.[42] The military is indeed moving toward fighting
in cyberspace.

The Virtual Battlefield

As was the case for industrial and financial firms in the civil sector, the
new power of computerized information and communication systems
transformed not only organizational forms, but the definition, inter-

pretation, and representation of organizational and managerial tasks. Mechanization and integration of the battlefield added to the historical planning and leadership requirements of command the need to organize, coordinate, and manage complex and interdependent sequences. At the same time, increased communications and logistics ability allowed commanders to seek control by tightening links from command centers to combatants, while claiming that the new systems would add to their flexibility and discretion.

With the addition of the new electronic capabilities, the entire, extended battle, from front to logistics, from close air support to strategic interdiction, could now be visualized and managed as a single, integrated whole. Just as the new industrial technologies gave operators more control over immediate task and process, the new weapons have given fighting troops more discretionary power ever at the level of their fighting "task." But in striking parallel to the restraints placed on industrial and office workers by the demands and requirements of their automated and integrated equipment, battlefield commanders now have less discretion than ever at the critical level of operations.

Computerization remains the key. According to U.S. Army Chief of Staff General Gordon Sullivan, "the digitalization of the battlefield— the electronic linking of every weapon system in the Battlespace—will allow the commander to synchronize all the elements of combat power."[43] Moreover, the strategies being adopted are not only those of modern business, but have a distinctly Taylorist flavor. What is sought is a fully networked army, with logistics designed "to anticipate and respond just in time to sustainment requirements." As with the similar strategies of the business world discussed in chapter 4, computerization is to substitute tight coupling for resiliency and buffering, and networking is to allow direct control to be exercised remotely from anywhere on the net.[44] Moreover, the logic and the feedback are nearly identical to those of the world of business, and very similar to those described in chapter 8 for weapons:

> As the leaders' visions are incorporated into doctrine and the organizationally correct position on operations, a positive feedback loop emerges such that up and coming senior officers expect to implement this kind of highly precise warfare. These expectations then channel their control efforts at lower levels of the organization. Just like any [business] managers, they will attempt to distribute people, resources, and tasks across

organizational structures, operations, and needs according to these images and assumptions.[45]

Command was historically an open cycle process: The commander set up the battle, gave instructions, provided for whatever contingencies could be planned for, and then issued the command to execute. After that, the ability to intervene was minimal. In contrast, control is a closed cycle process with feedback, analysis, and iteration; it was not possible even to consider the transition from command to command-and-control until modern technical means for intelligence and communication became available.[46] But it is possible, even in the military, to move to control without command.

The problems of modern command-and-control systems are legion. Among those identified are: overconfidence; information overload; high support requirements; overdependence on automated systems; hidden flaws and mistakes in technical systems; the aura of timeliness without its reality; and the illusion of command without its authority.[47] For these reasons, the military was at first reluctant to implement computerization completely into the formal process of command; computerized systems were at first intended more for the provision of expert advice than for making decisions. But the embedding of computers into newer military systems such as Aegis or JSTARS makes it increasingly difficult to distinguish between advice and actual command-and-control.

The computer revolution is no longer distinct from weapons and weapons system development. Computers are embedded elements of a whole new class of weapons, and of command and information systems.[48] Humans are still formally in charge. Yet there remains the fundamental and extrinsic problem of just how much command-and-control they can exert in the new combat environment. The rapid advance in technology continues to escalate the problem of weapons and system control at least as fast as it has increased the capability of the central command structure. The electronic battlefield is as short in decision time as it is high in information flows.[49] In an era of supersonic aircraft armed with high-speed missiles, quick-reacting radar-directed gun and missile batteries, and tank battles that may be won or lost on the first shot, there is simply not the time for centralized command systems to exercise real-time control over battlefield events.[50]

Although the arguments in the literature about the causes of the First World War continue, it is generally held that the technology of the time contributed greatly to its outbreak.[51] Mobilization of the logistically demanding armies of 1914 was entirely dependent upon the railways. As the tensions escalated during that summer, various governments began to work up their mobilization plans. In August, the anxious military convinced political leaders to allow mobilization to begin. At that point, the war had essentially begun. Once the technological process of mobilization had started, the decision to go to war was taken out of political hands. The military argued that the confusion, disorder, and other consequences of halting or delaying it would put the country at risk. Last-minute efforts to avoid the disaster that many felt was coming were of no avail.

Many analysts argue that the illusion of inevitability was just that. Although it has been widely held that the tight coupling of the mobilization systems effectively co-opted the political process once mobilization had been ordered, the belief by those in power that it was irreversible seems to have been a cognitive trap.[52] The governments of France, Russia, and Germany could have averted war by halting mobilization, even at the last minute, just as the USS *Vincennes* (and the Israeli Air Defense Command) could have decided to wait instead of firing to make sure that their prospective target was really hostile. But in both cases, the pressure to commit rapidly made the costs seem far too high.

In the Napoleonic Wars, committing to a process that would inevitably lead to battle was something that might be done days, or weeks, before the first shot was fired. In 1914, the commitment time to start the war was measured in days: during the war, commitment in combat was often measured in hours. The advancing soldiers were fully aware that the preprogrammed artillery barrage at the Somme had moved too far in front of them to be effective in keeping the Germans in their trenches, but they were committed; there was no way to cancel their orders, or their battle. On the electronic battlefield, the time from detection to commitment may soon be measured in fractions of seconds.

The introduction of computerized systems for force integration and communication, for weapons firing and control, or for command-and-control, makes rapid and effective intervention more possible. But the introduction of these systems also shortens the reaction time, possibly creating a framework where the human beings who are supposed to retain the ultimate discretion and judgment are effectively trapped in a logical decision loop in which they are no more likely to change the sequence of events than were the political leaders in August 1914.

It is in this context that the example of Iran Air Flight 655 or the shooting down of the Libyan airliner are disquieting illustrations of the potential vulnerabilities of future military C³I systems. In both cases, the pressure to commit within a short time did not allow the commanders to escape being captured by the representations created by their own electronic capabilities. The resulting combination of tight coupling and cognitive error is disturbingly reminiscent of the "logic trap" that determined the course of the First World War, or that which led to the U.S. debacle in Vietnam.[53]

In the new vision of the battlespace, commanders from the company level up to the commander in chief, linked by nearly instantaneous communications, can be kept informed of every battle almost on a moment-to-moment basis, and supplied continuously with a steady stream of detailed and up-to-date information on enemy dispositions, movements, and perhaps even intentions. The Force XXI document spells it out clearly: "Electronic connectivity between and among all echelons in the Army will result in such speed and precision in communications that the entire organization's situational awareness and agility will far exceed that of today's forces."[54]

Recognizing that the military of the next century is more likely to be engaged in flexible missions of limited scope than large, central wars, the response has been to increase not only effectiveness, but "efficiency." Despite all the claims to have studied, and learned from, *Auftragstaktik*, independence of action is rejected as too costly and too inefficient.

Electronics are no longer to be extrinsic to the realities of combat; information and communication flows will now be tightly integrated to allow planning in hours, rather than days, almost in "real time." Firepower will be concentrated, intense, and highly technical, and, in some arenas (tanks, airpower, surface fights at sea), the outcome of individual combat will be decided almost instantaneously by the response and accuracy of the electronics. Instead of uncertainty about disposition and movement, there will be AWACS aircraft, satellites, and ground positioning systems. Instead of the painstaking process of building cognitive maps of the state of battle through the interpretation of remotely transmitted messages and the observations of runners and other messengers, an electronically informed and direct map will be constructed and maintained in headquarters. No expense will be spared to ensure that the troops, increasingly scarce, and increasingly valuable, are not exposed to unnecessary risk.

Just as more and more business organizations are moving to a tightly coupled, highly interdependent organization whose resources are controlled and allocated horizontally across the network by a web of computerized communications and coordinated by computerized command-and-control systems, so, apparently, is the U.S. Army. As was discussed in chapter 7, even those long-term consequences that can be anticipated for such safety critical systems as air traffic control or nuclear power operation are enough to have slowed down the rate of implementation. In those cases, operators had sufficient prestige and influence to hold the designers off. But in the U.S. military, the promoters of technical change are by now almost completely in charge, and the "operators," the grunts who do the actual fighting, are likely to have almost no voice at all. The resulting surprises could be very unpleasant indeed.

Conclusion

The new image of the military of the twenty-first century is a totally integrated, electronically linked, fully computerized fighting force, trained for and fighting on an electronic battlefield. In the air and at sea, training for combat with computer simulators and games is already being taken as the equivalent of actual combat. Even the Army, historically the most traditional and conservative of the armed forces, is moving as fast in the direction of an electronic battlefield as budgets and system designs will allow toward "full integration of information-age technology [which] . . . will result in making operating force decisions from the individual soldier to the highest level of the Institutional Army."[55]

Such tight control goes against the lesson that confusion and disorder, Clausewitz's "fog of war," will remain the natural state of combat, however advanced, sophisticated, and precise the new systems might appear to be when tested in peacetime. Loosely coordinated small-group autonomy is inefficient, it calls for considerable logistic and maintenance independence and the ability of front commanders to marshall their own air support and artillery. Abandoning it for a more integrated doctrine that could prove tragically fragile in the face of an enemy capable of interfering with the elaborate command networks runs the great risk of trading off overall effectiveness for the sake of technical efficiency.

When computers were first introduced into the military, they were large and centralized mainframes, primarily for the command-and-control of nuclear forces. Having acquired computer literacy early and convincingly, the military set off on the active pursuit of ever smaller and more capable systems. These were intended at first for improving the capabilities of nuclear forces, including delivery systems. As powerful and portable computers became available, they were also introduced rapidly into those elements of other forces, particularly air forces, where technical advantage had been identified as a leading factor in combat. As van Creveld has pointed out, the simpler the fighting environment, the greater the military benefit of technical superiority.[56] To which he might have added, the greater the cost and the scarcer the weapons system, the more cost-effective is the investment in electronic capabilities.

But the rapid progress in computer power and miniaturization in the 1980s and 1990s made it possible to think of introducing computers and computerized systems into every element of combat, including the complex and often incoherent environment of ground battles. As recently as a decade ago, the computer was with few exceptions still an innovation in conventional ground warfare, an adjunct and augmentation to traditional ways of fighting. As with other aspects of computing in other, more civil settings, it was the embedding of the computer into the force structure, its disappearance as a separable and unusual object, that marked its growing importance. Albeit to varying degrees, and on different timetables, every component of U.S. military forces is now being designed and built around computerized weapons, systems, and C³I. The historical military that carried on almost unchanged structurally through the early years of the computer is now being almost totally deconstructed. What remains unclear is what will result from the still-ongoing reconstruction and redefinition of the meaning and purpose of U.S. military power in the age of computerized, smart machines.

The intervention of the military reformers during the 1980s can now be seen to have committed the United States not only to the doctrines and strategies of maneuver warfare, but also to a radical transformation of representation. The doctrines of *FM 100-5* and the tactics of AirLand Battle have evolved into Force XXI and similar plans for the next century that represent a commitment to the extensive use of electronics and other high-technology systems to keep casualties to a minimum as well as to new weapons and small units.

During the height of the defense reform debate, the reformers were sometimes referred to by their conservative colleagues as the Jedi Knights.[57] Many of the reformers were delighted. The image is not only that of autonomy, independence, and rebellion against bureaucratized imperial structures and large, clumsy, centralized militaries, but also of cleverness, of the creative use of flexible technical innovation, of the triumph of intelligent and forward-looking youth. But it should be remembered that every force has its dark side: Darth Vader was also a Jedi.

12.

Invisible Idiots

Introduction

The recent literature on the growing use of computers has drawn many critical studies of the relationship between the individual and the newly reconstructed society. Sherry Turkle has studied the transformative effect on human personality and culture by immersion in the new world of interactive computer technology.[1] Howard Rheingold has not only extolled the prospects of the new virtual community, but warned of the darker implications of immersion in virtual trivialities and the prospect of intrusive monitoring and the loss of privacy.[2] And Jeremy Rifkin has extended the traditional arguments over labor and the loss of jobs and skills into concern that we are entering a post-market world where all labor, at all levels, that is not directly concerned with manufacturing and supporting the computerized networks will become first devalued and then displaced.[3]

My specific concern, however, has not been the direct impact on the individual. What motivated the research that led to this book was that neither the significance nor the immediacy of the use of computers in business, the military, and other large organizations was receiving the same degree of attention. Both computerization of operation and control and the growth in the scope and capabilities of computerized networks are rapidly altering the nature, approach, and goals of large organizations, often transforming them into structures and webs that cannot be understood, let alone managed and operated, by unaided human beings.

From time to time there issues from the computer community some pronouncement about the increased capability of computers to enhance or emulate some realm of human activity that is meant to both startle and impress. Most typically, the ones that receive the greatest critical attention are not those that make particularly effective use of the mathematical, memory, or networking power of computers, but those that seemingly intrude into those realms that are uniquely human. Progress in artificial intelligence is one such, robotics another. The role of computers in creating and maintaining elaborate webs of differentiated activities, such as the coordination and scheduling of continent-wide organ transplants, or the managing of complex inventories, is at best relegated to the science journals or the business news, with almost no forethought about the long-term and systemic implications of the increased dependencies and vulnerabilities that are thereby created.

To some extent, this is because such long-term and structural effects are often diffuse and indirect. Consider, for example, the increasingly obvious statement that by some future year (say 2050), there will exist computer chess-playing programs that no human being will be able to beat. Many in the technical community seem to find such statements very profound, to represent a real and direct intrusion into the realm of human capabilities. Those of us who are more immersed in the social world of human responses and human interaction often find this puzzling, and respond simply: So what? What are the consequences? What are the implications? The puzzles of the world in which we live arise not only from individual behavior and capabilities, but from more complex, socially constructed webs of action, reaction, and interaction that make up the socio-political environment. What matters is not whether computers win, but how that will affect human perceptions of their role and place in the world.

As computerization of social and business organizations continues apace, however, the temptation to apply the "so what" factor is increasingly tempered with caution. Computers, networks, and the automation and interconnection they foster are no longer just the socially and technically constructed outputs of human activities; they have become part of the socio-economic-technical construction kit from which future societies will be assembled. If those who are designing, programming, installing, and implementing computerized systems for business, industry, finance, or the military show no greater appreciation for the relationships among and differences between personal, social, and technical objectives than they have showed in their pursuit of the computerized Grand Master, prospects for the future are alarming indeed.

Standardization and Slack

Gurus and acolytes of the information revolution argue that unlimited desktop power linked through global networks will enrich and enhance human life by providing individuals, even (or perhaps increasingly) isolated ones, with access to enormous bodies of information in unimaginable variety. But much of what passes for distributed information is eclectic, idiosyncratic, frequently disorganized, and often unreliable. To a great extent, it is large organizations that create, maintain, provide, and sometimes control the repositories of systematic, organized information, and, in large organizations, efficiency and standardization have a logic of their own. Whatever the faults of the "modern" hierarchical organization, those far down the chain from the top were always able to find enough leeway to create individual, differentiated means of operating within specified constraints. What the web of interconnection makes possible, and therefore makes probable, is a push for "efficiency," for standardization and compliance at an unprecedented level of detail.

Imagine a world in which every cook in every restaurant has an expert assistant to ensure that every dish prepared reliably tastes the same, anywhere you order it. Boring, perhaps, but efficient.[4] What about integrated global markets that are open only to the largest and most powerful global corporations? More than just probable. What about a world in which every supermarket not only tracks check-outs for managing inventory, but uses the information to change deliveries to stores to ensure that valuable shelf space is not taken up by items that move slowly, or erratically? Very real indeed, as the success of Wal-Mart will attest.[5] If present trends continue, the same means of managing space may soon also be applied to newly computerized libraries, and then perhaps to other overcrowded databases, turning them into Wal-Marts of the mind.

What about a fully re-engineered, computer-linked industry in which parts inventories and buffer stocks are held to a bare minimum, with a web of communications linking specialized shops all over the globe so that an order for any complicated good is turned into a network of specialized orders, calculated, coordinated, and integrated by a web of interconnected computers? Futuristic? Not really, for that is already the goal of many, based on the existing practice of just-in-time manufacturing.

In the longer term, however, what is more troubling is not the transformation of organizational structures, but the intrusion of automation into organizational management and operations, much of it promoted by technical experts who seem to view the interactive social world as an exercise in game theory—not chess, perhaps, but, however elaborate and complex, subject in principle to more efficient, effective, and rapid play through the intervention of computers and computer networks. Good management and operation is an art. All a computer can do is to efficiently manipulate a predesigned mathematical representation of a social activity according to a predetermined logic—as long as both rules and model are fixed.[6] In short, convert art to artifice.

In many realms of human activity, computers are now performing with precision and predictability many tasks that human limitations prevent human beings from doing as exactly, or as reliably. What is lost in many cases is not just variety, and specific human skills, but the capacity to nurture, enhance, and expand them through the messy processes of direct, trial-and-error learning. Computerization and automation are also wonderful promoters of the icon of technical efficiency, as opposed to the duplicative and often haphazard maintenance of sufficient extra resources to control or mitigate the effects of human mistakes. Of particular concern is the degree to which what is destroyed or discarded in the relentless pursuit of technical and operational efficiency is not waste or slop, but "slack," the human and material buffering capacity that allows organizations and social systems to absorb unpredicted, and often unpredictable, shocks.

The social costs in many of these cases may seem moderately but not critically serious. In the short term, that may be true. To those of us who study indirect and collective effects on human behavior and long-term trends in human interaction, however, the potential effects on the future structures, social formations, and organizations of human societies, the potential losses of social means for learning, social capacity for adaptation, and social space for innovation and creativity that are pointed at, if not actually represented by such cases, are more than a little disturbing.

Virtual Organizations in a Real World

Another recent development that has drawn considerable interest is virtual reality (VR). At first, the idea was confined primarily to the individual user. The primitive sensory-tactile "VR" sets in amusement arcades are only the first step to a promised world of virtual reality in which human beings can climb mountains, or walk on the moon, or duel, or make love, without risk and without physical harm. But transcending the body is not what is attracting commercial attention. To many, the goal of virtual space, like the goal of computer chess, is to use computers to go beyond the capacity of real, physical human beings, and, eventually, to move beyond simple representations of human space and into a wide variety of larger-scale social activities. The Internet and its future successors are already being promoted by their developers and enthusiasts as opening the door to the creation of extended virtual communities in which people can interact without the time-consuming and frequently messy processes of physical movement and physical intimacy.

If the many journals and articles written and read by the prophets and promoters of organizational computing are to be believed, the ultimate goal is to blend the presumed interpretive and logical skills designed into gaming machines such as computerized chess programs with the architecture and connectivity of the Internet, and then supply it with a variety of tactile and direct interfaces—not only to surpass but to transcend both the analytic and physical limitations of human beings. What most fail to realize is that in so doing, they will be deconstructing the historically socially constructed worlds of business, and of the military, transforming them into computer-constructed virtual spaces in which automated, computerized systems interpret human wants and needs and translate them into reality via adaptable automatic machinery.

The virtual factory will be able to take a customer order and turn out a customized automobile, or couch, within days, if not hours, using automated machinery and just-in-time delivery systems. The virtual corporation will be able to present to the world whatever face is contingently the most appropriate, adapting and configuring internally via computers and computerized networks from, perhaps, an oil company on Monday to a fertilizer company on Tuesday.[7] The virtual military will be able to throw together almost immediately the force mix appropriate to any crisis or need, set up a command-and-control structure, and apply force intelligently and rationally in pursuit of specific goals and objectives.[8] And if markets can be made any more virtual than they are already, they might perhaps trade in purely conceptual instruments that relate only to what people (and other computers) think might happen, or should happen, making and losing money as a pure computer game instead of being tied to the slow and cumbersome processes of real economic activity.[9]

Many critics have pointed out that the uncalculated risk in all of this is the risk of failure, either direct and mechanical failure of the machine through error or accident, or software failures owing either to limitations of the program or errors in programming. In cases such as nuclear plant operations, a few of the more farsighted have even pointed out the dangers of believing that human programmers, or any electronic analogue they concoct, can anticipate all contingencies or provide for all circumstances, and worry about how the computer, or the computerized controls, will respond to a circumstance that announces time and safety urgency but provides no input that quite fits the set of programmed responses or analytic techniques.

The case of glass cockpits raised another linked, but less direct concern about the possible loss of expertise that will occur if the computerization and automation of complex and risky systems not only prevents humans from gaining expertise, but interferes with their learning how to respond at all without computer aid. This too is the replacement of art with artifice, but in this case a very consequential one. Pilots and other operators live in a world of irreducible uncertainty, of "unknown unknowns," where they must deal with what was not known not to be known.[10] No computer can be programmed to deal with contingencies that cannot be anticipated. Coping with such "rogue" outcomes is in fact the art of the superb manager or master operator.[11] But who will master the virtual world of virtual corporations operating over virtual links? Indeed, who will operate and manage them?

Once, many years ago, as a student at the University of Chicago, I followed on a real, physical board a duel between two blindfolded chess masters—a game of real chess being played in virtual space. That was, and is, a tremendous display of human beings working beyond their normal limitations. What is now happening in the social and economic world as the widespread computerization of communication, information, management, and control pushes organizations and systems beyond human limits seems instead to be a virtual game being played with real pieces. The difference matters.

Conclusion

The long-standing search for an automated chess player was an understandable pursuit of the computer community, and perhaps a nearly perfect one for them. Chess is, after all, a highly structured, artificial game with finite rules and finite possibilities. It is more challenging to humans than most formal games because there are so many possibilities, and the strategies are so complex, by human standards, that proficiency (let alone expertise) is not easily gained. What is more, skill at chess is highly valued in academic and professional communities, such as those from which the designers of computer chess players tend to be drawn.

The design of a computer chess player that could defeat a human master was once an impressive accomplishment because of limitations on the size, speed, and algorithmic sophistication of the machines. But as a demonstration of machine intelligence, it is more mechanical than intelligent, its "intelligence" of relevance only in a universe where rules are finite and fixed, behavior bounded, and causal chains deterministic and simply linked. Sooner or later, the machines will be sufficiently large, and sufficiently fast, that they will be able to find brute force solutions to all possible chess moves, even without simplifying algorithms. At that point, no one will be able to beat them (nor will they be able to beat each other).

For those who find delight in the computer's ability to master skills once held by only a few human beings, that will be a meaningful, perhaps even an important achievement. For human beings who play chess with other human beings, for enjoyment, as a test of comparative cognitive mastery, that will be, or should be, of no importance whatsoever. Computers cannot really "play" chess at all, for they have no knowledge of what chess is, to a human, and no conception of why humans play it.[12] Chess as a human activity will remain an exploration of the ability to recognize patterns in the face of near limitless possibilities, and to learn how to act into an uncertain future not recklessly but with forethought and insight. But for others, the erosion of context, the knowledge that there is a machine that can play a better game from any position and make a better move in any situation, will strip the game of importance and meaning.

That people possessing operational skills corresponding to these are now threatened, even if only indirectly and unintentionally, by the new modes of automation is an immediate concern, but not a long-term one. The long-term consequences will arise from the web of secondary effects, ranging from the loss of the basis from which such skills can be constructed to the creation of a socio-technical dependency on operating at such high levels of efficiency and complexity that human beings will not be able to manage or control the effects, intended or unintended, whether the computers break down or not.

What I have called the "computer trap" is a shorthand for the elaborate, long-term, collective effects of the possibly irreversible and largely unexamined drive to computerize and network everything and anything whose efficiency or economic performance might thereby be improved. In the process, those who re-design and re-engineer the large-scale social and socio-technical systems that are essential for managing the complexities and structures of modern life seem to have little understanding of the potential vulnerabilities they are creating. Such effects are already being noted in the similar, persistent search to eliminate from hazardous systems all possible sources and causes of "human error." Whether those systems be military or industrial, financial or bureaucratic, the increased tightness of coupling, lack of redundancy, and speed of response, will make human intervention or control difficult at best when (and not if) something goes wrong—particularly for those systems whose means and mechanisms of operation are so deeply embedded in the computers that operate them that no human being fully understands them.

There is an apocryphal story about early efforts to construct intelligent machines for language translation. Having received a new pro-

gram to intertranslate English and Russian, the operators decided to
check the system by translating phrases from English to Russian and
then back again. To make the test doubly hard, some sentences and
phrases were deliberately chosen to be short, metaphoric, and free of
other clues as to interpretation and meaning. One of them was: "Out
of sight, out of mind." What came back into English, after retransla-
tion, was: "Invisible idiots."

As computers become more deeply embedded as the underlying
performers of a wide variety of social and organizational tasks, they
are also growing more and more invisible. It is all too easy to forget
that they are also idiots, having no information other than what has
been supplied them and capable of doing no more than what was programmed into them. And they are no more capable of understanding
or predicting indirect and long-term consequences than were their designers or programmers. They require constant, intelligent, and informed monitoring. Over time, they will be increasingly out of sight,
but they must never be out of mind. Otherwise it is we, and not the
computers, who will become invisible idiots.

Notes

Chapter 1
Introduction

1. It is reasonable to speculate that the reason she exists at all instead of being replaced by a voice-simulating computer system is because those holding the frequent flier card I hold are considered to be privileged customers, who therefore are given the luxury of personal service. Some forms of inefficiency are deliberate, and functional.

2. Although this same computer allows you to walk virtual shelves of an imaginary limitless stack sequentially, by catalog number, the process is not the same, nor, in my own experience, does it have the same richness or reward.

3. Winner, "Do Artifacts Have Politics?"

4. Toffler, *The Third Wave.*

5. Mazlish, *The Fourth Discontinuity.*

6. McCorduck, *Machines Who Think.*

7. Mazlish, *The Fourth Discontinuity*; Rabinbach, "Automata, Evolution, and Us," 9–10.

8. See, for example, Dunlop and Kling, eds., *Computerization and Controversy*, particularly their chapter "The Dream of Technical Utopianism." Other recent examples include Negroponte, *Being Digital*; Rheingold, *Virtual Reality.*

9. An excellent and empirical analysis is that of Thomas, *What Machines Can't Do*, who applied a power-process model to study the introduction of new techniques into a variety of firms. The empirical work of Shoshana Zuboff (*In the Age of the Smart Machine*) is also highly relevant.

10. Karlsen and Oppen, "Professional Knowledge." Also see chapter 7.

11. Karlsen and Oppen, "Professional Knowledge." Also see Rochlin and

von Meier, "Nuclear Power Operations." This will be discussed further in some detail in chapter 7.

12. See, for example, Thomas, *What Machines Can't Do*; Zuboff, *Age of the Smart Machine*; Rochlin and von Meier, "Nuclear Power Operations"; Rasmussen, Anderson, and Bernsen, eds., *Human-Computer Interaction*; Göranzon and Josefson, eds., *Knowledge, Skill and Artificial Intelligence*.

13. Turkle, *The Second Self*, 35ff.

Chapter 2
Autogomous Technology

1. Winner, *Autonomous Technology*.

2. A notable exception is the recent dissertation of Kären Wieckert, whose empirical and theoretical study of designers contrasts the "context of design" from the "context of use." Wieckert, "Design under Uncertainty."

3. I explore these ideas more fully in Rochlin, "Pris dans la toile" (Trapped in the web).

4. See, for example, Edwards, *Closed World*, Flamm, *Targetting the Computer*.

5. The fascinating story of the evolving relationship between the U.S. government, IBM, and MIT that grew out of the SAGE (Semi-Automatic Ground Environment) project is told in some detail in Edwards, *Closed World*, 142ff. Prior to its choice as prime contractor for SAGE, IBM had no experience at all in the computer field. By the time the SAGE contracts were played through, it was dominant.

6. One only has to attend a large computer conference to witness the size and makeup of the crowds who attend talks by such research leaders as Negroponte to verify this observation.

7. See, for example, the graphic description in Shurkin, *Engines of the Mind*, especially p. 171.

8. Davidow and Malone, *The Virtual Corporation*, 36ff.

9. Shurkin, *Engines of the Mind*, 301ff. Vacuum-tube computers were of course not only large in size but generated enormous amounts of heat (as a graduate student, I helped build one of the first transistorized computers in two relay racks at one end of a gigantic room that had more air conditioning capacity than the rest of the research building). More troublesome was the nongaussian distribution of failures as a function of lifetime, which guaranteed that failure of a new tube was in fact more probable than that of one that had

been in long use. See, for example, the excellent discussion in Edwards, *Closed World*, 109–110.

10. Shurkin, *Engines of the Mind*, 261.

11. Roberts, "The ARPANET."

12. Shurkin (loc. cit.) also has an excellent and entertaining history of the punched card, and of Herman Hollerith's punched-card census machines. Hollerith's company eventually merged with others to form the Computing-Tabulating-Recording (CTR) company. In 1914, CTR hired a young salesman named Thomas Watson, who soon took control. In 1924, CTR was renamed International Business Machines. Forty years later, the computer giant being led by Watson's son, Thomas Jr., was still promoting the use of Hollerith punched-card equipment. Hollerith's technology, patented in 1887, dominated the market for almost a century.

13. George Orwell's classic vision of the computer as an interactive observer in the service of a totalitarian state has reappeared in countless stories, novels, and films (*1984: A Novel*); indeed, repetition has rendered it almost rhetorical. An alternative form, the central computer that asserts control on its own, has been a popular theme in science fiction for some time, e.g., Jones, *Colossus*, which was later made into the movie *The Forbin Project*, or HAL, in *2001: A Space Odyssey*. The most creatively parodic vision of a computer-centralized dysfunctional society is probably the recent movie *Brazil* (Terry Gilliam, *Brazil*).

14. As the late David Rose of MIT once observed, dinosaurs had independent motor-control brains in their butts even larger than those in their head. When you kill a dinosaur, it takes a long time for the body to figure out it's dead.

15. Depending on the method of analysis, the real (constant-dollar) cost of a given amount of computing power has been falling at the rate of between 30 percent and 35 percent annually for the past thirty years (roughly a factor of ten every six years or so). A single transistor has fallen in price by a factor of 10,000 during that time; in contrast, the cost of a memory chip has remained almost constant since 1968—but their capacity has gone up by a factor of 4,000. The most remarkable progress, however, is an area that cannot be measured on monetary scales and has no analogue in any other industry. A single advanced large-scale integrated circuit chip selling for a few hundred dollars may have millions of microtransistors on it, and be capable of performance equal in capacity and exceeding in speed that of a mainframe computer of little more than a decade ago. It has become almost rhetorical by now to note that

if the automobile industry had made the same progress as the semiconductor industry since the mid-1960s, a fully functional Mercedes Benz would cost less than five dollars; it would also be smaller than a pinhead.

16. Interesting narratives of the development of the minicomputer can be found in Kidder, *Soul of a New Machine*, and Olson, *Digital Equipment Corporation*. Pearson, *Digital at Work*, is a beautifully illustrated history of DEC that complements the exhaustive historical inquiry of Rifkin and Harrar, *Ultimate Entrepreneur*.

17. Other companies such as Data General and SDS quickly followed DEC into the market (Kidder, *Soul of a New Machine*), but they never achieved the same level of success.

18. My own memories of being a sometimes reluctant player in the rapid development of the now famous Berkeley Standard Distribution (BSD) version of UNIX remain quite vivid. From time to time there would issue by message from the computer center an announcement of a new release of the editor, or the formatter, or even the terminal definition program, that drove us not only to despair but to the center to pick up the new documentation. More than one user found that a year's leave from Berkeley required extensive relearning before it was possible to come up to speed again.

19. Of all the narratives of the early history of the PC, none is more amusing, or more idiosyncratic, than that of the pseudonymous Robert X. Cringely (*Accidental Empires*).

20. This is the essence of the story narrated by Freiberger and Swaine in their superb history, *Fire in the Valley*.

21. Ibid., 31ff.

22. Ibid., 212.

23. I thank Kären Wieckert for this observation, and for her help in guiding me through the maze of the early days of computer and software development.

24. The definitive history of Xerox PARC and the failure to market the Alto is that of Smith and Alexander, *Fumbling the Future*.

25. In the apocryphal story, very popular at PARC, a nameless programmer, failing to realize the editor is in command mode, types out the word "edit." The editor promptly marks everything in the text (e), deletes it all (d), goes into insert mode (i), and types the single letter "t"—which is now all that remains of the day's work.

26. Smith and Alexander, *Fumbling the Future*, 93ff. The display was 808 by 606 pixels, 8.5 by 11 inches, a form of electronic paper. The first image ever put up on a bitmapped screen was the Sesame Street Cookie Monster.

27. It was also, in computing power terms, very, very expensive. To this day, many university computer centers running UNIX have only limited graphics capabilities to reduce the load on their multiuser, time-shared machines.

28. Apple devotees tend to be disproportionately concentrated in the fields of education and research. To some extent, this is a reinforcing feedback loop, since as a result quite a bit of software specialized to those fields, particularly that making use of elaborate graphics, was developed for Apple machines. But it is also interesting to note that these are the people who have traditionally accepted their dependence, e.g., on near-monopoly mainframe or minicomputer companies, as the cost of getting what they want, and are not intimidated by a machine whose inner workings are not open or visible to them.

29. DOS stands for disk operating system, but PC-DOS (the version created for IBM) and MS-DOS (the generic form) also include a basic input-output system whose open standardization is even more important for the development of software.

30. Some have argued that IBM never did think this line of reasoning through, but just assumed that they would come to dominate the market because, after all, they *were* IBM. It has also been pointed out that many of the top executives at IBM never really believed that the personal computer would amount to much, and may therefore not have been paying that much attention to the details.

31. I omit here the entire history and evolution of specialized workstations for graphics and other design applications, such as those of Sun, Hewlett-Packard, and Silicon Graphics. Not only is their market fairly specialized, the machines, systems, and demands on user competence and training are closer in design and specification to minicomputers than micros, even if the cost differential has narrowed over time. I also omit discussion of IBM's OS/2, a PC operating system with many strengths that was poorly supported, and is fading into comparative insignificance.

32. It is also ironic to note that as Windows evolves from an interface into an operating system, it is becoming as complex and almost as obscure as Apple's latest System 7.5.

33. Indeed, Microsoft's attempts to dominate all aspects of software, from operating system to applications of every type and, perhaps, even telephone access to the Internet, have not only drawn the attention of government regulators, but caused some concern among users about their growing dependence upon a single company.

34. More powerful desktop or graphics workstations such as those from

Sun and Xerox are basically miniaturized minicomputers, and tend to run their own OS or some variant of UNIX. The two dominant systems for desktops at the moment are Apple's System 7.5 for the Macintosh and Microsoft's MS-DOS and Windows. Other machines such as the Apple II and the Amiga have relatively small, specialized market shares, as do other PC operating systems such as Digital Research's DR-DOS, or OS/2.

35. For those who follow this stuff, 1995 was the year of irony. Apple moved to open up its system, not only allowing but encouraging clone makers, introducing a more compatible chip, and adopting a PC interface bus standard (PCI) for some of its new machines. On the PC side, Microsoft's desire to completely dominate the software market was being matched by Intel's drive to gain control over the hardware through a combination of aggressive marketing and buying up memory chip production.

36. See, for example, Rifkin and Harrar, *Ultimate Entrepreneur*, 213ff. Dan Bricklin designed VisiCalc specifically for the Apple II; Mitch Kapor created Lotus 1-2-3 specifically for the IBM PC.

37. As of July 1995, IBM belonged to about 1,000 standards organizations. Cavender, "Making the Web Work for All."

38. Hughes, "Evolution of Large Technical Systems"; Hughes, *Networks of Power*. Although similar to the arguments of Hughes and others in its account of the social nature and context of technologies, the arguments advanced here take a perspective that is oriented more around intraorganizational factors than toward the external interplay of organizations with knowledge, markets, and regulatory practice. Both of these approaches differ epistemologically and methodologically from social constructionist schools in their central focus on organizations and institutions rather than individuals as central elements of interactions. See, for example, Bijker, Hughes, and Pinch, eds., *Social Construction of Technological Systems*.

39. Hughes, *Networks of Power*, for example, has pointed out the importance for technical development of "reverse salients," in which the further expansion or improvement of the system that is desired or sought is held up by the requirement for new techniques or methods.

40. David, "The Dynamo and the Computer." David argues that one would expect productivity gains to increase markedly at about the 70 percent adoption point. What is disputed about computers in business is just what the actual adoption point is. Although office computing only represents 2–3 percent of net capital investment (compared with perhaps 20–30 percent for the electricity case he studied), it is not clear that this is an appropriate measure.

41. Landauer, *Trouble with Computers*, 103–104.

42. For a wonderful exposition of the difference between deliberate consequences and intended ones, see Osborn and Jackson, "Leaders, Riverboat Gamblers."

43. Even for those cases that have been criticized as examples of "autonomous" technology, out of human control, a careful look shows that it is the users and not the developers and promoters who are driving the system. See, for example, Winner, *Autonomous Technology*.

44. Landauer, *Trouble with Computers*, especially at 118ff. For another perspective, see also Wurman, *Information Anxiety*.

45. Landauer, *Trouble with Computers*, 115ff.

46. Ibid., 338–339.

47. Ibid., 169.

48. Ibid. The first example is on p. 170, the second on p. 318.

49. Wieckert, "Design Under Uncertainty." In a recent review of a new portable disk drive for personal computers in *Byte*, Stan Miastkowski commented: "Rather than use the old engineer-driven 'build neat stuff and they will come' design philosophy, Iomega queried end user focus groups, asking potential customers what they wanted most in a removable-media drive." This was noted as being desirable, but not at all common ("Portable-Data Stars," *Byte*, August 1995: 129–131).

50. According to Kären Wieckert, whose dissertation focuses on this problem: "Surprisingly, there has been little careful study of the behavior of actual designers confronting *authentic* design dilemmas generated by concerns from the context of use, creating representations of those concerns, or resolving those concerns through the artifacts they are designing" (Wieckert, "Design Under Uncertainty," 12). The notable exception is her dissertation, whose empirical studies of the design process in three organizations are complemented by a subtle theoretical argument that separates and compares the "context of design" and the "context of use." That she has also been a professional designer of expert systems makes the study all the more unique, and more valuable.

51. See, for examples, Winograd and Flores, *Understanding Computers*; Norman, *Things That Make Us Smart*. This approach has been used extensively in Scandinavia. See, for example, Ehn, *Work-Oriented-Design*.

52. Wieckert, "Design Under Uncertainty," 107ff.

53. Ibid., 108.

54. Suchman, "Working Relations."

Chapter 3
Networks of Connectivity: Webs of Dependence

1. Looking for the three-letter combination "art," for instance, brought up every word that had an art in it: artifact; cuisinart; smart; cart; fart; and so on.

2. Strangely enough, this is to some extent true even for users who for other reasons preferred the Macintosh because it was simpler to use and otherwise more user-friendly.

3. Baker, "Discards."

4. To put a final twist on this, the last two people we hired as computer system operator in my institute were students in the "library" school. We used to get them from computer science. Since that time, the School of Library and Information Science has become the School of Information and Managegement Science; most of the book-librarians are gone.

5. See, for example, Baker, "Discards." An excellent review of the automation of Berkeley's library and the removal of the card catalogue may also be found in Stoll, *Silicon Snake Oil*, 193–202. The new San Francisco library has since joined the list of those who have used the former catalog cards as a decorative motif.

6. Baker, "Discards."

7. Reports of searches that either end up totally missing the item sought or return hundreds of entries are not totally exaggerated (nor are cases where a mistake in data entry, such as misspelling a name, makes finding the item nearly impossible). The other day I logged on in search of a set of hearings on organized crime in Chicago. After nearly half an hour of frustrating attempts at searching the database, I just gave up. But I couldn't believe the category, or the hearings, did not exist. So I went to the card catalog (which still survives in our Government Documents collection) and found them almost instantly, listed, as it turns out, under the subject heading of "Organized Crime, Illinois, Chicago." It seems that our search program could not manage to skip the Illinois when scanning the database.

8. See, for example, Wurman, *Information Anxiety*; Strassman, *Information Payoff*.

9. That is, if the databases were fixed. Unfortunately, the amount of information that is available seems to be growing even faster, paralleling the famous problem of trying to count the human race by parading them past a single point. According to Honan ("At the National Archives"), the U.S. National Archives are already receiving about one million megabytes per year.

10. Beniger, *Control Revolution*; Chandler, Jr., *Visible Hand*; Scott Morton, ed., *Corporation of the 1990s*.

11. Flamm, *Targetting the Computer*. Also see the excellent discussion on DARPA's origins and goals in Edwards, *Closed World*. Originally called the Advanced Research Projects Agency (ARPA), the D for Defense was added to its name in 1972. President Kennedy gave it a wide mandate to pursue research that made it (by design) more independent than most military-related research organizations.

12. Flamm, *Targetting the Computer*, 57ff.

13. In an ordinary mainframe, or mini, of the time, jobs had to be entered and executed sequentially. Physically, this could mean a long wait even for a small task; socially, it meant that the computer was an external rather than an interactive tool. In timesharing, computing time is cut up into slices that are allocated to users by some internal rule. Each connected user can operate as if they had a (sometimes much slower) machine that was their own.

14. The initial impetus appears to have come from President Johnson, who was worried about the confusion and lack of coordination among the computer systems used by the three armed services. By 1969, ARPANET had three nodes up, one for each service. Today it has thousands. But the Government Accounting Office still issues several reports a year criticizing the confusion and lack of coordination among the computer systems used by the three armed services. Some problems cannot be solved with technology.

15. Krol, *Whole Internet*, 11. As it became increasingly realized that much of the threat to existing telecommunications came not from physical destruction but from the ravages of electromagnetic pulses, DARPA and other governments increased their funding for other technical solutions and more robust means of communications. Among other things, this led to rapid improvements in fiber-optics technology, which then led back to a further transformation of computer networking capabilities.

16. Roberts, "The ARPANET."

17. Flamm, *Targetting the Computer*, 59–60. Protocols are the rules by which the packets are constructed, assembled, and sent. They may include such information as source, destination, packet length, bit-code, and other information designed to monitor and detect the integrity of the packet to check for transmission errors.

18. Krol, *Whole Internet*, 21ff. The TCP is particularly important for extended, decentralized national networks, since the idea of multiple paths for transmission means that the packets may not be received in the same sequence

in which they were sent. TCP will recognize this and wait until the whole sequence has arrived before declaring the message to be complete.

19. Flamm, *Targetting the Computer*, 61.

20. In order to organize the users coherently so that they do not interfere with each other, its designers came up with was the tree-like hierarchy of directories and subdirectories that PC users now take almost completely for granted, with the additional constraint of restricted access between individual branches.

21. At least that is how it appears to the user. In many advanced operating systems, the "copying" or "moving" of files takes place by changing the address or permission settings (pointers) rather than by physically copying the file bit-by-bit from one location to another.

22. The excitement of that period, and the eagerness with which graduate students in particular spread the gospel of UNIX and electronic mail, is hard to recapture. As the saying goes, "You would have had to have been there at the time."

23. Recognizing the achievement, the Association for Computing Machinery awarded three Xerox PARC researchers the 1984 Software Systems Award for the invention of distributed personal computing. By that time, the Alto was history, and the PARC project team broken up.

24. Flamm, *Creating the Computer*, 239.

25. See, for an excellent example, Negroponte, *Being Digital*.

26. Stoll, *Silicon Snake Oil*; Turkle, *Life on the Screen*.

27. Krol, *Whole Internet*, contains a wealth of information about Internet access and rules, especially for independent users.

28. The best definition is perhaps the general one of Quarterman: "The *Internet* is an internetwork of many networks all running the TCP/IP protocol suite, connected through gateways, and sharing common name and address spaces. It exists to facilitate sharing of resources at participating organizations and collaboration among researchers, as well as to provide a testbed for new developments in networking." Quarterman, *The Matrix*, 278.

29. The name, which is a formalization of a technical description, appears to be more a matter of history than intent; the original ARPANET was sometimes referred to as the ARPA internet (because it was an association, or intertie, between and among other networks).

30. As pointed out by Denning, "ARPANET After 20 Years," the Research Internet had taken over so many of ARPANET's functions at the time of its dissolution that many users never even noticed.

31. The 1993 figures are from Eckhouse, "INTERNET." John Markoff had estimated the number at ten million some four months earlier ("Turning the Desktop PC").

32. This is somewhat easier for so-called "client-server" LANs using a central, dedicated microcomputer to handle LAN traffic and common programs than for a peer-to-peer network such as the PARC design for Ethernet. On the other hand, client-server networks are increasingly more popular, particularly in medium-sized laboratories or businesses.

33. Are they really part of the Internet or just attachments? The response of some is that because the Internet is so self-organized, self-designed, and self-regulated, they are if they want to be. See, e.g., Krol, *Whole Internet*, 13. Krol's metaphor for the Internet is that of a (very Protestant) church, a sort of free association that is entirely voluntary, but very demanding of beliefs and compliance if you do join.

34. Markoff, "A Web of Networks."

35. According to a recent story (Cavender, "Making the Web Work for All"), the goals of a new consortium formed to promote the use of the World Wide Web and make it "more democratic," are to set better and stricter standards, including protocols, specifications, and software. According to Tim Berners-Lee, who first invented the Web, and now directs and coordinates the new consortium that is trying to bring some order and standards to it, what is needed is more order, structure, and harmony. IBM, Microsoft, AT&T, and Sony are among the first corporate members.

36. Rockart and Short, "The Networked Organization."

37. This is the central argument of Beniger's splendid work of history and analysis, *Control Revolution*.

38. Korzeniowski ("The IS Tug-of-War") uses as an example Florida Power and Light, which at one time had more than 3,000 users running a "hodge-podge" of LANs with a variety of incompatible network protocols that included Novell, DEC, IBM SNA, and TCP/IP.

39. Although IBM tried to promote its own system, Token Ring, users found Ethernet to be faster and more reliable.

40. Rockart and Short, "Networked Organization," 213.

41. Korzeniowski, "The IS Tug-of-War."

42. Abate, "Someone Could Be Watching."

43. I apologize to those who consider this analogy to be hoary and overworked, but I think that in this case it is quite appropriate. See, for example, Flink, *Automobile Age*.

44. See, for example, Juhlin, "Information Technology."

45. Wieckert, "Design Under Uncertainty"; Suchman, "Working Relations."

46. See, for example, Scott Morton, *Corporation of the 1990s*.

Chapter 4
Taylorism Redux?

1. See, for example, Negroponte, *Being Digital*; Stoll, *Silicon Snake Oil*; Kelly, *Out of Control*.

2. Thomas, *What Machines Can't Do*; Zuboff, *Age of the Smart Machine*; Noble, *Forces of Production*.

3. Of the many works in this field, those particularly relevant to the arguments developed in this book are Toffler, *Third Wave*; Hughes, *Networks of Power*; Beniger, *Control Revolution*; Chandler, *Visible Hand*; Scott Morton, *Corporation of the 1990s*; Chandler, Jr., *Scale and Scope*; Fogel, *Railroads*; Merkle, *Management and Ideology*; Thompson, *Organizations in Action*.

4. Hirschhorn, *Beyond Mechanization*.

5. Doray, *A Rational Madness*, 34ff.

6. Classic examples of early integration include not only the well-known case of the railroad, but the creation of the giants of the meatpacking industry. See, for example, Chandler, *Visible Hand*; Cronon, *Nature's Metropolis*.

7. Doray, *A Rational Madness*, 61ff.

8. Taylor, "Principles of Scientific Management."

9. Davidow and Malone, *Virtual Corporation*, 164ff.

10. Merkle, *Management and Ideology*; Waring, *Taylorism Transformed*.

11. Doray, *A Rational Madness*. Also Harvey, *Condition of Postmodernity*, 228ff.

12. Doray, *A Rational Madness*.

13. Beniger, *Control Revolution*, 298.

14. As so cleverly, and beautifully, expressed by Charlie Chaplin. Chaplin and Goddard, *Modern Times*.

15. Beniger, *Control Revolution*, 298–299.

16. Noble, *Forces of Production*, 16; Rabinbach, *Human Motor*, 238ff.

17. Beniger, *Control Revolution*, 295.

18. Doray, *A Rational Madness*, 34ff.

19. Beniger, *Control Revolution*.

20. Dreyfus and Dreyfus, *Mind Over Machine*.

21. This level of expertise and tacit knowledge not only persists, but is nur-

tured in some modern organizations, particularly those managing the safety-critical operation of highly complex and fast reacting systems. See, for examples, Rochlin and von Meier, "Nuclear Power Operations"; La Porte, "United States Air Traffic System"; Rochlin, "Essential Friction."

22. Zuboff, *Age of the Smart Machine*.

23. Waring, *Taylorism Transformed*.

24. Merkle, *Management and Ideology*, 76. The ability to quantify the value to a firm of such "nonproductive" activities was one of the great motives for the development of transaction cost economics.

25. Rabinbach, *Human Motor*; Noble, *America by Design*.

26. In a final twist, the management techniques of General Motors as put forth by Alfred P. Sloan resulted in the gradual disappearance of even those individual entrepreneur-innovator-owners such as Henry Ford in favor of those whose major skill was running large, formal organizations.

27. Harvey points out that Taylorism never made major inroads in Europe between the wars because of the relatively greater strength of labor movements there and the lack of major immigration or movements of workers to provide leverage against them (*Postmodernity*, 128).

28. Barnard, *Functions of the Executive*; Scott, *Organizations*.

29. Zuboff, *Age of the Smart Machine*; Merkle, *Management and Ideology*; Waring, *Taylorism Transformed*.

30. The most splendid, and durable, presentation is Barnard, *Functions of the Executive*.

31. Scott, *Organizations*; Perrow, *Complex Organizations*.

32. Thompson, *Organizations*.

33. Baxter, *Scientists against Time*.

34. The flavor of those early days is wonderfully captured by Emery and Trist, "Socio-Technical Systems." Both the book and the article remain among the most important basic statements of the principles of socio-technical systems analysis.

35. Perrow, *Complex Organizations*.

36. Waring, *Taylorism Transformed*, 25. In a sense, this was a completion of the agenda of integration that had preoccupied managers since the nineteenth century, and therefore, by extension, of the search for control as described by Beniger, *Control Revolution*.

37. The term comes from Zuboff, *Age of the Smart Machine*, by analogy with and extension of workplace automation by more dedicated and single-purpose computers.

38. Scott Morton, *Corporation of the 1990s*, 8.

39. Davidow and Malone, *Virtual Corporation*, 10.

40. See, for examples, Marenco, "Effects of Rationalization"; McColloch, *White Collar Workers*.

41. McColloch, *White Collar Workers*.

42. Ibid., 116.

43. Braverman, *Labor and Monopoly Capital*.

44. Osterman, "Impact of IT on Jobs and Skills," 231ff.

45. Management and control in white-collar and office settings has been studied extensively by the research group at the University of California at Irvine. See, for example, Dunlop and Kling, *Computerization and Controversy*; Danziger and Kraemer, *People and Computers*; Danziger and others, *Computers and Politics*.

46. Monger, *Mastering Technology*, 84–85.

47. The term "scientific management" is rarely used by those who declare their field to be management science. They sharply contrast their use of models of limited rationality in the open- or natural systems approach with the formal, closed-system perspectives of the historical scientific management school. Nevertheless, the modern focus on "optimal" solutions seems quite reminiscent of the Taylorist approach. See, for example, Davidow and Malone, *Virtual Corporation*, 186.

48. Scott Morton, *Corporation of the 1990s*, 14; Rifkin, *End of Work*, 104. The best account of the historical development of the just-in-time strategy is that of Womack, Jones, and Roos, *Machine That Changed the World*.

49. Thomas, *What Machines Can't Do*; Zuboff, *Age of the Smart Machine*.

50. Davidow and Malone, *Virtual Corporation*. The span of control can nevertheless be impressive. If General Motors indeed had the fifteen levels of management attributed to it, and eight people reporting to each manager at each level, in principle, more than thirty billion employees could be controlled (p. 171). A more reasonable organization with eight levels and six people reporting directly at each level could still control more than 1.5 million. The point is that a even a relatively low-level manager, sitting at level four (from the top), with four levels below, would be passing up to the next level the summed and integrated information from more than a thousand subordinates.

51. Although this is not surprising in the context of the traditional neo-Marxist literature on deskilling, it is true even of the more sophisticated and sympathetic studies such as that of Thomas, *What Machines Can't Do*; Zuboff, *Age of the Smart Machine*; Nadis and MacKenzie, *Car Trouble*.

52. Beniger, *Control Revolution*; Noble, *Forces of Production*; Hirschhorn, *Beyond Mechanization*.

53. Zuboff, *Age of the Smart Machine*.

54. To make the distinction clear in a complex setting, an "automatic pilot" is a simple servo device that keeps an airplane on a specified heading at a specified speed and altitude, compensating for winds and other factors. An automatic navigation system, on the other hand, is fed a desired course from one point to another, and also controls the aircraft to keep it on the predetermined flight plan. The former device automates flight, the latter "informates" it.

55. Similar results were found in the detailed empirical studies of Thomas, *What Machines Can't Do*.

56. See, for example, the review by Osterman, "Jobs and Skills."

57. Zuboff, *Age of the Smart Machine*, 246ff.

58. Ibid., 238ff.

59. Howard, *Brave New Workplace*.

60. See, for example, Donald Chisholm, *Coordination without Hierarchy*.

61. See, for example, Danziger and Kraemer, *People and Computers*.

62. As is beautifully represented in the movie *Brazil* (see chapter 2, note 13).

63. Zuboff, *Age of the Smart Machine*; Thomas, "Politics of Growth."

64. Lerman and Salzman, "Deskilling and Declassing"; Wood, ed., *Degradation of Work?*; Wood, ed., *Transformation of Work?* Also see the recent effort by Rifkin (*End of Work*) to extend this debate about the displacement and deskilling of labor to the "white-collar" class in what he calls a "postmarket" era.

65. Hirschhorn, *Beyond Mechanization*, 71.

66. Dreyfus and Dreyfus, *Mind Over Machine*.

67. It is quite remarkable that although the author has heard this same description given at various times to mathematicians, performing artists, physicists, and automobile mechanics, it remains a distinction much more familiar in practice than in the analytic literature.

68. Göranzon, "Practice of Use of Computers." The original text was published in Swedish, in Göranzon, *Datautveckslingsens Filosofi*. The text here is Göranzon's translation of 1988.

69. Most of us possess at least some realm of expertise even in the practice of daily life, perhaps as a teacher or cook, singer or carpenter, or even driving or riding a bicycle. That such skills are in general not highly valued is a trenchant critique of the values of modern technical societies.

70. Janik, "Tacit Knowledge."

71. The notional "jellybean factory" is an artifice developed by my colleague at Berkeley, Karlene Roberts of the Haas School of Business, as the diametrical opposite of reliability-demanding, safety-critical, and socially, environmentally, or politically important operations.

72. That is, in fact, one of the things that went wrong at Bhopal. See, for instance Shrivastava, *Bhopal: Anatomy of a Crisis*.

73. Braun, Feuerstein, and von Grote-Janz, "Organ-Technick"; Braun and Joerges, "How to Recombine Large Technical Systems." A similar system now exists in the United States, but has not been so extensively studied.

74. Hughes, *Networks of Power*.

75. Scott Morton, *Corporation of the 1990s*.

76. Beniger, *Control Revolution*; Chandler, *Visible Hand*; Chandler, *Scale and Scope*; Gras, *Grandeur et Dépendance*.

77. Davidow and Malone, *Virtual Corporation*.

78. Rochlin, "Trapped by the Web." Also see Rifkin, *End of Work*.

79. "Shrinking of the Big Board."

Chapter 5
Computer Trading

1. "Anyone Know a Cure for Hiccoughs?"

2. Compare, for example, to Hans Moravec, "Pigs in Cyberspace." The term first gained wide currency in the cyberpunk science-fiction literature, e.g., Gibson, *Neuromancer*.

3. See, for example, "The Screen Is the Future, Master."

4. See, for example, Garbade and Silber, "Technology."

5. Landauer, *Trouble with Computers*, 33. As an interesting sidenote, Landauer also cites Franke ("Technological Revolution") as showing that bank productivity stagnated during the 1970s, when computerization was taking place rapidly for the ostensible purpose of increasing it.

6. U.S. Congress, Office of Technology Assessment, *Electronic Bulls and Bears*.

7. Liquidity means that exchanges should provide a means for every seller to find a buyer, and vice-versa. The larger and more varied the trading volume on an exchange, the more likely that such transactions could be completed. But for markets to be efficient, transactions should be rapid. Here also, increased capacity and sophistication of constitutive technologies (even such simple

ones as the telephone) helped the exchanges to grow without delays or bottle-necks that would impede liquidity.

8. This is, of course, especially true for secondary markets that trade in futures or other paper rather than issued securities or bonds.

9. Salsbury, "Emerging Global Systems."

10. Although Salsbury points out that this was suspended following the October 1987 debacle because of the risk it posed to market makers in a rapidly falling market, Reuters and others are still pursuing the idea.

11. Meyer and Starbuck, "Interactions Between Ideologies."

12. Harvey, *Postmodernity*, 163. The growth of paper entrepreneurialism had already been noted in the early 1980s: See, e.g., Reich, *Next American Frontier*.

13. Some Wall Street analysts maintain that electronic arbitrage is actually to be preferred. Writing in *Science*, M. Mitchell Waldrop quotes trader Michael Alex on the counter-argument: "Think what it means when you execute a program trade without using the computer system. The broker has to take the orders for (500) different stocks and give it to all these runners. The runners go screaming out onto the floor, pushing up to the specialists' desks and shouting. That alone can create panic" (Waldrop, "Computers Amplify Black Monday").

14. Remarkably, and despite the concern shown by technology assessors and some market analysts, the computer science and other technical communities seem to have overlooked these issues almost completely. Many recent books and articles surveying the role of computers in the future "information society" fail to mention security, bond, or currency markets at all. See, for example, Weinberg, *Computers in the Information Society*.

15. Computer trading programs based on historical trend analysis tend to converge, and are therefore likely to behave similarly given similar inputs. Market responses are therefore likely to be exaggeratedly large, perhaps dangerously so, despite regulatory attempts to suspend program trading on large movements.

16. "Is Your Stockbroker User-Friendly?"

17. Crudele, "Volatility"; Sloan, "Why Stocks Fell."

18. Bennett, "More Wild Stock Swings Expected."

19. A good deal of this chronology is adapted from Rosen, "Crashing in '87." Also see OTA, *Bulls and Bears*.

20. Rosen, "Crashing in '87."

21. A "specialist" or market-maker is an exchange member who takes special responsibility for providing liquidity and smoothing transactions for one

or a few specific stocks in exchange for a unique and profitable role as dealer. They not only find buyers and sellers, but use their own capital to absorb shares to ensure a smoothly functioning market. A growing concern is that specialists are not sufficiently capitalized to stabilize against the large blocks being moved by the trading programs of large institutional investors, as was nearly the case during the Black Monday crash of October 19, 1987. See, for example, OTA, *Bulls and Bears*, chapter 3.

22. For example, Wells Fargo alone acting on behalf of a giant pension fund fed in thirteen separate bundles of more than $100 million each. By the end of the day, the $1.4 billion represented more than 5 percent of the total trading. "What Caused the Meltdown?"

23. See, for example, French, "Efficiency of Computer Systems." Ironically French's firm survived October 19 very well by shutting down its computers and trading almost exclusively from the floor, using its floor-trained, experienced personnel. There is a lesson in there somewhere about the displacement of such people by computer systems in the future, but few, if any, of the market firms are paying attention to it. Also see OTA, *Bulls and Bears*, chapter 3.

24. Rosen, "Crashing in '87."

25. "Terrible Tuesday."

26. Rosen, "Crashing in '87."

27. For an analysis of the role of arbitrage on October 19, see, e.g., "What Caused the Meltdown." A similar fluctuation occurred in the spring of 1988 (de Maria, "Dow Up Just 1.99 in Wild Day").

28. Historically, market pundits have never lacked for causal explanations of market activity. It is therefore quite remarkable how common, and readily accepted, it now is for news reports of the day's market action to attribute the moves solely to program trading—accepting without question the notion that computerized trading is now as much determinative as responsive.

29. U.S. Congress, Office of Technology Assessment, *Trading Around the Clock*.

30. This somewhat Pollyanna conclusion is not uncommon among market traders and analysts, who see the new technologies as adding to their capabilities, efficiency, and profits. The same set of beliefs is expressed by the many authors collected in Lucas and Schwartz, as well as repeatedly in journals such as *The Economist* and the *Wall Street Journal*. The underlying myths are powerful and enduring.

31. Indeed, it is not even clear whether the link between technological change and increased dominance by large and powerful parties is indirect

rather than direct. Many critics of capitalist economic systems go even further and argue that technological change is a means by which large and powerful actors directly seek to increase their dominance under the guise of sharing authority or power with the less wealthy and less advantaged. See, e.g., Noble, *Forces of Production*; Harvey, *Postmodernity*; Noble, *America by Design*; Jameson, *Postmodernism*.

32. In formal terms, this closely resembles the dynamic models of structuration developed by Giddens (*Central Problems in Social Theory*; "Structuralism"). For other applications of similar ideas to socio-technical systems, see, for examples, Thomas, *What Machines Can't Do*; Barley, "Technology as an Occasion for Structuring"; Barley, "Alignment of Technology."

33. This is hardly surprising, since the predictive tools of policy analysis are rarely able to deal with extensive social transformations, particularly those in which technical and social changes interact strongly.

34. The SEC regulates trading in securities and assets, and tends to be more cautious in dealing with innovation than the CFTC, which, as regulator of contracts generally used for hedging and speculation, has tended to seek to be flexible and responsive to new approaches and ideas.

35. Crudele, "Market Being Manipulated." The opening of the Chicago futures exchange to electronic trading, for example, allowed a maneuver by which a large investor could rapidly buy large quantities of futures, hoping thereby to trigger the programs of other traders to buy the underlying securities on the NYSE. When the stock rises, the manipulator can quickly sell his futures, getting out with a profit before the NYSE can respond.

36. OTA, *Bulls and Bears*, 13, and chapter 3.

37. Ibid., 12.

38. Barley, "New World of Work."

39. Although it was not until May 8, 1996, in the middle of what several traders described as the most volatile week in memory, that the NYSE was to invoke both the uptick and the downtick limitations on computer trading in the same day.

40. Louis, "Heavy Stock Trading Jams Broker's Lines."

41. The full story of Nasdaq on that July day very much resembled the trials and tribulations set out by Viorst and Cruz in *Alexander and the Terrible, Horrible, No Good, Very Bad Day*. I thank Alexander Rochlin for having brought this to my attention.

42. Harvey, *Postmodernity*, 163; Reich, *Next American Frontier*.

43. Secondary instruments such as futures or "derivatives" such as option

indices are essentially bets on the future performance of interest rates, or the indices of exchanges dealing in "real" goods, securities, bonds, or other financial instruments. Although derivative markets are by definition zero-sum (every seller must find a buyer, and anyone's loss is someone else's gain), they have attracted considerable concern because of their leveraging effect and their potential volatility. In principle, there is never any net gain or loss in a derivative market; in practice, individual investors or firms can lose large amounts of money very quickly.

44. Which does not seem to have stopped Congress from at least considering attempts to regulate and control the accessibility and flow of pornography over the Internet, or the use of certain forms of data encryption.

45. Rochlin, "Trapped by the Web."

46. For an exemplary discussion of the knowledge burden, the costs to an organization of keeping itself informed and up to date on the activities it is trying to monitor or control, see Demchak, *Military Organizations*.

Chapter 6
Jacking into the Market

1. Hansell, "Rogue Traders."

2. "A Falling Star: The Collapse of Barings."

3. "Demise of Barings."

4. Lacking the ability to actually regulate, many states are considering a complete ban on trading in derivatives and other speculative instruments by government agencies and entities.

5. "Bankers Marched in Two by Two."

6. Hansell, "Rogue Traders."

7. Gibson, *Neuromancer*.

8. Kurtzman, *Death of Money*. Things may not be quite as bad as portrayed by Kurtzman, but the overall construction is accurate.

9. Rheingold, *Virtual Reality*, 369.

10. Passell, "Fast Money."

11. As quoted in Rheingold, *Virtual Reality*, 369, "The value of currencies are no longer determined by trade volumes or any of the physical activities normally associated with industrial economies." Also see note 8 above.

12. Rheingold, *Virtual Reality*, 371.

13. The possibilities of electronic theft or fraud, as well as the possible consequences of electronic or network failures, seem to have attracted more press than analytic attention, even though some instances have already occurred. For an excellent summary, see Passell, "Fast Money."

14. The literature on encryption, the Clipper Chip, and the public domain "Pretty Good Privacy" code is enormous. Among the more useful reviews are. U.S. General Accounting Office, *Information Superhighway*; U.S. Congress. Senate, Committee on Judiciary, *Administration's Clipper Chip*. For a somewhat different view, see Garfinkel, *PGP, Pretty Good Privacy*.

15. Provided the humans do choose to act as dampers, in the historical mold, and not as amplifiers of the trends as they have done in several previous market crashes.

16. The chaos literature has also grown to enormous proportions. Among the more directly relevant are Trippi, *Chaos*; Sherry, *Technical Analysis*; Peters, *Chaos and Order*; Chorafas, *Chaos Theory*. Good overviews may be found in Kauffman, *At Home in the Universe*; Waldrop, *Complexity*; Holden, *Chaos*.

17. Waldrop, "Black Monday."

18. Holusha, "Disruption."

19. For example, several of the authors in Lucas, Jr. and Schwartz, eds., *Challenge of Information Technology*.

20. Rosen, "Crashing in '87."

21. Harvey, *Postmodernity*; Jameson, *Postmodernism*.

22. OTA, *Trading around the Clock*, 32.

23. See, for example, Lamiell, "Global Stock Index."

24. Stoll, *Silicon Snake Oil*, 92ff.

25. OTA, *Trading around the Clock*.

26. Edwards, "The Crash."

27. OTA, *Bulls and Bears*, 57–58. The NYSE now requires program traders to cease entering orders into its electronic trading system when the Dow advances or declines more than fifty points; however, it does not prevent the traders from entering orders manually. By mid-1996, the circuit breaker had been triggered on downticks or (more rarely) upticks more than sixty times.

28. OTA, *Trading Around the Clock*, 73ff.

29. As Winner, "Artifacts," so lucidly points out, people continue to believe that they can control the things they have made.

30. Wilson, "Dead Hand."

31. Harvey, *Postmodernity*, 162–163.

32. Passell, "Fast Money."

33. Adam Smith, "Derivatives," WNET, July 21, 1995; "The Rocket Scientists," July 28, 1995.

Chapter 7
Expert Operators and Critical Tasks

The first of the two pilot quotes used as an epigraph to this chapter is taken from *Aviation Week & Space Technology*, May 4, 1992: 2. The second is taken from Phillips, "Man-Machine Cockpit Interface" (note 32 below).

1. For a further description of our work, see, for example, Roberts, ed., *New Challenges*; Rochlin, Todd La Porte, and Roberts, "Self-Designing High-Reliability Organization"; La Porte and Consolini, "Working in Practice but Not in Theory"; and the collection of articles in the special "Future Directions in HRO Research" issue of *Journal of Contingencies and Crisis Management* 4, no. 2 (June 1996), edited by Gene I. Rochlin.

2. Rochlin and others, "Self-Designing High-Reliability Organization"; Roberts and Rousseau, "Having the Bubble"; Rochlin, "Informal Organizational Networking." Note that the bubble is not a metaphor for the cognitive map or representation; rather, "having the bubble" expresses the state of being in control of one. The term seems to derive from earlier times, when the sighting of guns, and the movement of the ship, was read from mechanical level-reading devices consisting of a bubble of air in a curved tube full of fluid, much like the familiar carpenter's spirit level.

3. As is true in other areas where integrative expertise passes over into mastery, not all officers are equally adept, and the ship tries to make sure the best are on duty at the most critical times.

4. To declare publicly that you have "lost the bubble" is an action that is deemed praiseworthy in the Navy because of the potential cost of trying to fake it. Depending upon the situation, either one or more of the other people in the center will feel they have enough of the bubble to step in, or everyone will scramble to try and hold the image together by piecemeal contributions. As a rule, even a few minutes of relief will allow the original officer to reconstruct the bubble and continue.

5. La Porte and Consolini, "Working in Practice but Not in Theory"; Roberts and Rousseau, "Having the Bubble"; Schulman, "Analysis of High-Reliability Organizations."

6. Similar behavior is cited by Perby, "Computerization and Skill in Local Weather Forecasting," for Swedish weather forecasters, and by Zuboff, *Age of the Smart Machine*, 53, 64ff, for operators of complex industrial facilities.

7. Similar expressions have been found in other empirical work in similar situations. See, for example, Thomas, *What Machines Can't Do*, 213ff; Gras, Moricot, Poirot-Delpech, and Scardigli, *Faced with Automation*, 23.

8. Rochlin and von Meier, "Nuclear Power Operations." This "quote" is actually summarized from comments made during an extended interview with three nuclear power plant operators in Europe—where the professional consultants are more likely to be bearded and less likely to have practical, hands-on experience than in the United States.

9. Gras and others, *Faced with Automation*, 37.

10. But compare these interviews with those of Zuboff, *Age of the Smart Machine*, or of Thomas, *What Machines Can't Do*. The people they interviewed expressed pretty much the same range of concerns in situations that were conceptually similar, if somewhat less exacting. Many have four-year college degrees or more, some in engineering or other professional disciplines, and almost all consider regular schooling and retraining as part of the process of maintaining their skills in a changing world.

11. Much of the discussion has taken place at professional conferences whose proceedings are sometimes not as well known as those directed as specific issues such as plant safety or aviation accidents. Interesting articles addressing these points may be found in Göranzon and Josefson, *Knowledge, Skill and Artificial Intelligence*, and in Bauersfeld, Bennett, and Lynch, *Striking a Balance*. Among the other relevant literature containing a number of useful sources and references are Bainbridge, "Ironies of Automation"; Roth, Mumaw, and Stubler, "Human Factors Evaluation Issues."

12. I adopt here the conventional terminology of dividing risk (exposure to the potential for human harm) as the product of the particular potential harm for any event (hazard), which depends only on the character of the physical artifacts and processes, multiplied by the probability that any particular sequence or event will occur. In simple notation, risk = hazard × probability. In more complex systems, where many hazards are present, this is usually expressed as (total risk) = sum (individual hazards × individual probabilities):

$$R_{total} = \sum_i r_i p_i$$

Engineered safety can involve either the reduction of hazard or a reduction in the probability of occurrence. Operators are there not only to try to reduce probabilities, but to manage sequences once they start and control or mitigate their effects. See, for example, Clarke, *Acceptable Risk?*; Ralph, ed., *Probabilistic Risk Assessment*.

13. See, for examples, Gras and others, *Faced with Automation*; "Automated Cockpits: Keeping Pilots in the Loop"; Foushee and Lauber, "Effects of Flight Crew Fatigue on Performance"; Hollnagel, Cacciabue, and Bagnara, "Workshop Report"; Hopkins, "Through the Looking Glass"; Squires, "The 'Glass Cockpit' Syndrome."

14. Fisher, "Experience, Not Rules, Led Airliner Crew in Emergency." Also see *Aviation Week and Space Technology*, March 6, 1989, 18.

15. Weiner, "Jet Carrying 290 Crashes in Iowa."

16. Parker, "Pilots Added Page to DC-10 Manual."

17. Malnic and Kendall, "Struggle to Gain Control of Jet Told."

18. Hughes, "Human Factors Are Critical in Computer-Driven Systems."

19. For a discussion in the aviation context, see Wiener, "Fallible Humans and Vulnerable Systems." Also see Bainbridge, "Ironies of Automation"; Hollnagel and others, "Limits of Automation in Air Traffic Control"; Vortac, Edwards, Fuller, and Manning, "Automation and Cognition in Air Traffic Control."

20. For the purpose of simplicity, I continue to refer in this section to "pilot" error rather than distinguishing errors made by individuals in command from those that arose as part of overall crew performance. In many cases, however, it is difficult to separate the two factors. See, for example, Foushee and Lauber, "Flight Crew Fatigue"; Weick, "Vulnerable System."

21. Foushee and Lauber, "Flight Crew Fatigue."

22. Historical examples include such disparate events as the crimping of DC-10 controls by a cargo door collapse and such external events as lightning (rare) or severe and unexpected wind shear (not uncommon). A recent example is the Lauda Air crash in Thailand in 1991, when an engine control computer deployed a thrust reverser during full power climb-out from the Bangkok airport.

23. "Air Crashes: Murders and Mistakes."

24. "Crash that Killed 92 in India Is Attributed to Pilot Error." Crossette, "Crash of Indian Airlines Plane Kills 89."

25. "Airliner Crashes in France." According to a report in Internet newsgroup comp.risk (RISK 14.74: June 28, 1993), "In France-Soir of Monday 10th May the Commission of Enquiry into the crash of an A320 near Strasbourg on 20th January 1992 . . . is about to deliver its final report. The conclu-

sion on the cause of the accident is "pilot error." The main error was the confusion of the "flight-path angle" (FPA) and "vertical speed" (V/S) modes of descent, selected on the Flight Management and Guidance System (FMGS) console. The pilots were inadvertently in V/S when they should have been in FPA mode. The error was not noticed on the console itself, due to the similarity of the number format display in the two modes. The other cues on the Primary Flight Display (PFD) screen and elsewhere (e.g., altitude and vertical speed indicator) were not noticed since the pilots were overloaded following a last-minute change of flight plan, and presumably were concentrating on the Navigational Display." In this regard, it is interesting to note that another A320 pilot, landing at Frankfurt, refused to switch from Runway 25R to Runway 25L because "my copilot would have had to make something like 12 reprogramming steps with the computer, and I was not in the position to properly monitor what he was doing" (*Aviation Week & Space Technology*, February 3, 1992: 29).

26. Weick, "Organizational Culture as a Source of High Reliability." In Weick's lexicon, "errors" are lapses in judgment or performance in a decision environment where time and information are adequate and ambiguity low. Mistakes arise from specific individual judgments made in a context where the information is presented poorly, or presented in such a way as to interfere with rather than aid the exercise of informed judgment in the time, or with the information, available. See, for example, Rochlin, "Defining High-Reliability Organizations in Practice"; Weick, "Collapse of Sensemaking in Organizations."

27. See, for example, the detailed analysis of the Tenerife disaster in Foushee and Lauber, "Flight Crew Fatigue"; Weick, "Tenerife."

28. Gras and others, *Faced with Automation*, 24.

29. There was redundancy of all systems, of course, but it was in the form of multiple systems rather than complementary ones (e.g., hydraulics in case of electronic failures). There were also vivid memories both of the Florida 727 crash where all three engines failed owing to a common-mode mistake in maintenance, and of the Sioux City accident, where the disintegrating engine severed the lines of all three hydraulic systems because they were all routed through the same part of the fuselage.

30. I thank Alain Gras for having helped me condense a very extensive literature into this brief summary. Also see *Aviation Week*, "Keeping Pilots in the Loop"; Squires, "Glass Cockpit Syndrome."

31. "Airbus May Add to A320 Safeguards." Having set the aircraft on auto-

matic pilot in a landing approach, the pilot in charge was instructing the trainee in the left seat while the airspeed dropped dangerously low. Although the computerized autopilot compensated to prevent a stall, it did it so smoothly that neither pilot was concerned. By the time they did notice, there was not enough energy or thrust to bring the aircraft out of its glide path in time. The overconfidence syndrome was being seen frequently enough to warrant a special conference. Limits were placed on the controls to prevent pilots from overcontrolling, given the lack of tactile feedback, and more (computerized) alarms were added to notify pilots of dangerous excursions within the flight envelope.

32. Phillips, "Man-Machine Cockpit Interface."

33. Hughes, "Mixed Reviews to Glass Cockpits."

34. Stix, "Along for the Ride?" Also see Gras, Moricot, Poirot-Delpech, and Scardigli, *Le Pilote, le Contrôleur, et l'Automate*.

35. One side effect of this was a major debate among pilots as to whether a future aircraft would be better off with two-man crews to divide the work, even at the expense of increased weight, that continues to the present day. Just as the Navy has both the two-seat F-14 and the single-seat F-18, the Air Force has the two-seat F-15 and the single-seat F-16. In both cases, the two-seat aircraft is larger, heavier, and thought to possess an extra measure of sophistication that makes it superior under some circumstances.

36. The question of expertise went a long way toward explaining why the average German pilot had such a short life in the air while a very few had victories numbering in the hundreds. As was explained by several of the German aces after the war, the training given to new pilots, especially toward the end when losses were mounting, was neither as lengthy nor as extensive as that given by the British or Americans, making them more vulnerable. But the few pilots who had survived (some since the Spanish Civil War) and were still fighting had become so expert that they were practically invulnerable in combat, barring equipment problems or serious mistakes. By rotating their pilots home after a fixed number of missions, the Americans raised morale and improved their training, but they also systematically removed from combat those few who had become truly expert.

37. After several crashes of high-performance aircraft were attributed to the controls flying the plane into a regime where the pilot blacked out because of the g-loads, the computers were programmed to put limits on what the pilots could order the aircraft to do—prefiguring the limits placed on commercial aircraft when they also went to fly-by-wire.

38. Hughes, "Mixed Reviews to Glass Cockpits."

39. Phillips, "Man-Machine Cockpit Interface"; Hughes, "Mixed Reviews to Glass Cockpits."

40. Gras and others, *Faced with Automation*.

41. It has been suggested that this is at least partially because so many of the analysts, engineers, regulators, and politicians involved spend a great deal of their time flying from one place to another.

42. Phillips, "Man-Machine Cockpit Interface."

43. Most notable were the series of articles in *Aviation Week*, "Keeping Pilots in the Loop." Also see Stix, "Along for the Ride?"

44. Squires, "Glass Cockpit Syndrome." Squires's analysis also extended to the Iran Air incident, as discussed in chapter 9.

45. Because of the limitations placed on flight evolutions and maneuvers by the automatic control systems of the newer airliners, pilots complain that they will not be able to fly the aircraft out of a bad situation in an emergency unless they are given the power to override the limits. The matter is still being discussed.

46. Schulman, "Analysis of High-Reliability Organizations," provides an interesting comparison of air traffic control, nuclear plant operations, and a conventional power plant.

47. La Porte and Consolini, "Working in Practice but Not in Theory."

48. La Porte, "U.S. Air Traffic System."

49. See, for example, La Porte, "U.S. Air Traffic System"; La Porte and Consolini, "Working in Practice but Not in Theory"; Hollnagel and others, "Limits of Automation in Air Traffic Control"; Vortac and others, "Automation and Cognition." The U.S. General Accounting Office, the Federal Aviation Administration, and NASA have also addressed these issues in a long series of publications. For a parallel analysis of the situation in Europe, see Gras and others, *Faced with Automation*; Gras and others, *Le Pilote, le Contrôleur, et l'Automate*.

50. Hirschhorn, *Beyond Mechanization*, 92ff.

51. En route control centers must be distinguished from terminal centers that manage the airspace only in the immediate vicinity of airports, and those that manage the traffic on the ground, not only by the scope of their operational area but by the diversity of their tasks.

52. Vortac and others, "Automation and Cognition," 632.

53. This was equally true in France, where the strips also were both symbols of operator culture and status and a link to traditional ways of forming cognitive maps. See, for example, Gras and others, *Faced with Automation*, 64–65.

54. An excellent summary of recent work is Hollnagel and others, "Limits of Automation in Air Traffic Control."

55. The question in air traffic control has always been "when" and not "if" the operator has to step in and take over control manually, which supports the observations of the Berkeley research group that air traffic control has the characteristics of a "high-reliability organization." See, for example, La Porte, "U.S. Air Traffic System"; Rochlin, "Defining High-Reliability Organizations in Practice." Even Vortac and others, "Automation and Cognition," who found no significant decline in performance or cognitive integration in controllers operating a simulation of the new automated system, were very cautious about how to implement their findings.

56. Hollnagel and others, "Limits of Automation in Air Traffic Control."

57. Henderson, "Automation System Gains Acceptance." The new system was designed in collaboration with the NASA Ames Research Center, which also did much of the path-breaking human factors interface work on automated cockpits.

58. Rochlin and von Meier, "Nuclear Power Operations." Zuboff, *Age of the Smart Machine* made very similar observations about operators of complex chemical plants.

59. Beare and others, "Human Factors Guidelines."

60. See, for example, Norman, *Things That Make Us Smart*, 142ff.

61. Roth and others, "Human Factors for Advanced Control Rooms." This is quite similar to the observations of Hollnagel and others, "Limits of Automation in Air Traffic Control," about aviation.

62. Roth and others, "Human Factors for Advanced Control Rooms."

63. Bainbridge, "Ironies of Automation."

64. Hollnagel and others, "Limits of Automation in Air Traffic Control," 564.

65. Zuboff, *Age of the Smart Machine*, 65.

66. See, for example, the excellent discussion in Norman, *Things That Make Us Smart*, especially at pages 142ff and 225ff.

67. As James Beniger has pointed out, this is nothing new. The tendency to turn information techniques put into place primarily to ensure safety into a means to exert control for greater efficiency was manifest as early as the 1850s, when the telegraph, first put on the lines to prevent collisions, was turned into a mechanism for dispatch; Beniger, *Control Revolution*, 226ff.

68. Scott Morton, *Corporation of the 1990s*, 14.

69. Norman, *Things That Make Us Smart*, 225ff.

70. For a discussion of the interactive process in this context, and its relation to formal theories of structuration (e.g., Giddens, *Central Problems in Social Theory*), see Thomas, *What Machines Can't Do*, 225ff.

71. One engineer even described operator beliefs derisively as being little more than operator "black magic," implying that the issue was as much one of social class and education as operating realities.

Chapter 8
Smart Weapons, Smart Soldiers

The quote from then DARPA Director Richard S. Cooper used as an epigraph to this chapter is taken from Henderson, *Cohesion: The Human Element in Combat*.

1. Demchak, *Military Organizations*, 80ff.

2. See, for examples, Zuboff, *Age of the Smart Machine*; Strassman, *Information Payoff*; Noble, *Forces of Production*; McColloch, *White-Collar Workers in Transition*; Bainbridge, "Ironies of Automation."

3. For sweeping surveys of all or part of this long history, see, for example, van Creveld, *Technology and War*; McNeill, *Pursuit of Power*; Dupuy, *Weapons and Warfare*.

4. It is interesting to note that many of our European colleagues skip over the Civil War, taking the history of military technology from the Napoleonic Wars to the Franco-Prussian War, and then to World War I. Because of this emphasis on European history and technical innovation, they often date the era of industrial warfare from the end of the nineteenth century instead of its middle.

5. On land, that is. That part of the war fought at sea still greatly resembled that of Napoleonic time, with the slight but remarkably prescient exception of the experiments with ironclads and submersibles.

6. Beaumont and Snyder, "Combat Effectiveness: Paradigms and Paradoxes." Also see Mcnaugher, *The M-16 Controversies*.

7. Strachan, *European Armies and the Conduct of War*.

8. Dupuy, *Weapons and Warfare*, 196.

9. It should be noted that both the cowboys and the Indians of the "Old West" had no such compunctions and disdained the Army's rifle in favor of the Spencer and later equivalents such as the famed 1866 Winchester. The apocryphal story was that the victorious Sioux did not even bother gathering

up the single-shot Springfields that littered the ground after the Battle of Little Big Horn. It was not until 1903 that the Army was to produce even a bolt-loaded magazine rifle of its own, the 1903 Springfield, that was to remain the standard infantry weapon right into the Second World War. The same struggle between accuracy and rate of fire (culture vs. technology) was to take place over the relative merits of the M-14 and M-15 rifles, leading ultimately to the use of the flawed M-16 in Vietnam.

10. Ellis, *Social History of the Machine Gun*, 63ff.

11. As noted by Armstrong, *Bullets and Bureaucrats*, 137, American critics of the machine gun enunciated four major objections to the large-scale employment of the weapon:

> 1. Machine guns, unlike the infantry rifle, could not be relied upon to score a hit with each separate shot and, therefore, wasted ammunition.
> 2. It was difficult to determine the range from the gun to its target.
> 3. The weapon was mechanically unreliable . . . [jams].
> 4. Machine guns used large amounts of ammunition in an era when ammunition resupply was difficult.

Points 1, 3, and 4 were essentially the same arguments used against the repeating rifle. British and French general staffs used the same reasoning, adding to it the notion that it went against the grain and tradition of infantry movements on the battlefield—even though the lessons of the Civil War showed that the next war would be fought in trenches, not on open fields. The misperceptions and ideological biases of the period from 1865 through 1914 are also discussed extensively by Ellis, *Social History of the Machine Gun*.

12. Ellis, *Social History of the Machine Gun*, and Armstrong, *Bullets and Bureaucrats* suggest that this was a form of neocolonial racism. It would cost the British dearly.

13. Morison, *Men, Machines, and Modern Times*.

14. Beard, *Developing the ICBM*, 233.

15. Ellis, *Social History of the Machine Gun*, 53ff.

16. A few examples among many are van Creveld, *Technology and War*; McNeill, *Pursuit of Power*; Dupuy, *Weapons and Warfare*; Ellis, *Social History of the Machine Gun*; Deitchman, *Advance of Technology*; O'Connell, *Of Arms and Men*; Rosen, *Winning the Next War*; Shimshoni, "Technology, Military Advantage, and World War I; Smith, ed., *Military Enterprise and Technological Change*.

17. The great exception, of course, was Germany. Prohibited by the Ver-

sailles treaty from building a large army, German rearmament in the 1930s was forced to focus on the new ideas and technologies as an offset to prohibitions against raising a large army.

18. Baxter, *Scientists against Time*; Jones, *Wizard War*; Bush, *Modern Arms and Free Men*.

19. Indeed, postwar analysis of the German effort showed that their remarkable innovation, particularly in aviation, seriously compromised their war effort by interfering with mass production. See, for example, Millett Murray, eds., *Second World War*; van Creveld, *Fighting Power*.

20. References are too numerous to mention, as the war itself, its crucial battles, the performance of soldiers, and the individual categories of weapons systems have all spawned enormous literatures—even when restricted to categories touching primarily on technology. Of recent books, Carver, *Twentieth-Century Warriors*, is a good place to start. Also useful are van Creveld, *Technology and War*; Dupuy, *Weapons and Warfare*; O'Connell, *Of Arms and Men*; Hadley, *Straw Giant*.

21. Brodie, ed., *Absolute Weapon*, 76.

22. This history and its subsequent continuation through Korea and Vietnam into the present is discussed in admirable detail in Hadley, *Straw Giant*.

23. In fact, ENIAC, the first large-scale digital computer, had been built specifically to improve ballistic firing tables; only later was it pressed into service by the designers of the atomic bomb.

24. Edwards, "History of Computers and Weapons Systems."

25. Armacost, *Weapons Innovation*. The quoted portion is from Buchan, "Age of Insecurity." The entire quote is taken from Beard, *Developing the ICBM*, 13.

26. See, for example, Hadley, *Straw Giant*; Gibson, *Perfect War*; van Creveld, *Command in War*.

27. Hadley, *Straw Giant*, 177.

28. During the hundreds of sorties that took place during the Rolling Thunder campaigns of 1965–1968, a legend was said to have appeared among Navy and Air Force pilots that "the world was composed of two spring-loaded hemispheres, hinged somewhere under the Atlantic and held together by the Thanh Hoa bridge" (Gibson, *Perfect War*, 364). The irony is that the North Vietnamese never bothered to try repairing the bridge. There was a ford a few miles upstream.

29. Other PGMs were in fact available to the U.S. forces, but the lack of valuable targets made their use somewhat problematic. There may be occasions

and circumstances where it makes sense to fire a $25,000 missile at a $2,000 truck, but that is not a tactic to be applied as a matter of course during a protracted and dispersed conflict.

30. See Gibson, *Perfect War*, for some of the contrary arguments.

31. This, too, resulted in an outpouring of critical literature. For examples that treat individual weapons or systems in some depth, see Beard, *Developing the ICBM*; Betts, ed., *Cruise Missiles*; Coulam, *Illusions of Choice*; Dörfer, *Arms Deal*; Bellin and Chapman, *Computers in Battle*; Fallows, *National Defense*; Kaldor, *The Baroque Arsenal*; Luttwak, *Pentagon and the Art of War*; Rasor, ed., *More Bucks, Less Bang*.

32. For an unusually in-depth study of the new political economy of military procurement, see Kotz, *Wild Blue Yonder*.

33. See, for example, Fallows, *National Defense*; Spinney, *Defense Facts of Life*.

34. Although the debate was essentially over in the United States by the mid-1980s, it was picked up in the European context as part of the continuing argument about defensive versus offensive postures for NATO. See, for example, Clark, Chiarelli, McKittrick, and Reed, eds., *Defense Reform Debate*. Deitchman, *Advance of Technology*, provides a good summary at pp. 223ff. The internal debate that shook the Pentagon in the 1970s was revealed publicly in Fallows, *National Defense*; the famed briefing by Chuck Spinney upon which Fallows drew was later published as *Defense Facts of Life*.

35. Nelan, "Revolution at Defense."

36. van Creveld, *Technology and War*, 318.

37. The main direct risk of excessive sophistication and standardization is the vulnerability to surprise of having few systems with little variety. See, e.g., van Creveld, *Technology and War*; Luttwak, *Art of War*.

38. For a superb and detailed review of the organizational and cultural costs not only of weapon system complexity, but also of the computer systems that are designed to maintain it, see Demchak, *Military Organizations*.

39. See, for example, Perry, "Defense Investment Strategy." The extent to which this was true even for so-called conventional forces and postures was largely masked in the public debate by the continuing arguments over nuclear weapons control and the Strategic Defense Initiative. But the money spent on these high-profile programs was considerably less than that being spent on force modernization and technical improvements.

40. The preceding is in part based on comments made by John Lehman, former Secretary of the Navy, at a colloquium at the Institute of International Studies, University of California, Berkeley, April 16, 1991.

41. For a superb exposition of this linkage, see Edwards, *Closed World.*

42. De Lauer, "Force Multiplier."

43. For a discussion of complexity in military organizations, see Demchak, *Military Organizations*; Binkin, *Defense Manpower*; Bracken, *Command and Control of Nuclear Forces.*

44. Binkin, *Defense Manpower*, 38.

45. Ibid., 43ff.

46. Demchak, *Military Organizations*. The rest of this paragraph is based largely on the study of implications for the Army of the complexity of the M-1 Abrams main battle tank. Binkin, *Defense Manpower*, tells two similar stories. In the 1970s, the Navy introduced a general-purpose automatic test equipment suite known as VAST, for Versatile Avionics Shop Test; 70 percent of VAST time was spent in self-diagnosis of its own problems. The first variant of the built-in test and fault-isolation capability of the F-16 advanced fighter detected only half of the faults that occurred; 45 percent of the faults reported were false positives.

47. Winner, "Artifacts."

48. Demchak, *Military Organizations.*

49. See, e.g., van Creveld, *Technology and War*; Margiotta and Sanders, eds., *Technology.*

50. "The essence of AirLand Battle is to defeat the enemy by conducting simultaneous offensive operations over the length and breadth of the battlefield . . . AirLand Battle doctrine is centered on the combined arms team, fully integrating the capabilities of all land, sea, and air combat systems, and envisions rapidly shifting and concentrating decisive combat power, both fire and maneuver, at the proper time and place on the battlefield" (U.S. Department of Defense, *Persian Gulf War*). The demands for coordination, integration, and synchronization, in real time, in the face of an enemy trying to interfere with electronic and command-and-control systems as well as combat units, are immense.

51. Gibson, *Perfect War*, 23.

Chapter 9
Unfriendly Fire

1. The complete story of the Wampanoag is wonderfully told by Morison, *Men, Machines and Modern Times.*

2. Ibid., 111ff.

3. Douglas, "Navy Adopts the Radio," 131.

4. Deitchman, *Advance of Technology*, 244–245.

5. There is a long list of books on technical innovation in the military, of which those of Deitchman, *Advance of Technology*, Rosen, *Winning the Next War*, Smith, *Military Enterprise and Technological Change*, and van Creveld, *Technology and War*, are of particular interest because of their multiple case studies and comparative sensitivity to organizational issues.

6. Morison, *Men, Machines and Modern Times*, 144. The U.S. and other navies still maintain a few of the tall ships for training cadets. Because of the special problems of command at sea, navies are in many ways the most traditional of military services, and the most self-conscious about their culture.

7. Morison, *Men, Machines and Modern Times*, 117.

8. Deitchman, *Advance of Technology*, 245.

9. The phrase comes from Zvi Lanir, who, along with Chris C. Demchak, contributed greatly to my thinking about computers and cognition in the military. The details that follow are taken from Lanir, "Reasonable Choice of Disaster."

10. Lanir points out that the investigators were fortunate in having access to all radio transmissions, Egyptian and Israeli, as well as the cockpit flight recorders. Therefore, it was not so easy to follow the usual practice of seeking to assign causality to a single human action or a single point of failure, as was the case with the shooting down of Korean Air Lines Flight 007 over Kamchatka. Although more details about the failures of Soviet air defenses are now being revealed, arguments about cause raged for many years.

11. This is very similar to Barry Turner's observation that human societies are inherently "negentropic," and therefore capable of self-organizing disasters out of ordinary conditions and circumstances. See, for example, Turner, *Man-Made Disasters*.

12. Because the United States was not at that time formally at war with Iraq, and regarded Iran as the more hostile to its interests, AWACS were in the habit of reporting Iraqi aircraft as potential strike support rather than hostile—a decision reinforced by occasional overflights of U.S. ships by Iraqi aircraft in the past.

13. U.S. Congress. House of Representatives, Committee on Armed Services, *Iraqi Attack on the U.S.S. Stark*.

14. U.S. Congress, *Iraqi Attack on the U.S.S. Stark*. For an excellent, concise description, see Vlahos, "*Stark* Report."

15. This section is based on Rochlin, "Iran Air Flight 655."

16. Most of the detail in this section is obtained directly from Fogarty, *Formal Investigation into the Circumstances Surrounding the Downing of a Commercial Airliner by the U.S.S. Vincennes (CG49) on July 3, 1988*, hereinafter referred to as the "Fogarty report."

17. The Aegis Display System data could not be extracted, precluding any positive confirmation of actions taken at the CO and TAO consoles.

18. This was much clearer in the perusal of the Fogarty report than it was in subsequent news stories.

19. To quote the Fogarty report directly: "The data from USS *Vincennes* tapes, information from USS *Sides* and reliable intelligence information, corroborate the fact that [Iran Air Flight 655] was on a normal commercial air flight plan profile, in the assigned airway, squawking Mode III 6760, on a continuous ascent in altitude from takeoff at Bandar Abbas to shoot-down."

20. *Washington Post*, 30 April 1990. The Legion of Merit, the U.S. armed forces second highest award, was presented to Captain Rogers and Lieutenant Commander Lustig (the weapons officer) for meritorious conduct and "heroic achievement" on July 3, 1988. The citations did not mention the downing of the Iran Air flight at all.

21. Admiral Crowe was reported to have concluded that airport officials at Bandar Abbas "should not have allowed the flight to take off while a firefight was going on some miles away" (*New York Times*, August 20, 1988). Then Vice President George Bush was quoted as saying: "I will never apologize for the United States—I don't care what the facts are." For these and similar quotes, see, e.g., George Wilson, "The Risks of Shooting First" (*Washington Post*, January 28, 1989). It should, however, be noted that the Navy's conclusion that Captain Rogers was justified in firing in presumptive self-defense was widely shared on Capitol Hill. See, e.g., *Congressional Quarterly*, July 9, 1988, 1905ff.

22. It is rare that such investigations touch on the broader and more systemic level in which the actors, individually and collectively, were placed in a situation in which the probability that they could exercise proper judgment was greatly reduced. See, for example, Weick, "Mann Gulch Disaster."

23. This arises from the usually praiseworthy desire to expedite inquiry while evidence is fresh and untainted. The problem lies not with the speed of the first inquiry, but with the closing of the book on the entire incident once this hurried and summary court, held in the combat area, far from other sources of information and analysis, is concluded.

24. The version of the Fogarty report released to the press on August 19 was

cleansed of classified material, and of potentially damaging references to specific individuals.

25. Fogarty report, 45.

26. Baruch Fischoff, Robert Helmreich, Richard Nisbett, Richard Pew, and Paul Slovic each presented testimony "on behalf of the American Psychological Association." These are summarized in U.S. Congress. Senate, Committee on Armed Services, *Downing of an Iranian Airliner by the U.S.S. Vincennes*.

27. Testimony of Baruch Fischoff before the Committee on Armed Services, U.S. House of Representatives, on behalf of the American Psychological Association, October 6, 1988.

28. Testimony of Robert L. Helmreich before the Committee on Armed Services, U.S. House of Representatives, on behalf of the American Psychological Association, October 6, 1988. Also see Squires, "Glass Cockpit Syndrome."

29. See, for example, Perrow, *Complex Organizations*. This crucial distinction is rarely made in the policy debate over the military and its equipment, or even for analogous systems such as nuclear power plants or chemical refineries.

30. Unfortunately, Aegis cruisers may well have been so designed. The CIC is located high up in the superstructure, behind the Aegis radar panels rather than in the small and already cramped main hull. Aegis cruisers, with their light displacement and narrow beam, roll easily, and the CIC location multiplies the effects of the ship's motion on those fighting it. Their primary mission is that of long-range air defense of an aircraft carrier Battle Group in blue-water operations. Thus, they represent yet another move in naval warfare away from the close grappling of ancient days through cannon, rifled guns, and aircraft to remote combat fought at extreme ranges by electronics.

31. Byron, "Surface Navy."

32. In principle, this is also the position of the Department of Defense. Yet the U.S. General Accounting Office found that the DoD was generally not complying with its own *Directive 5000.3* requirement that testing should be conducted under conditions realistically simulating combat stress. See, for example, U.S. General Accounting Office, *Weapons Testing*.

33. See, for example, Jeff Cohen and Normal Solomon, "Today's News Next Year, Maybe," *San Francisco Examiner*, July 12, 1992, A11.

34. Demchak, *Military Organizations*; Roberts, *New Challenges*; Rochlin and others, "Self-Designing High-Reliability Organization"; La Porte and Consolini, "Working in Practice but Not in Theory"; Perrow, *Normal Accidents*; Sagan, *Limits of Safety*.

35. Zuboff, *Age of the Smart Machine*, 196.

36. The match between oral culture and action orientation has also been documented in naval flight operations. See Rochlin and others, "Self-Designing High-Reliability Organization"; Rochlin, "Informal Organizational Networking."

Chapter 10
The Logistics of Techno-War

1. Covault, "Desert Storm Reinforces Military Space Directions." The epigraph to this chapter is a direct quote made while General McPeak was still Chief of Staff of the U.S. Air Force.

2. Secretary of Defense for Manpower, Logistics, and Reserve Affairs from 1981 to 1985, as quoted by Morrison, "Logistic War's Long, Long Lines."

3. The fundamental question of the quantity-quality debate was whether the United States should spend, for example, a $400 million procurement budget by buying ten advanced fighter aircraft at $40 million each or forty at $10 million each. The "quantity" side emphasized survival of the force in the face of possible surprises or unexpected vulnerabilities; the "quality" side emphasized survival of the individual and the need therefore to maintain an edge over opponents. The substance of the debate is much too long to summarize here. Some useful readings are Rosen, *Winning the Next War*; Hadley, *Straw Giant*; Bellin and Chapman, *Computers in Battle*; Fallows, *National Defense*; Luttwak, *Art of War*; Spinney, *Defense Facts of Life*; Clark and others, *Defense Reform Debate*; Binkin, *Defense Manpower*; Barnaby and Borg, eds., *Emerging Technologies and Military Doctrine*. What is most interesting is that the recognition by the United States in the 1970s that it had to choose at all was caused not so much by the economic constraints that surfaced in the 1990s as by the exponentially rising cost of state-of-the-art technology in military systems once technology rather than use became the driving force in weapons acquisition.

4. Deitchman, *Advance of Technology*, 246ff. Also see van Creveld, *Technology and War*; Luttwak, *Art of War*; Spinney, *Defense Facts of Life*; Binkin, *Defense Manpower*; Chapman, "High-Technology Weapons"; Gansler, *Defense Industry*.

5. See, for example, the extended discussions in Weigley, *American Way of War*.

6. Ibid., 128ff.

7. This is the main thrust of *American Way of War*. There were certainly a number of technical triumphs on the Allied side in the Second World War, many of which, including cryptography and systems analysis as well as nuclear weapons, contributed greatly to the outcome. But few of these affected the actual fighting, particularly on the ground. Only when the tide of war had turned, and there was spare production capacity, was the possibility of seeking new weapons for the individual soldier, sailor, or airman given serious consideration.

8. Many comparative evaluations of Allied and German performance in both World Wars have come to the conclusion that man-for-man and unit-for-unit the German forces fought more effectively—unless they were similarly constrained. See, for example, Millett and Murray, *Military Effectiveness*; Dupuy, *Genius for War*; Sarkesian, ed., *Combat Effectiveness*. The Germans, for example, had better and more innovative weapons, and, surprisingly to many, were more practiced in nurturing cohesion in combat, even at the end of the war. The American rhetorical posture of precision shooting and bombing, technical superiority, and troop nurture did not match the reality of mass bombing, sketchy training, and the freezing of many design and training innovations to encourage mass production at maximum volume.

9. See, for example, Kennedy, *Great Powers*.

10. An excellent summary of Britain's dilemma following the Second World War is given by Barnett in *Audit of War*.

11. For a concise history of military-funded support of strategic and other forms of computing, see Edwards, *Closed World*; Bellin and Chapman, *Computers in Battle*.

12. This section draws heavily on Rochlin and Demchak, *Lessons of the Gulf War*. Since that time, several other major reviews of the Gulf War have come to similar conclusions. See especially, Department of Defense, *Persian Gulf War*; Freedman and Karsh, *Gulf Conflict*; Mazarr, Snider, and Blackwell, Jr., *Desert Storm*.

13. For a brief review, see Rochlin and Demchak, "The Gulf War: Technological and Organizational Implications."

14. That this was a popular theme may be seen by glancing at "America at War," *Newsweek*, Spring/Summer 1991.

15. For example, Air Force General Merrill McPeak, as quoted in the *Washington Post*, March 15, 1991; Morrocco, "Gulf War Boosts Prospects." Even long after the Gulf war, the argument for moving to more reliance on air forces and

sophisticated weapons systems as a fundamental element of U.S. military forces for all theaters of war persists. See, for example, "Air Dominance Called Key to U.S. Defense." One of the things that got forgotten in this rush to technology was that those emphasizing quantity had called for less expensive technology, not less altogether; the cruise missile was one of the favored systems.

16. Department of Defense, *Persian Gulf War*.

17. Mazarr and others, *Desert Storm*, 4ff. See, also, Freedman and Karsh, *Gulf Conflict*, who argue that the victory was due more to "traditional" failings on the Iraqi side than to the coalition's technological superiority.

18. Cohen, "Air War in the Persian Gulf."

19. Department of Defense, *Persian Gulf War*, 416ff.

20. Ibid., 444ff.

21. Blackwell, *Thunder in the Desert*, 229. Other estimates range up to three or four weeks' supply, arguing that the intensity of the first four days could not have continued. Indeed, it probably could not have: In a situation reminiscent of Patton in France in 1944, the speed of the armored attack during the four days of the ground war far exceeded the ability of the logistics system to supply it. In addition, the ground war was being fought almost twenty-four hours a day; simple exhaustion would soon have forced a slower tempo.

22. The lack of effective BDA was pointed out as one of the critical shortcomings of U.S. technology during the entire period. See, for example, Department of Defense, *Persian Gulf War*, where it is mentioned in several places as one of the more pressing future needs.

23. Postol, "Lessons of the Gulf War."

24. Schmitt, "Israel Plays Down Effectiveness of Patriot Missile."

25. Mazarr and others, *Desert Storm*, 107. They also cite one reference as having likened the F-16 to a big computer game that needed more disk space.

26. Hughes, "Small Firm Acted Quickly." In only twenty-four days, a small Texas firm produced three thousand infrared beacons for $3.2 million as AFID (Antifratricide Identification Devices). They worked in Kuwait and Iraq primarily because suppression of Iraqi air prevented using the beacons to target coalition forces.

27. "Word Perfect Called to Action."

28. "Let's Clear the Air on Stealth."

29. Lenorovitz, "Air National Guard." As many as fifteen coalition aircraft were lost to small arms or man-carried infrared missiles, including several British Tornados (*Newsweek*, "America at War," 76–77). Note that these were the mission profiles for which the Tornados were designed.

30. Although friendly fire casualties averaged 5 percent for previous American wars, nine of seventeen British soldiers killed in action in Iraq were victims of by friendly fire. Of the American deaths, 35 of the 146 soldiers killed (25 percent), and 72 of the 467 wounded (15 percent) were friendly fire casualties (Department of Defense, *Persian Gulf War*, 589ff.). All of the damaging hits on M1A1 tanks turned out to be from friendlies. Despite efforts to seek new identification technologies, the report also states that the combination of longer-range weapons, low-visibility and night fighting, high-kill-probability weapons and ammunition, and the necessity to engage rapidly and (almost) automatically to survive on the modern battlefield will greatly complicate efforts to devise better methods for battlefield identification.

31. Schmitt, "Unforeseen Problems." Friendly fire losses were common even in the Second World War. However, the costs and scarcity of the new technology aircraft, and the amount of time and training their pilots receive, makes them far more valuable assets, on a comparative basis, than individual aircraft of earlier wars—perhaps one might use the analogy of losing a whole flight or wing (which is quite different in terms of effectiveness from losing a number of individual aircraft). The point is that even with the best of modern technology, such incidents *still* occur. The difference is that in the modern era of very expensive and sophisticated weapons and very highly trained crews, the cost of even a single incident is very high.

32. Department of Defense, *Persian Gulf War*; Rochlin and Demchak, "Lessons of the Gulf War"; Rochlin and Demchak, "Gulf War"; U.S. General Accounting Office, *Operation Desert Storm*.

33. Department of Defense, *Persian Gulf War*, 389.

34. "As You Were?" According to *Newsweek*, "America at War": "Schwartzkopf had to improvise a credible defense from whatever he could scratch up. At one point he phoned the Navy to ask what Iraqi targets the USS *Wisconsin* could hit with its sea-launched Tomahawk cruise missiles. The answer came back: zero. The Tomahawks must be programmed with electronic terrain maps to home in on their targets. The CIA and DIA, preoccupied with monitoring the Soviet Union's withdrawal of conventional forces in Eastern Europe, hadn't programmed their satellites to make such maps for Iraq. The maps didn't arrive until the end of August."

35. Rochlin and Demchak, "Gulf War."

36. See, for example, David F. Bond, "Troop and Materiel Deployment Missions"; Bond, "Army Speeds Helicopter Enhancements." "The Army beefed up Apache maintenance at unit and higher levels with personnel from the

AH-64 manufacturer, McDonnel Douglas Helicopter Co. Army personnel levels were below those authorized and were insufficient to support a wartime tempo of operations. The AH-64 maintenance training base was geared simply to support the continued fielding of Apache units. AH-64 readiness had been low during much of the aircraft's lifetime in the field, *and the Army brought in contractor support rather than take chances in wartime*" [Emphasis supplied].

37. Department of Defense, *Persian Gulf War*, 439.

38. Ibid., App. N, especially at 599–600.

39. Lt. General James S. Cassity, as quoted in Department of Defense, *Persian Gulf War*, 559.

40. Klass, "Gulf War Highlights Benefits."

41. Department of Defense, *Persian Gulf War*, especially 337ff.

42. Richelson, "Volume of Data."

43. Department of Defense, *Persian Gulf War*, 560.

44. Most of the preceding was digested from *Persian Gulf War*, App. K, "Command, Control, Communications, and Space."

45. The inability of the Iraqis to appreciate the situation they were in is dramatically apparent from the lack of any attempt to exploit the open availability of GPS data, or to interfere with the signals, even though most analysts credit them with the capability in principle.

46. The "product displacement cycle" represents the gradual transfer of technology down the hierarchy of industrialized nations. Because labor costs also decline as one moves down the chain, the country at the top must continue to innovate technologically to maintain its markets. And, because the dominant power almost always also favors a liberal (open) trading system, it cannot otherwise protect itself without incurring serious costs. Thus, the "technological imperative" of product innovation can be seen to be a political-economic as well as socio-technical consequence of the structure of the international system.

47. See, for example, Demchak, *Military Organizations*; Rochlin, "Informal Organizational Networking"; Rochlin and Demchak, "Gulf War"; Demchak, "Fully Networked Battlespace."

48. Michener, *Bridges at Toko-ri*.

49. Ellis, *Social History of the Machine Gun*.

50. Mazarr and others, *Desert Storm*.

51. Ibid., 97.

52. See, for example, U.S. Department of the Army, *Force XXI*.

Chapter 11
C³I in Cyberspace

The version of the famous Moltke quote used an epigraph to this chapter is taken from van Creveld, *Command in War*, 146.

1. O'Connell, *Of Arms and Men*; Weigley, *American Way of War*; Dupuy, *Genius for War*; John Keegan, *Face of Battle*.

2. van Creveld, *Command in War*; March and Weissinger-Baylon, *Ambiguity and Command*.

3. van Creveld, *Command in War*, 6.

4. One measure of complexity used in formal organization theory can be characterized broadly as the product $N \times D \times I$, where N is the number of interacting units, D their functional differentiation, and I the measure of interdependency between and among them. See La Porte, ed., *Organized Social Complexity*. For a direct application of this formalism to military organization, see Demchak, *Military Organizations*.

5. This also extends to the various combinations of C and I that are bandied about at various times for various reasons, ranging from the simple C^2 to acronymic neobarbarisms such as C^4I^2 (for command, control, communications, intelligence, and information). See, for example, Orr, "Combat Operations."

6. See, for example, the many usages set out in Beniger, *Control Revolution*.

7. Landau and Stout, Jr., "To Manage Is Not to Control."

8. See, for example, Orr, "Combat Operations," 58ff.

9. Demchak, "Fully Networked Battlespace"; Morton, "The Softwar Revolution."

10. Although that is not always the case. Because of the time it took to communicate over long distances, the historic Battle of New Orleans was fought after the peace treaty concluding the War of 1812 had already been signed.

11. This is the historical origin of the claim by naval captains for unusual powers of independence and command, including the right to execute offenders and perform marriages at sea.

12. Strachan, *European Armies*, 37ff.

13. Ibid., 41ff. The lowly potato was perhaps the first portable field ration. Since it could be carried along with the ordinary foot soldier, was durable, and did not spoil easily, it played a major role in the transformation.

14. van Creveld, *Fighting Power*; Dupuy, *Genius for War*.

15. Of course, in war, nothing is certain, or generalizable. There were also times and places where lack of coordination was fatal, or at least disastrous.

Napoleonic infantry and artillery squares were effective, but more rigid than most. Nevertheless, the generalization still holds. No better description could be found than Tolstoy's description of Borodino, or van Creveld's masterly analysis of Königgrätz.

16. For a more detailed exposition, see Donnelly, "Friction and Warfare."

17. Weigley, *American Way of War*, 143ff.

18. Strachan, *European Armies*; Dupuy, *Genius for War*. The latter argues that the Prussian success may have been due more to the breech loading needle gun and the more intelligent use of the railroads for massing forces.

19. van Creveld, *Command in War*, 146.

20. Prefiguring U.S. experience a century later, Moltke's main problem was that his superiors in Berlin had no such compunctions, and kept up a steady stream of queries, comments, criticisms, and attempts at intervention. Hence the epigraph at the head of this chapter.

21. Strachan, *European Armies*, 141.

22. van Creveld, *Command in War*, 166.

23. Keegan, *Face of Battle*, 267.

24. Strachan, *European Armies*, 140ff.; van Creveld, *Command in War*, 168ff.

25. van Creveld, *Command in War*, 183.

26. van Creveld, *Fighting Power*, 167.

27. The term comes from Jones, *Wizard War*. Although the book reveals only the details of allied cryptography efforts, and not the equally important work done in the areas of radar, systems and operations research, communications, and other electronics (such as proximity fusing), the term has come to be applied to the secret allied scientific effort generally.

28. Rhodes, *Atomic Bomb*.

29. The definitive postwar statement of this new approach was that of Bush, *Modern Arms and Free Men*.

30. Thompson, *Organizations in Action*.

31. van Creveld, *Command in War*, 232ff. Gibson's *Perfect War* may be the single best book on how American managerial and technocratic assumptions led to a systemic defeat.

32. Chapman, "High-Technology Weapons," 78ff.

33. As quoted by Chapman, "High-Technology Weapons," 61.

34. Bellin and Chapman, *Computers in Battle*, 78ff.

35. Jacky, "Strategic Computing Program."

36. Ibid., 181–182.

37. Dupuy, *Genius for War*.

38. For example: "Horizontal technology integration across today's weapons systems is a cost-effective means to achieve the five Force XXI objectives and dominate the 21st Century battlefield" (Department of the Army, *Force XXI*, 14).

39. For an excellent discussion of the implications of tight coupling, see Perrow, *Normal Accidents*.

40. Chapman, "High-Technology Weapons," 91–92.

41. Nelan, "Revolution at Defense"; *Newsweek*, "America at War"; *San Francisco Chronicle*, "Air Dominance"; Morton, "Softwar."

42. Admiral William Owens, vice-chairman of the Joint Chiefs of Staff, as cited by Morton, "Softwar Revolution," S8. Also see Department of the Army, *Force XXI*.

43. The quotes from General Sullivan are taken from Demchak, "Information Age Army."

44. Demchak, "Information Age Army."

45. Ibid.

46. Coakley, *Command and Control*.

47. Ibid.; Coakley, ed., C^3I.

48. Deitchman, *Advance of Technology*; Bellin and Chapman, *Computers in Battle*; Din, ed., *Arms and Artificial Intelligence*.

49. Chapman, "High-Technology Weapons," 70.

50. See, for example, Lanir, Fischoff, and Johnson, "Military Risk-Taking."

51. Although it did not necessarily create it. The recent debate over the comparative roles of technology, offensive doctrine, and politics has been quite animated. See, for examples, Shimshoni, "Technology, Military Advantage, and World War I"; Posen, *Military Doctrine*; Sagan, "1914 Revisited"; Snyder, "Civil-Military Relations"; Snyder, *Ideology of the Offensive*; Trachtenberg, "Meaning of Mobilization"; Van Evera, "Cult of the Offensive."

52. A notable exception is Trachtenberg, "Meaning of Mobilization," who argues that the preemption of politics by the technology of mobilization does not stand up to close scrutiny. This article provoked an animated exchange of letters in *International Security* (vol. 15, no. 1) that continued and expanded the arguments without ever resolving them.

53. I thank Zvi Lanir for this provocative and useful analogy.

54. Department of the Army, *Force XXI*, 6.

55. Ibid., 29. Also see Morton, "Softwar Revolution."

56. van Creveld, *Technology and War*, 228.

57. Mazarr and others, *Desert Storm*, 153.

Chapter 12
Invisible Idiots

1. Turkle, *Life on the Screen*.
2. Rheingold, *Virtual Community*.
3. Rifkin, *End of Work*.
4. There will, of course, always be human chefs and other personalized human services available to individuals in a high enough socio-economic class. Indeed, the scarcer such resources become, the more valuable, and the more likely that high-income individuals will pay for them as visible signs of status. This can easily be generalized to a wide variety of other human-centered activities that are otherwise displaced by computerization and automation. See, for example, Hirsch, *Social Limits to Growth*.
5. See, for example, Rifkin, *End of Work*, 104ff.
6. Moravec, "Pigs in Cyberspace."
7. Davidow and Malone, *Virtual Corporation*.
8. Demchak, "Information Age Army."
9. Adam Smith, "Derivatives."
10. Demchak, *Military Organizations*.
11. Karlsen and Oppen, "Professional Knowledge"; Gullers, "Automation—Skill—Apprenticeship."
12. Negroponte, *Being Digital*.

Bibliography

Abate, Tom. "Someone Could Be Watching . . ." *San Francisco Chronicle*, May 12, 1996, B-1.

"Air Crashes: Murders and Mistakes." *The Economist*, January 14, 1989, 54–55.

"Air Dominance Called Key to U.S. Defense." *San Francisco Chronicle*, June 23, 1993, A3.

"Airbus May Add to A320 Safeguards, Act to Counter Crew Overconfidence." *Aviation Week & Space Technology*, April 30, 1990, 59.

"Airliner Crashes in France; 11 of 96 on Board Survive." *New York Times*, January 21, 1992, A3(N), A3(L).

"America at War." *Newsweek*, Spring/Summer 1991.

"Anyone Know a Cure for Hiccoughs?" *The Economist*, November 1, 1986.

Armacost, Michael H. *The Politics of Weapons Innovation: The Thor-Jupiter Controversy*. New York: Columbia University Press, 1969.

Armstrong, David A. *Bullets and Bureaucrats: The Machine Gun and the United States Army, 1861–1916*. Westport, Conn.: The Greenwood Press, 1982.

"As You Were?" *The Economist*, March 9, 1991, 26–27.

"Automated Cockpits: Keeping Pilots in the Loop." *Aviation Week & Space Technology*, March 23, 1992, 48–71.

Bainbridge, Lisanne. "Ironies of Automation." In *New Technology and Human Error*, edited by Jens Rasmussen, Keith Duncan, and Jacques Leplat, 271–286. New York: John Wiley and Sons, 1987.

Baker, Nicholson. "Discards." *The New Yorker*, April 4, 1994, 64–86.

"The Bankers Marched in Two by Two . . ." *The Economist*, April 6, 1996, 75–76.

Barley, Stephen R. "The Alignment of Technology and Structure through Roles and Networks." *Administrative Science Quarterly* 35, no. 1 (March 1990): 61–103.

———. "The New World of Work." Research paper. Washington D.C.: The British North-American Committee, 1995.

Barley, Stephen R. "Technology as an Occasion for Structuring: Evidence from Observations of CT Scanners and the Social Order of Radiology Departments." *Administrative Science Quarterly* 31 (March 1986): 78–108.

Barnaby, Frank, and Marlies ter Borg, eds. *Emerging Technologies and Military Doctrine: A Political Assessment.* New York: St. Martin's Press, 1986.

Barnard, Chester I. *The Functions of the Executive.* Cambridge, Mass.: Harvard University Press, 1938.

Barnett, Correlli. *The Audit of War: The Illusion and Reality of Britain as a Great Nation.* London: MacMillan, 1986.

Bauersfeld, Penny, Tiny Bennett, and Gene Lynch. *Striking a Balance: Conference on Human Factors in Computing Systems, Monterey Calif., 1992.* New York: Association for Computing Machinery, 1992.

Baxter, James Phinney. *Scientists against Time.* Boston: Little, Brown, 1946.

Beard, Edmund. *Developing the ICBM: A Study in Bureaucratic Politics.* New York: Columbia University Press, 1976.

Beare, A. N., C. D. Gaddy, W. E. Gilmore, J. C. Taylor, R. R. Fray, and S. M. Divakaruni. "Human Factors Guidelines for Fossil Power Plant Digital Control System Displays." In *IEEE Fifth Conference on Human Factors and Power Plants* (Monterey, Calif., June 7–11), edited by Edward W. Hagen, Institute of Electrical and Electronics Engineers, 248–253. New York: IEEE, 1992.

Beaumont, Roger A., and William P. Snyder. "Combat Effectiveness: Paradigms and Paradoxes." In *Combat Effectiveness: Cohesion, Stress, and the Volunteer Military*, edited by Sam C. Sarkesian, 20–56. Beverly Hills: Sage Publications, 1980.

Bellin, David, and Gary Chapman. *Computers in Battle: Will They Work?* New York: Harcourt Brace Jovanovich, 1987.

Beniger, James R. *The Control Revolution: Technological and Economic Origins of the Information Society.* Cambridge, Mass.: Harvard University Press, 1986.

Bennett, Robert A. "More Wild Stock Swings Expected." *New York Times*, January 25, 1987, 12.

Betts, Richard K., ed. *Cruise Missiles: Technology, Strategy, Politics.* Washington, D.C.: The Brookings Institution, 1981.

Bijker, Wiebe, Thomas P. Hughes, and Trevor Pinch, eds. *The Social Construction of Technological Systems: New Directions in the Sociology and History of Technology.* Cambridge, Mass.: Harvard University Press, 1987.

Binkin, Martin. *Military Technology and Defense Manpower.* Washington, D.C.: The Brookings Institution, 1986.

Blackwell, James. *Thunder in the Desert: The Strategy and Tactics of the Persian*

Gulf War. New York: Bantam, 1991.

Bond, David F. "Army Speeds Helicopter Enhancements in Response to Desert Storm Problems." *Aviation Week and Space Technology* 134, no. 13 (April 1, 1991): 24–25.

──────. "Troop and Materiel Deployment Missions Central Elements in Desert Storm Success." *Aviation Week and Space Technology* 134, no. 16 (April 22, 1991): 94–95.

Bracken, Paul. *The Command and Control of Nuclear Forces*. New Haven, Conn.: Yale University Press, 1983.

Braun, Ingo, Gerhard Feuerstein, and Johann von Grote-Janz. "Organ-Technick: Technik und Wissenschaft im Organtransplantationswesen." *Soziale Welt* 4 (1991): 445–472.

Braun, Ingo, Gerhard Feuerstein, Johann von Grote-Janz, and Bernward Joerges. "How to Recombine Large Technical Systems: The Case of European Organ Transplantation." In *Changing Large Technical Systems*, edited by Jane Summerton, 25–52. Boulder, Colo.: Westview Press, 1994.

Braverman, Harry. *Labor and Monopoly Capital: The Degradation of Work in the Twentieth Century*. New York: Monthly Review Press, 1975.

Brodie, Bernard, ed. *The Absolute Weapon*. New York: Harcourt, Brace, 1946.

Buchan, Alastair. "The Age of Insecurity." *Encounter* 20 (June 1963), 5.

Bush, Vannevar. *Modern Arms and Free Men: A Discussion of the Role of Science in Preserving Democracy*. New York: Simon and Schuster, 1949.

Byron, Captain John L. "The Surface Navy Is Not Ready." *Proceedings of the Naval Institute* (December 1987): 34–40.

Carver, Michael. *Twentieth-Century Warriors*. New York: Weidenfeld & Nicolson, 1987.

Cavender, Sasha. "Making the Web Work for All." *San Francisco Sunday Examiner and Chronicle*, July 16, 1995, B5–B6.

Chandler, Alfred D., Jr. *Scale and Scope: The Dynamics of Industrial Capitalism*. Cambridge, Mass.: The Belknap Press, 1990.

──────. *The Visible Hand: The Managerial Revolution in American Business*. Cambridge, Mass.: Harvard University Press, 1977.

Chaplin, Charlie, and Paulette Goddard. "Modern Times." Comedy Film. Hollywood, Calif.: Paramount, 1936.

Chapman, Gary. "The New Generation of High-Technology Weapons." In *Computers in Battle: Will They Work?*, edited by David Bellin and Gary Chapman, 61–100. New York: Harcourt Brace Jovanovich, 1987.

Chisholm, Donald. Coordination without Hierarchy: Informal Structures in

Multiorganizational Systems. Berkeley and Los Angeles: University of California Press, 1989.

Chorafas, Dimitris N. *Chaos Theory in the Financial Markets: Applying Fractals, Fuzzy Logic, Genetic Algorithms, Swarm Simulation & the Monte Carlo Method to Manage Market Chaos and Volatility.* Chicago: Probus, 1994.

Clark, Asa A. IV, Peter W. Chiarelli, Jeffrey S. McKittrick, and James W. Reed, eds. *The Defense Reform Debate.* Baltimore, Md.: The Johns Hopkins University Press, 1984.

Clarke, Lee. *Acceptable Risk?* Berkeley and Los Angeles: University of California Press, 1989.

Coakley, Thomas P., ed. *C³I: Issues of Command and Control.* Washington, D.C.: National Defense University Press, 1991.

————. *Command and Control for War and Peace.* Washington, D.C.: National Defense University Press, 1991.

Cohen, Eliot A. "The Air War in the Persian Gulf." *Armed Forces Journal International*, June 1993, 10–14.

Coulam, Robert F. *Illusions of Choice: The F-111 and the Problem of Weapons Acquisition Reform.* Princeton, N.J.: Princeton University Press, 1977.

Covault, Craig. "Desert Storm Reinforces Military Space Directions." *Aviation Week and Space Technology* 134, no. 14 (April 8, 1991): 42–47.

"Crash That Killed 92 in India Is Attributed to Pilot Error." *New York Times*, January 12, 1991, 4.

Cringely, Robert X. [pseud.]. *Accidental Empires.* Reading, Mass.: Addison-Wesley, 1992.

Cronon, William. *Nature's Metropolis: Chicago and the Great West.* New York: W.W. Norton, 1991.

Crossette, Barbara. "Crash of Indian Airlines Plane Kills 89." *New York Times* 139, February 15, 1990, A3.

Crudele, John. "Market Being Manipulated, So Watch Out." *San Francisco Examiner*, May 26, 1991, D-2.

————. "Volatility Tied to Wide Use of Computers to Set Trading Patterns." *New York Times*, September 13, 1986, 1.

Danziger, James N., William H. Dutton, Rob Kling, and Kenneth L. Kraemer. *Computers and Politics: High Technology in American Local Governments.* New York: Columbia University Press, 1982.

Danziger, James N., and Kenneth L. Kraemer. *People and Computers: The Impacts of Computing on End Users in Organizations.* New York: Columbia University Press, 1986.

David, Paul A. "The Dynamo and the Computer: An Historical Perspective on the Modern Productivity Paradox." *American Economic Review* 80, no. 2 (1990): 355–361.

Davidow, William S., and Michael S. Malone. *The Virtual Corporation.* New York: Harper Collins, 1992.

De Lauer, Richard D. "The Force Multiplier." *IEEE Spectrum* 19 (October 1982): 36.

De Maria, Lawrence. "Dow Up Just 1.99 in Wild Day." *New York Times*, April 22, 1988, C1.

"The Demise of Barings." *The Economist*, July 22, 1995, 66.

Deitchman, Seymour J. *Military Power and the Advance of Technology: General Purpose Military Forces for the 1980s and Beyond.* Boulder, Colo.: Westview Press, 1983.

Demchak, Chris C. *Military Organizations, Complex Machines: Modernization in the U.S. Armed Services.* Ithaca, N.Y.: Cornell University Press, 1991.

———. "Fully Networked Battlespace: Uncertainty and the 'Information Age' Army." Euro XIV Operations Research Conference, Jerusalem, Israel, July 1995. To be published in JCCM, March 1996.

Denning, Peter J. "The ARPANET after 20 Years." *American Scientist* 77, no. 6 (November–December 1989): 530–534.

Din, Allan M., ed. *Arms and Artificial Intelligence: Weapons and Arms Control Applications of Advanced Computing.* New York: Oxford University Press, 1987.

Donnelly, Chris. "Friction and Warfare." In *The Necessity of Friction*, edited by Nordal Akerman, 87–122. Heidelberg: Springer-Physika Verlag, 1993.

Doray, Bernard. *From Taylorism to Fordism: A Rational Madness.* Translated by David Macey. London: Free Association Books, 1988.

Dörfer, Ingemar. *Arms Deal: The Selling of the F-16.* New York: Praeger, 1983.

Douglas, Susan J. "The Navy Adopts the Radio: 1899–1919." In *Military Enterprise and Technological Change*, edited by Merritt Roe Smith, 117–174. Cambridge, Mass.: MIT Press, 1985.

Dreyfus, Hubert L., and Stuart E. Dreyfus. *Mind over Machine: The Power of Human Intuition and Expertise in the Era of the Computer.* New York: The Free Press, 1986.

Dunlop, Charles, and Rob Kling, eds. *Computerization and Controversy.* San Diego, Calif.: Academic Press, 1991.

Dupuy, Trevor N. *The Evolution of Weapons and Warfare.* London: Jane's, 1980.

———. *A Genius for War: The German Army and the General Staff, 1807–1945.*

Englewood Cliffs, N.J.: Prentice Hall, 1977.

Eckhouse, John. "INTERNET." *San Francisco Chronicle*, June 1, 1993, C1.

Edwards, Franklin R. "The Crash: A Report on the Reports." In *The Challenge of Information Technology for the Securities Markets: Liquidity Volatility, and Global Trading*, edited by Henry C. Lucas, Jr. and Robert A. Schwartz, 86–111. Homewood, Ill.: Dow Jones-Irwin, 1989.

Edwards, Paul N. *The Closed World: Computers and the Politics of Discourse in Cold War America*. Inside Technology. Cambridge, Mass.: MIT Press, 1996.

———. "A History of Computers and Weapons Systems." In *Computers in Battle: Will They Work?*, edited by David Bellin and Gary Chapman, 45–60. New York: Harcourt Brace Jovanovich, 1987.

Ehn, Pelle. *Work-Oriented Design of Computer Artifacts*. Stockholm: Almqvist and Wiksell International, 1988.

Ellis, John. *The Social History of the Machine Gun*. New York: Arno Press, 1981.

Emery, Frederick E., and Eric L. Trist. "Socio-Technical Systems." In *Systems Thinking*, edited by Frederick E. Emery, 281–296. London: Penguin Books, 1960.

"A Falling Star: The Collapse of Barings." *The Economist*, March 4, 1995, 19–21.

Fallows, James. *National Defense*. New York: Random House, 1981.

Fisher, Lawrence M. "Experience, Not Rules, Led Airliner Crew in Emergency." *New York Times*, March 4, 1989, 1.

Flamm, Kenneth. *Creating the Computer: Government, Industry, and High Technology*. Washington, D.C.: The Brookings Institution, 1988.

———. *Targetting the Computer: Government Support and International Competition*. Washington, D.C.: The Brookings Institution, 1987.

Flink, James J. *The Automobile Age*. Cambridge, Mass.: MIT Press, 1988.

Fogarty, Rear Admiral William M. "Formal Investigation into the Circumstances Surrounding the Downing of a Commercial Airliner by the U.S.S. *Vincennes* (CG49) on July 3, 1988." Washington, D.C.: U. S. Department of the Navy. July 1988.

Fogel, Robert. *Railroads and American Economic Growth: Essays in Econometric History*. Baltimore, Md.: The Johns Hopkins University Press, 1964.

Foushee, H. Clayton, and John K. Lauber. "The Effects of Flight Crew Fatigue on Performance: A Full-Mission Simulation Study." In *New Challenges to Understanding Organizations*, edited by Karlene Roberts, 151–172. New York: Macmillan, 1993.

Franke, Richard H. "Technological Revolution and Productivity Decline: Computer Introduction into the Financial Industry." *Technology Forecasting and Social Change* 31 (1987): 143–154.

Freedman, Lawrence, and Efraim Karsh. *The Gulf Conflict 1990–1991: Diplomacy and War in the New World Order*. Princeton, N.J.: Princeton University Press, 1993.

Freiberger, Paul, and Michael Swaine. *Fire in the Valley: The Making of the Personal Computer*. Berkeley, Calif.: Osborne/McGraw-Hill, 1984.

French, James. "The Efficiency of Computer Systems Under Stress: The View from an Institutional Trading Desk." In *The Challenge of Information Technology for the Securities Markets: Liquidity Volatility, and Global Trading*, edited by Henry C. Lucas, Jr. and Robert A. Schwartz, 232–234. Homewood, Ill.: Dow Jones-Irwin, 1989.

Gansler, Jacques S. *The Defense Industry*. Cambridge, Mass.: MIT Press, 1980.

Garbade, Kenneth D., and William L. Silber. "Technology, Communication, and the Performance of Financial Markets." *The Journal of Finance* 23, no. 3 (June 1978): 819–832.

Garfinkel, Simson. *PGP, Pretty Good Privacy*. Sebastopol, Calif.: O'Reilly and Associates, 1995.

Gibson, James William. *The Perfect War*. New York: Vintage, 1988.

Gibson, William. *Neuromancer*. London: Gollancz, 1984.

Giddens, Anthony. *Central Problems in Social Theory: Action, Structure and Contradiction in Social Analysis*. Berkeley and Los Angeles: University of California Press, 1979.

―――. "Structuralism, Post-structuralism, and the Production of Culture." In *Social Theory Today*, edited by Anthony Giddens and Jonathan H. Turner, 195–223. Stanford, Calif.: Stanford University Press, 1987.

Gilliam, Terry, director. *Brazil*. Produced by Arnon Milchan, Joseph P. Grace, and Patrick Cassavetti. Screenplay: Terry Gilliam, Tom Stoppard, and Charles McKeown. Music: Michael Kamen. London: Embassy International Pictures, 1985.

Göranzon, Bo. "The Practice of Use of Computers. A Paradoxical Encounter between Different Traditions of Knowledge." In *Knowledge, Skill and Artificial Intelligence*, edited by Bo Göranzon and Ingela Josefson, 9–18. New York and Berlin: Springer-Verlag, 1988.

Göranzon, Bo, and Ingela Josefson, eds. *Knowledge, Skill and Artificial Intelligence*. Foundations and Applications of Artificial Intelligence. Berlin: Springer-Verlag, 1988.

Gras, Alain. *Grandeur et Dépendance: Sociologie des Macro-Systèmes Techniques.* Sociologie d'aujourd'hui. Paris: Presses Universitaire de France, 1993.

Gras, Alain, Caroline Moricot, Sophie L. Poirot-Delpech, and Victor Scardigli. *Faced with Automation: The Pilot, the Controller, and the Engineer.* Translated by Jill Lundsten. Paris: Publications de la Sorbonne, 1994.

Gras, Alain, Caroline Moricot, Sophie L. Poirot-Delpech, and Victor Scardigli. *Le Pilote, le Contrôleur, et l'Automate.* Paris: Editions de l'IRIS, 1991.

Gullers, Peter. "Automation—Skill—Apprenticeship." In *Knowledge, Skill and Artificial Intelligence,* edited by Bo Göranzon and Ingela Josefson, 31–38. New York and Berlin: Springer-Verlag, 1988.

Hadley, Arthur T. *The Straw Giant: A Report from the Field.* New York: Random House, 1986.

Hansell, Saul. "For Rogue Traders, Yet Another Victim." *New York Times,* February 28, 1995.

Harvey, David. *The Condition of Postmodernity.* Oxford: Basil Blackwell, 1990.

Henderson, Breck W. "Automation System Gains Acceptance." *Aviation Week & Space Technology* (November 23, 1992): 97–98.

Henderson, William Darryl. *Cohesion: The Human Element in Combat.* Washington, D.C.: National Defense University Press, 1985.

Hirsch, Fred. *The Social Limits to Growth.* Cambridge, Mass.: Harvard University Press, 1978.

Hirschhorn, Larry. *Beyond Mechanization.* Cambridge, Mass.: MIT Press, 1984.

Holden, Arun V. *Chaos.* Princeton, N.J.: Princeton University Press, 1986.

Hollnagel, Erik, Peter C. Cacciabue, and S. Bagnara. "Workshop Report: The Limits Of Automation in Air Traffic Control and Aviation." *International Journal of Human-Computer Studies* 40, no. 3 (March 1994): 561–566.

Holusha, John. "The Painful Lessons of Disruption." *New York Times,* March 17, 1993, C1.

Honan, William H. "At the National Archives, Technology's Flip Side." *New York Times,* October 1, 1995, 17.

Hopkins, Harry. "Through the Looking Glass: Electronic Flight Instruments—the 'Glass Cockpit'—Have Been in Service for a Decade." *Flight International* 141, no. 4321 (June 9, 1992).

Howard, Robert. *Brave New Workplace.* New York: Viking, 1985.

Hughes, David. "Human Factors Are Critical in Computer-Driven Systems." *Aviation Week & Space Technology* 131, no. 25 (December 18, 1989): 104–105.

———. "Pilots, Research Studies Give Mixed Reviews to Glass Cockpits." *Aviation Week & Space Technology* 136, no. 12 (March 23, 1992): 50–51.

————. "Small Firm Acted Quickly to Design, Field Infrared Beacons for Vehicles." *Aviation Week & Space Technology* 134, no. 20 (May 20, 1991): 54–56.

Hughes, Thomas P. "The Evolution of Large Technical Systems." In *The Social Construction of Technological Systems*, edited by Wiebe E. Bjiker and Thomas P. Hughes, 51–82. Cambridge, Mass.: MIT Press, 1987.

————. *Networks of Power: Electrification in Western Society 1880–1930*. Baltimore, Md.: The Johns Hopkins University Press, 1983.

"Is Your Stockbroker User-Friendly?" *The Economist*, October 25, 1986, 79–81.

Jacky, Jonathan. "The Strategic Computing Program." In *Computers in Battle: Will They Work?*, edited by David Bellin and Gary Chapman, 171–208. New York: Harcourt Brace Jovanovich, 1987.

Jameson, Frederic. *Postmodernism, or, The Cultural Logic of Late Capitalism*. Durham, N.C.: Duke University Press, 1991.

Janik, A. "Tacit Knowledge, Working Life and Scientific Method." In *Knowledge, Skill and Artificial Intelligence*, edited by Bo Göranzon and Ingela Josefson, 53–66. New York and Berlin: Springer-Verlag, 1988.

Jones, Dennis Feltham. *Colossus*. New York: Berkley, 1985.

Jones, R. V. *The Wizard War: British Scientific Intelligence, 1939–1945*, 1st American ed. New York: Coward, McCann & Geoghegan, 1978.

Juhlin, Oskar. "Information Technology Hits the Automobile? Rethinking Road Traffic as Social Interaction." In *Changing Large Technical Systems*, edited by Jane Summerton, 291–311. Boulder, Colo.: Westview Press, 1994.

Kaldor, Mary. *The Baroque Arsenal*. New York: Hill and Wang, 1981.

Karlsen, T. K., and Maria Oppen. "Professional Knowledge and the Limits of Automation in Administrations." In *Knowledge, Skill and Artificial Intelligence*, edited by Bo Göranzon and Ingela Josefson, 139–149. New York and Berlin: Springer-Verlag, 1988.

Kauffman, Stuart A. *At Home in the Universe: The Search for Laws of Self-organization and Complexity*. New York: Oxford University Press, 1995.

Keegan, John. *The Face of Battle*. Harmondsworth, Middlesex: Penguin, 1978.

Kelly, Kevin. *Out of Control: The Rise of Neo-Biological Civilization*. Reading, Mass.: Addison-Wesley, 1994.

Kennedy, Paul. *The Rise and Fall of the Great Powers*. New York: Random House, 1987.

Kidder, Tracy. *The Soul of a New Machine*. Boston: Little, Brown, 1981.

Klass, Philip J. "Gulf War Highlights Benefits, Future Needs of EW Systems." *Aviation Week & Space Technology* 135, no. 16 (October 21, 1991): 34–37.

Korzeniowski, Paul. "The IS Tug-of-War." *Infoworld*, December 21, 1992, 40–41.

Kotz, Nick. *Wild Blue Yonder: Money, Politics, and the B-1 Bomber*. New York: Pantheon, 1988.

Krol, Ed. *The Whole Internet: User's Guide and Catalog*. Sebastabol, Calif.: O'Reilly & Associates, 1992.

Kurtzman, Joel. *The Death of Money: How the Electronic Economy Has Destabilized the World's Markets and Created Financial Chaos*. New York: Simon and Schuster, 1993.

La Porte, Todd R. "The United States Air Traffic System: Increasing Reliability in the Midst of Rapid Growth." In *The Development of Large Technical Systems*, edited by Renate Mayntz and Thomas P. Hughes, 215–244. Boulder, Colo.: Westview Press, 1988.

————, ed. *Organized Social Complexity*. Princeton, N.J.: Princeton University Press, 1975.

La Porte, Todd R., and Paula M. Consolini. "Working in Practice but Not in Theory: Theoretical Challenges of 'High-Reliability Organizations'." *Journal of Public Administration Research and Theory* 1 (1991): 19–47.

Lamiell, Patricia. "Global Stock Index Here, but Market Isn't." *San Francisco Examiner*, January 10, 1993, E-7.

Landau, Martin, and Russell Stout, Jr. "To Manage Is Not To Control: Or the Folly of Type II Errors." *Public Administration Review* 39 (March/April 1979): 148–156.

Landauer, Thomas K. *The Trouble with Computers: Usefulness, Usability, and Productivity*. Cambridge, Mass.: The MIT Press, 1995.

Lanir, Zvi. "The Reasonable Choice of Disaster—The Shooting Down of the Libyan Airliner on 21 February 1973." *Journal of Strategic Studies* 12, no. 4 (December 1989): 479–493.

Lanir, Zvi, Baruch Fischoff, and Stephen Johnson. "Military Risk-Taking: C³I and the Cognitive Function of Boldness in War." *Journal of Strategic Studies* 11, no. 1 (March 1988): 96–114.

Lenorovitz, Jeffrey M. "Air National Guard Unit's F-16 Pilots Say Small Arms Fire Is the Primary Threat." *Aviation Week and Space Technology* 134, no. 8 (February 25, 1991): 42–44.

Lerman, Robert I., and Harold Salzman. "Deskilling and Declassing: Wither the Middle Stratum?" *Society* 25, no. 6 (September–October, 1988).

"Let's Clear the Air on Stealth." *Aviation Week & Space Technology*, May 20, 1991, 9.

Louis, Arthur M. "Heavy Stock Trading Jams Broker's Lines." *San Francisco Chronicle*, July 20, 1995, B1.

Lucas, Henry C., Jr., and Robert A. Schwartz, eds. *The Challenge of Information*

Technology for the Securities Markets: Liquidity, Volatility, and Global Trading. Homewood, Ill.: Dow Jones-Irwin, 1989.

Luttwak, Edward N. *The Pentagon and the Art of War.* New York: Simon and Schuster, 1984.

Malnic, Eric, and John Kendall. "Struggle to Gain Control of Jet Told." *Los Angeles Times* 108, July 22, 1989, 18.

March, James G., and Roger Weissinger-Baylon. *Ambiguity and Command: Organizational Perspectives on Military Decision-Making.* Marshfield, Mass.: Pitman, 1986.

Marenco, Claudine. "The Effects of the Rationalization of Clerical Work on the Attitudes and Behavior of Employees." In *Employment Problems of Automation and Advanced Technologies,* edited by Jack Steiber, 412–428. New York: St. Martin's Press, 1966.

Margiotta, Franklin D., and Ralph Sanders, eds. *Technology, Strategy and National Security.* Washington, D.C.: National Defense University Press, 1985.

Markoff, John. "Turning the Desktop PC into a Talk Radio Medium." *New York Times,* March 4, 1993, A1.

———. "A Web of Networks, an Abundance of Services." *New York Times,* February 28, 1993, F-8.

Mazarr, Michael J., Don M. Snider, and James A. Blackwell, Jr. *Desert Storm: The Gulf War and What We Learned.* Boulder, Colo.: Westview Press, 1993.

Mazlish, Bruce. *The Fourth Discontinuity.* New Haven, Conn.: Yale University Press, 1993.

McColloch, Mark. *White-Collar Workers in Transition: The Boom Years, 1940–1970.* Westport, Conn.: Greenwood Press, 1983.

McCorduck, Pamela. *Machines Who Think: A Personal Inquiry into the History and Prospects of Artificial Intelligence.* San Francisco: W. H. Freeman, 1979.

McNaugher, Thomas L. *The M-16 Controversies: Military Organizations and Weapons Acquisition.* New York: Praeger, 1984.

McNeill, William H. *The Pursuit of Power: Technology, Armed Force, and Society Since A.D. 1000.* Chicago: University of Chicago Press, 1982.

Merkle, Judith A. *Management and Ideology: The Legacy of the International Scientific Management Movement.* Berkeley and Los Angeles: University of California Press, 1980.

Meyer, Alan D., and William H. Starbuck. "Interactions between Ideologies and Politics in Strategy Formation." In *New Challenges to Understanding Organizations,* edited by Karlene H. Roberts, 99–116. New York: Macmillan, 1993.

Miastkowski, Stan. "Portable-Data Stars." *Byte,* August 1995, 129–131.

Michener, James A. *The Bridges at Toko-ri.* New York: Random House, 1953.

Millett, Allan R., and Williamson Murray, eds. *The Second World War.* Military Effectiveness. Boston: Allen & Unwin, 1988.

Monger, Rod F. *Mastering Technology: A Management Framework for Getting Results.* New York: The Free Press, 1988.

Moravec, Hans. "Pigs in Cyberspace." In *Thinking Robots, an Aware Internet, and Cyberpunk Librarians,* edited by R. Bruce Miller and Milton T. Wolf, 15–22. Chicago: Library and Information Technology Association, 1992.

Morison, Elting. *Men, Machines, and Modern Times.* Cambridge, Mass.: MIT Press, 1966.

Morrison, David C. "Logistic War's Long, Long Lines." *National Journal* 23, no. 8 (March 2, 1991): 514–515.

Morrocco, John D. "Gulf War Boosts Prospects for High Technology Weapons." *Aviation Week and Space Technology* 134, no. 11 (March 18, 1991): 45–47.

Morton, Oliver. "The Softwar Revolution." *The Economist,* June 10, 1995, S1–S20.

Nadis, Steve, and James MacKenzie. *Car Trouble.* Boston: Beacon Press, 1993.

Negroponte, Nicholas. *Being Digital.* New York: Alfred A. Knopf, 1995.

Nelan, Bruce W. "Revolution at Defense." *Time,* March 18, 1991, 25–26.

Noble, David F. *America by Design: Science, Technology and the Rise of Corporate Capitalism.* New York: Oxford University Press, 1977.

———. *Forces of Production: A Social History of Industrial Automation.* New York: Alfred A. Knopf, 1984.

Norman, Donald A. *Things that Make Us Smart: Defending Human Attributes in the Age of the Machine.* Reading, Mass.: Addison-Wesley, 1993.

O'Connell, Robert L. *Of Arms and Men: A History of War, Weapons, and Aggression.* New York: Oxford University Press, 1989.

Olson, Kenneth H. *Digital Equipment Corporation: The First Twenty-Five Years.* Newcomen publication no. 1179. New York: Newcomen Society in North America, 1983.

Orr, George E. Airpower Research Institute. "Combat Operations C³I: Fundamentals and Interactions." Research Report AU-ARI-82-5. Maxwell Air Force Base, Alabama: Air University Press, July 1983.

Orwell, George. *1984: A Novel.* New York: New American Library, 1950.

Osborn, Richard N., and Daniel H. Jackson. "Leaders, Riverboat Gamblers, or Purposeful Unintended Consequences in the Management of Complex, Dangerous Technologies." *Academy of Management Journal* 31, no. 4 (December 1988): 924–947.

Osterman, Paul. "The Impact of IT on Jobs and Skills." In *The Corporation of the 1990s*, edited by Michael S. Scott Morton, 220–243. New York: Oxford University Press, 1991.

Parker, Laura. "Pilots Added Page to DC-10 Manual: For 41 Harrowing Minutes, Cockpit Team Improvised in Flying Jet." *Washington Post* 112, July 23, 1989, A1.

Passell, Peter. "Fast Money." *New York Times Magazine*, October 18, 1992, 42ff.

Pearson, Jamie Parker. *Digital at Work: Snapshots from the First Thirty-Five Years*. Burlington, Mass.: Digital Press, 1992.

Perby, Maja-Lisa. "Computerization and Skill in Local Weather Forecasting." In *Knowledge, Skill and Artificial Intelligence*, edited by Bo Göranzon and Ingela Josefson, 39–52. New York and Berlin: Springer-Verlag, 1988.

Perrow, Charles. *Complex Organizations: A Critical Essay*, 3rd ed. New York: Random House, 1986.

———. *Normal Accidents: Living with High-Risk Technologies*. New York: Basic, 1984.

Perry, William J. "Defense Investment Strategy." *Foreign Affairs* 68, no. 2 (Spring 1989): 72–92.

Peters, Edgar E. *Chaos and Order in the Capital Markets: A New View of Cycles, Prices, and Market Volatility*. New York: John Wiley and Sons, 1991.

Phillips, Edward H. "Pilots, Human Factors Specialists Urge Better Man-Machine Cockpit Interface." *Aviation Week & Space Technology* 136, no. 12 (March 23, 1992): 67–68.

Posen, Barry R. *The Sources of Military Doctrine*. Ithaca, N.Y.: Cornell University Press, 1984.

Postol, Theodore A. "Lessons of the Gulf War Experience with Patriot." *International Security* 16, no. 3 (Winter 1991/1992): 119–171.

Quarterman, John S. *The Matrix: Computer Networks and Conferencing Systems*. Burlington, Mass.: Digital Press, 1990.

Rabinbach, Anson. "Automata, Evolution, and Us." *The Times Literary Supplement*, no. 4754 (May 13, 1994): 9–10.

———. *The Human Motor: Energy, Fatigue and the Origins of Modernity*. Berkeley and Los Angeles: University of California Press, 1992.

Ralph, Robert, ed. *Probabilistic Risk Assessment in the Nuclear Power Industry: Fundamentals and Applications*. New York: Pergamon Press, 1988.

Rasmussen, Jens, H. B. Anderson, and N. O. Bernsen, eds. *Human-Computer Interaction*. London: Erlbaum, 1991.

Rasor, Dina, ed. *More Bucks, Less Bang: How the Pentagon Buys Ineffective Weap-*

ons. Washington, D.C.: Fund for Constitutional Government, 1983.

Reich, Robert. *The Next American Frontier*. Baltimore, Md.: The Johns Hopkins University Press, 1983.

Rheingold, Howard. *Virtual Reality*. New York: Simon and Schuster, 1991.

――――. *The Virtual Community: Homesteading on the Electronic Frontier*. Reading, Mass.: Addison-Wesley, 1993.

Rhodes, Richard. *The Making of the Atomic Bomb*. New York: Simon and Schuster, 1986.

Richelson, Jeffrey T. "Volume of Data Cripples Tactical Intelligence System." *Armed Forces Journal International* (June 1992): 35–37.

Rifkin, Glenn, and George Harrar. *The Ultimate Entrepreneur: The Story of Ken Olsen and Digital Equipment Corporation*. Chicago: Contemporary Books, 1988.

Rifkin, Jeremy. *The End of Work: The Decline of the Global Labor Force and the Dawn of the Post-Market Era*. New York: G. P. Putnam's Sons, 1995.

Roberts, Karlene H., ed. *New Challenges to Understanding Organizations*. New York: Macmillan, 1993.

Roberts, Karlene H., and Denise M. Rousseau. "Research in Nearly Failure-Free, High-Reliability Systems: Having the Bubble." *IEEE Transactions on Engineering Management* 36, no. 2 (May 1989): 132–139.

Roberts, Lawrence G. "The ARPANET and Computer Networks." In *A History of Personal Workstations*, edited by Adele Goldberg, 143–167. New York: ACM Press, 1988.

Rochlin, Gene I. "Defining High-Reliability Organizations in Practice: A Taxonomic Prologomena." In *New Challenges to Understanding Organizations*, edited by Karlene H. Roberts, 11–32. New York: Macmillan, 1993.

――――. "Essential Friction: Error Control in Organizational Behavior." In *The Necessity of Friction*, edited by Nordal Akerman, 196–234. Heidelberg: Physica-Verlag, 1994.

――――. "Informal Organizational Networking as a Crisis Avoidance Strategy: U.S. Naval Flight Operations as a Case Study." *Industrial Crisis Quarterly* 3 (1989): 159–176.

――――. "Iran Air Flight 655: Complex, Large-Scale Military Systems and the Failure of Control." In *Responding to Large Technical Systems: Control or Anticipation*, edited by Renate Mayntz and Todd R. La Porte, 95–121. Amsterdam: Kluwer, 1991.

――――. "Pris dans la toile: réseaux, mutations et conformité à l'ère de l'informatique" (Trapped in the web: networking, transformation, and conformance in the information age). *FLUX: International Scientific Quarterly on Networks and Territories*, no. 22, (October–December 1995): 17–30.

Rochlin, Gene I., and Chris C. Demchak. "The Gulf War: Technological and Organizational Implications." *Survival* 33, no. 3 (May/June 1991): 260–273.

———. *Lessons of the Gulf War: Ascendant Technology and Declining Capability.* Policy Papers in International Affairs. Berkeley: Institute of International Studies, University of California, Berkeley, 1991.

Rochlin, Gene I., and Alexandra von Meier. "Nuclear Power Operations: A Cross-Cultural Perspective." *Annual Review of Energy and the Environment* 19 (1994): 153–187.

Rochlin, Gene I., Todd R. La Porte, and Karlene H. Roberts. "The Self-Designing High-Reliability Organization: Aircraft Carrier Flight Operations at Sea." *Naval War College Review* 40, no. 4 (Autumn 1987): 76–90.

Rockart, John F., and James E. Short. "The Networked Organization and the Management of Interdependence." In *The Corporation of the 1990s*, edited by Michael S. Scott Morton, 189–219. New York: Oxford University Press, 1991.

Rosen, Michael. "Crashing in '87: Power and Symbolism in the Dow." In *Organizational Symbolism*, edited by Barry A. Turner, 115–136. New York: Walter de Gruyter, 1990.

Rosen, Stephen Peter. *Winning the Next War: Innovation and the Modern Military.* Ithaca, N.Y.: Cornell University Press, 1991.

Roth, Emilie M., Randall J. Mumaw, and William F. Stubler. "Human Factors Evaluation Issues for Advanced Control Rooms: A Research Agenda." In *IEEE Fifth Conference on Human Factors and Power Plants* (Monterey, Calif., June 7–11), edited by Edward W. Hagen, Institute of Electrical and Electronics Engineers, 254–260. New York: IEEE, 1992.

Sagan, Scott D. "1914 Revisited: Allies, Offense, and Instability." *International Security* 11, no. 2 (Fall 1986): 151–176.

———. *The Limits of Safety: Organizations, Accidents, and Nuclear Weapons.* Princeton, N.J.: Princeton University Press, 1993.

Salsbury, Stephen. "Emerging Global Computer and Electronic Information Systems and Their Challenge to World Stockmarkets." *FLUX: International Scientific Quarterly on Networks and Territories*, no. 7 (January–March 1992): 27–42.

Sarkesian, Sam C., ed. *Combat Effectiveness: Cohesion, Stress, and the Volunteer Military.* Beverly Hills: Sage Publications, 1980.

Schmitt, Eric. "Israel Plays Down Effectiveness of Patriot Missile." *New York Times*, October 31, 1991, A5.

Schmitt, Eric. "Unforeseen Problems in Air War Forced Allies to Improvise Tactics." *New York Times*, March 10, 1991, 1.

Schulman, Paul. "The Analysis of High-Reliability Organizations: A Comparative Framework." In *New Challenges to Understanding Organizations*, edited by Karlene Roberts, 33–54. New York: Macmillan, 1993.

Scott Morton, Michael S., ed. *The Corporation of the 1990s; Information Technology and Organizational Transformation*. New York: Oxford University Press, 1991.

Scott, W. Richard. *Organizations: Rational, Natural, and Open Systems*. Englewood Cliffs, N.J.: Prentice Hall, 1981.

"The Screen Is the Future, Master." *The Economist*, October 24, 1992, 85–86.

Sherry, Clifford J. *The New Science of Technical Analysis: Using the Statistical Techniques of Neuroscience to Uncover Order and Chaos in the Markets*. Chicago: Probus, 1994.

Shimshoni, Jonathan. "Technology, Military Advantage, and World War I: A Case for Military Entrepreneurship." *International Security* 15, no. 3 (Winter 1990/91): 187–215.

"The Shrinking of the Big Board." *The Economist*, February 16, 1991, 67.

Shrivastava, Paul. *Bhopal: Anatomy of a Crisis*. Cambridge, Mass.: Ballinger, 1987.

Shurkin, Joel. *Engines of the Mind: A History of the Computer*. New York: W. W. Norton, 1984.

Sloan, Leonard. "Why Stocks Fell So Quickly: Anxiety, with Computer Spin." *New York Times*, September 14, 1987, 1.

Smith, Adam. "Derivatives." TV Show. New York: WNET, July 21, 1995.

———. "The Rocket Scientists." TV Show. New York: WNET, July 28, 1995.

Smith, Douglas K., and Robert C. Alexander. *Fumbling the Future: How Xerox Invented, Then Ignored the First Personal Computer*. New York: William Morrow and Company, 1988.

Smith, Merritt Roe, ed. *Military Enterprise and Technological Change*. Cambridge, Mass.: MIT Press, 1985.

Snyder, Jack. "Civil-Military Relations and the Cult of the Offensive, 1914 and 1984." *International Security* 9, no. 1 (Summer 1984): 108–146.

———. *The Ideology of the Offensive: Military Decision Makers and the Disasters of 1914*. Ithaca, N.Y.: Cornell University Press, 1984.

Spinney, Franklin C. *Defense Facts of Life: The Plans/Reality Mismatch*. Boulder: Westview Press, 1985.

Squires, Sally. "The 'Glass Cockpit' Syndrome: How High Technology and Information Contribute to Fatal Mistakes." *Washington Post* 111 (October 11, 1988): W7.

Stix, Gary. "Along for the Ride?" *Scientific American*, July 1991, 94–106.

Stoll, Clifford. *Silicon Snake Oil: Second Thoughts on the Information Highway*. New York: Doubleday, 1995.

Strachan, Hew. *European Armies and the Conduct of War*. London: George Allen & Unwin, 1983.

Strassman, Paul A. *Information Payoff: The Transformation of Work in the Electronic Age*. New York: The Free Press, 1985.

Suchman, Lucille A. "Working Relations of Technology Production and Use." *Computer Supported Cooperative Work* 2 (1994): 21–39.

Taylor, Frederick Winslow. "The Principles of Scientific Management." In *Classics of Organization Theory*, edited by Jay M. Shafritz and J. Steven Ott, 66–80. Chicago: The Dorsey Press, 1987.

"Terrible Tuesday: How the Stock Market Almost Disintegrated." *Wall Street Journal*, November 20, 1987, 1.

Thomas, Frank. "The Politics of Growth: The German Telephone System." In *The Development of Large Technical Systems*, edited by Renate Mayntz and Thomas P. Hughes, 179–214. Boulder, Colo.: Westview Press, 1988.

Thomas, Robert J. *What Machines Can't Do: Politics and Technology in the Industrial Enterprise*. Berkeley and Los Angeles: University of California Press, 1994.

Thompson, James D. *Organizations in Action*. New York: McGraw-Hill, 1967.

Toffler, Alvin. *The Third Wave*. New York: Bantam, 1980.

Trachtenberg, Marc. "The Meaning of Mobilization in 1914." *International Security* 15, no. 3 (Winter 1990/91): 120–150.

Trippi, Robert R. *Chaos and Nonlinear Dynamics in the Financial Markets: Theory, Evidence and Applications*. Chicago: Irwin Professional Publishing, 1995.

Turkle, Sherry. *Life on the Screen: Identity in the Age of the Internet*. New York: Simon and Schuster, 1995.

———. *The Second Self: Computers and the Human Spirit*. New York: Simon and Schuster, 1984.

Turner, Barry A. *Man-Made Disasters*. London: Wykeham, 1978.

United States. Department of the Army. *Force XXI . . . America's Army of the 21st Century*. Fort Monroe, Virginia: DACS-LM, U.S. Army, 1995.

United States. Department of Defense. *Conduct of the Persian Gulf War: Final Report to Congress*. Washington, D.C.: U.S. Government Printing Office, April 1992.

United States Congress. House of Representatives. Committee on Armed Services. *Report on the Staff Investigation into the Iraqi Attack on the U.S.S. Stark*. Washington, D.C.: U.S. Government Printing Office, 1987.

United States Congress. Office of Technology Assessment. *Electronic Bulls and Bears: U.S. Securities Markets & Information Technology*. OTA-CIT-469. Washington, D.C.: U.S. Government Printing Office, September 1990.

———. Office of Technology Assessment. *Trading around the Clock: Global Securities Markets and Information Technology*. OTA-BP-CIT-66. Washington D.C.: U.S. Government Printing Office, July 1990.

———. Senate. Committee on Armed Services. *Investigation into the Downing of an Iranian Airliner by the U.S.S.* Vincennes. Hearing Before the Committee on Armed Services, United States Senate, 100th Congress, second session. Washington, D.C.: U.S. Government Printing Office, 1989.

———. Senate. Committee on Judiciary. *The Administration's Clipper Chip Key Escrow Encryption Program*. Hearing Before the Subcommittee on Technology and the Law of the Committee on the Judiciary, United States Senate, 103rd Congress, second session. Washington, D.C.: U.S. Government Printing Office, 1995.

United States General Accounting Office. *Information Superhighway: An Overview of Technology Challenges*. Report GAO/AIMD-95-23. Washington, D.C.: U.S. GAO, January 1995.

———. *Operation Desert Storm: The Services' Efforts to Provide Logistics Support for Selected Weapons Systems*. Report GAO/NSIAD-91-321. Washington, D.C.: U.S. GAO, September 1991.

———. *Weapons Testing: Quality of DOD Operational Testing and Reporting*. Report GAO/PEMD-88-32BR. Washington, D.C.: U.S. GAO, July 1988.

van Creveld, Martin. *Command in War*. Cambridge, Mass.: Harvard University Press, 1985.

———. *Fighting Power: German and U.S. Army Performance, 1939–1945*. Westport, Conn.: Greenwood Press, 1982.

———. *Technology and War: From 2000 b.c. to the Present*. New York: The Free Press, 1989.

Van Evera, Stephen. "The Cult of the Offensive." *International Security*, 1984.

Viorst, Judith, and Ray Cruz. *Alexander and the Terrible, Horrible, No Good, Very Bad Day*. New York: Atheneum, 1972.

Vlahos, Michael. "The *Stark* Report." *Proceedings of the Naval Institute* (May 1988): 64–67.

Vortac, O. U., M. B. Edwards, D. K. Fuller, and C. A. Manning. "Automation and Cognition in Air Traffic Control: An Empirical Investigation." *Applied Cognitive Psychology* 7, no. 7 (December 1993): 631–651.

Waldrop, M. Mitchell. *Complexity: The Emerging Science at the Edge of Order and*

Chaos. New York: Simon and Schuster, 1992.

———. "Computers Amplify Black Monday." *Science* 238, October 30, 1987, 602–604.

Waring, Stephen P. *Taylorism Transformed: Scientific Management Theory since 1945*. Chapel Hill, N.C.: The University of North Carolina Press, 1991.

Weick, Karl E. "The Collapse of Sensemaking in Organizations: The Mann Gulch Disaster." *Administrative Science Quarterly* 38, no. 4 (December 1993): 628–652.

———. "Organizational Culture as a Source of High Reliability." *California Management Review* 29, no. 2 (Winter 1987): 112–127.

———. "The Vulnerable System: An Analysis of the Tenerife Air Disaster." In *New Challenges to Understanding Organizations*, edited by Karlene Roberts, 173–198. New York: Macmillan, 1993.

Weigley, Russell. *The American Way of War*. New York: Macmillan, 1973.

Weinberg, Nathan. *Computers in the Information Society*. Boulder, Colo.: Westview Press, 1990.

Weiner, Eric. "Jet Carrying 290 Crashes in Iowa; 150 Aboard Are Said to Survive." *New York Times* 138, July 20, 1989, A1.

"What Caused the Meltdown?" *The Economist*, December 19, 1987, 65.

"Why London?" *The Economist*, May 4, 1991, 15–16.

Wieckert, Kären Elizabeth. "Design under Uncertainty: Engaging the Context of Use in the Design of Expert Systems." Ph.D. diss., University of California, Irvine, 1995.

Wiener, Earl L. "Fallible Humans and Vulnerable Systems: Lessons Learned from Aviation." In *Information Systems: Failure Analysis*, edited by John A. Wise and Anthony Debons, 163–182. NATO Advanced Science Institute Series F: Computer and Systems Sciences, vol. 32. Berlin: Springer Verlag, 1987.

Wilson, James Q. "The Dead Hand of Regulation." *The Public Interest* 25 (Fall 1971): 54–78.

Winner, Langdon. *Autonomous Technology: Technics Out-of-Conrol as a Theme in Political Thought*. Cambridge, Mass.: MIT Press, 1977.

———. "Do Artifacts Have Politics?" *Daedalus* (Winter 1980): 121–136.

Winograd, Terry, and Fernando Flores. *Understanding Computers and Cognition*. Reading, Mass.: Addison-Wesley, 1986.

Womack, James P., Daniel T. Jones, and Daniel Roos. *The Machine That Changed the World: The Story of Lean Production*. New York: Rawson Associates, 1990.

Wood, Stephen, ed. *The Degradation of Work? Skill, Deskilling and the Labour Pro-*

cess. London: Hutchinson, 1981.

————, ed. *The Transformation of Work? Skill, Flexibility and the Labour Process*. London: Unwin Hyman, 1989.

"Word Perfect Called to Action for Desert Storm." *WordPerfect Report*, May 1991, 9.

Wurman, Richard Saul. *Information Anxiety: What to Do When Information Doesn't Tell You What You Need to Know*. New York: Doubleday, 1989.

Zuboff, Shoshana. *In the Age of the Smart Machine: The Future of Work and Power*. New York: Basic, 1988.

Index

academics, 137, 138

"Adam Smith" (WNET television program), 106–7

Advanced Research Projects Agency (ARPA), 38, 138, 171, 200. *See also* Defense Advanced Research Projects Agency (DARPA)

Aegis electronic fire-control system, 156, 157, 167, 204; and stress, 164–65

Agincourt, Battle of, 185

Airbus 320, 114, 115, 116, 125

Air Canada Flight 767, 113

aircraft cockpits, automated, 112–19, 120, 125, 233n.54. *See also* "glass cockpit" syndrome

AirLand Battle, 148, 186, 200, 201, 209

airline reservations systems, 3–4, 38

air traffic control, 68, 99, 109–10, 119–22, 124, 125–26, 129; and manual control, 121–22

alienation, 7; and "information anxiety," 37; of workers, 52

Alto, The, 24

American Psychological Association (APA), 164, 165

Apple Computer, 6; Apple I, 22; Apple II, 22; and development of microcomputer, 23, 24–26, 27, 28; Macintosh, 24, 25; System 7, 27

Army Signal Corps, 138

ARPANET, 39–40, 44. *See also* Defense Advanced Research Projects Agency (DARPA)

artificial intelligence, 17, 211, 216

artisanal production, 7, 8

assembly line, 53

AT&T, 20, 21

Auftragstaktik, 201, 206

Autonomous Technology (Winner), 15

autonomy: and computer operating systems, 26–27; human, 11; of library users, 37–38; military, 208; of worker, 9–10

aviation, commercial, 122, 158–59, 160–61, 165, 206

Babbage, Charles, 17

Baker, Nicholson, 36. *See also* library catalogs: card

banking, 61, 75; electronic, 4, 92, 93; and electronic foreign exchange, 100; use of mainframe computers in, 76, 77

bar-coding systems, 4, 62

Barings P.L.C., 91–92, 106

Barnard, Chester I., 58

battlefield: of the future, 187; virtual, 200, 202–3, 204

Beard, Edmund, 139

Bell Laboratories, 20, 21, 39, 40, 41, 42

black-box electronics, 145–46, 160, 179

bombers, 151, 152–53

bookkeepers, 61

box office reservations systems, 38

Braverman, Harry, 62

British Midland Corporation, 114, 115

Brodie, Bernard, 137

"bubble," 109–10, 122, 128, 240n.4

Bulge, Battle of, 197

business: adopts systems analysis model, 59–69; computerization of, 8–9, 10; computer networking in, 46–48. *See also* banking; computer trading

California, 21, 22, 92, 106

cathode ray tube (CRT) display, 124

centralization: caused by computerized trading, 77, 78–80

centralized computers, 6. *See also* mainframe computers

Chemical Bank, 92

chemical plant operations, 125

chemical weapons, 200

chess, 211, 213, 214, 216–17

Chicago Stock Exchange, 100

Citron, Robert L., 92, 93

Civil War, 132–33, 136, 170, 193–94

Clausewitz, Karl von, 193, 194, 207

Clearing House Interbank Payments System (CHIPS), 95, 105

closed systems management, 58

cognitive maps, 109, 111–12, 126, 128–29, 206–7

combat systems, integrated, 201–2

command: as analogogous to modern management, 188, 189–91; complicated by automation, 201–2; in factory, 189; open cycle process of, 204

command-and-control, 174, 189–90, 192, 200, 207; in Civil War, 193; enhancement of, between the wars, 197; in Gulf War, 177–80, 181–82; problems

with, 204, 205–6; in World War II, 199

command centers, military, 109–10

Command, Control, Communications, and Intelligence (C³I), 145, 180–82, 185, 188, 200, 206, 208

Committee on Armed Services, Staff Report of, 155

Commodity Futures Trading Commission (CFTC), 86

communications: for expert operators, 123–24; in Gulf War, 180–81; in World War I, 194–95, 196–97. *See also* Command, Control, Communications, and Intelligence (C³I)

compatibility, computer, 28, 32, 46

computer-aided decision making, 7, 127

computer-aided graphic design (CAD), 23–24

computer-aided machinery, 8, 125

computer industry: development cycles in, 15–16

computer networks, 34, 48–49; in universities, 35–38. *See also* computer trading; global networks; Local Area Networks (LANs); mainframe computers

computer operating systems, 20–21, 23, 24–27, 39

computer programs: early days of, 22, 26, 27–28

computers: diffusion of, 29–32; early fear of, 6

Computer Systems Research Group (U.C. Berkeley), 41

computer trading: and call system, 78; and creation of new financial instruments, 89; and global markets, 96; and global network, 77–78, 88–89; and Stock Market Crash of 1987, 83–85, 86; vulnerability of, 96–99

computer trap, 217; defined, xii–xiii

computer users, 36–37; versus designers,

32–34, 129–30
conservatism, 169, 170; of military, 132, 133, 134, 150–51; of U.S. government, 136
consultants: and lack of experiential knowledge, 110
control: and changes in workplace hierarchies, 8–9; closed cycle process of, 204; through computerization, 9–10; defined, 189–90; of information technology, 49–50; via logistics, 182; managerial, 46, 47–48, 49–50, 53–54; organizational, 13; on virtual battlefield, 207–8; of workers, 48; in World War I, 196–97
Cooper, Richard, 131
Cooper, Robert S., 200
corporation, virtual, 214–15
cost-effectiveness, 186, 208
craft production, 8, 51, 53, 56–57, 68
Creveld, Martin van, 195, 199, 208
Cronin, David, 112
cyberpunk, 94, 96
cyberspace, 12, 13, 75, 94, 96, 188, 202

data: management programs for, 4; processing of, 7; storage and retrieval of, 37–38
David, Paul, 29
Davidow, William S., 60
decentralization, 8; of markets, 82, 87
decision analysis, 190
decision making, computer-aided, 7, 127
Defense Advanced Research Projects Agency (DARPA), 131, 200; and development of networks, 38–40. *See also* AR-PANET
defunctionalization: of workers, 66–67
Deitchman, Seymour J., 151–52
DeLauer, Richard D., 144
democratization: via computerization, 8, 9–10
Department of Defense, 149, 172, 180

dependency, 7; and computer interfaces, 25, 35–36; of military, on automation, 191, 201, 202; on MS-DOS and Windows, 26–27; on spreadsheets, 28
designers: and insensitivity to user concerns, 32–34, 110–12, 129–30. *See also* programmers
deskilling, 131; of workers, 52–53, 56, 57, 61, 64, 65–66; in workplace, 7
determinism, technical, 11
diagnostics, computer-aided, 124, 125
digital computers, 3, 6; in business, 8; demand for, 31; development of, 16–18
Digital Equipment Company (DEC): and development of minicomputers, 20, 22, 23, 25; and Internet, 41
discretion, 203, 206
Dreyfus, Hubert L., 67
Dreyfus, Stuart E., 67

Economist, The (periodical), 73, 74, 82
efficiency, 8, 11, 126–27, 183, 206, 212, 213; costs of, 4; versus effectiveness, 206, 208; in library research, 37; and modernity, 7; of smart weapons, 131
Eisenhower, Dwight D., 138, 140
electric utility grid management, 110
electronic mail, 40, 41
electronic warfare, 12, 174–77; and cognitive framing errors, 152; consequences of, 186, 205–9; and product displacement cycle, 182–83; and redefinition of effectiveness, 184; and transformation of warfare, 184–88. *See also* C^3I; combat systems, integrated; Iran Air Flight 655; Persian Gulf War; USS *Stark*; USS *Vincennes*
empowerment, 27; through computerization, xiii, 5, 8–9; of individual, 8–9; through Internet, 43; of library users, 35; via networked office, 47–48; of office workers, 49; of worker, 60

encryption, 96–98

encyclopedias, 37

error: cognitive framing, 152–54; human, 125, 126, 162; operator, 165; pilot, 112–14

Ethernet, 40, 42–43, 47

Eurotransplant, 70, 71

expertise, 10, 13, 180; displaced by global market trading, 106; experiential, 11, 12; loss of, 215; naval, 134; pilot, 244n.36; of skilled operators, 111–12, 113–14; "true," xiii, 67–68

expert systems, 127–28

factory: traditional, 189; virtual, 214

Federal Aviation Administration (FAA), 119–20, 122

Federal Reserve, 95

feedback, 203–4; and global markets, 98; used in control, 190

Field Manual (FM) 100–5 (U.S. Army Field Manual), 148, 199, 200, 201

Financial Futures Exchange (London), 100

financial instruments, secondary, 92

Fogarty, William M., 163, 164

Follow-On Forces Attack (FoFa), 148

Force XXI, 209

Ford, Henry, 53, 55

Fordism, 58

foreign exchange, 95. *See also* computer trading

France, 193, 194, 197, 205

Franco-Prussian War, 194

Frederick the Great, 192

friendly fire, 258n.30

game theory, 190, 213

Gatling gun, 133, 134

generation gap: financial, 93, 107; among securities traders, 86

Germany, 178, 205

Gibson, James Wilson, 148–49

Gibson, William, 94, 104

"glass cockpit" syndrome, 116–19, 165, 215

global markets, 82, 87, 96–103; social effects of, 104–5

global networks, 51, 80–81; and computer trading, 77–78, 88–89, 212

Globex, 100

Gomez, Victor, 92

Gopher, 36

government contracts, 18. *See also* Defense Advanced Research Projects Agency

Grant, James, 105

Grant, Ulysses S., 194, 197–98

Gras, Alain, 110–11

Great Britain, 135, 171

Greenspan, Alan, 106

Guadalcanal, 136

Gulf War. *See* Persian Gulf War

Gullers, Peter, 67–68

gunnery: continuous aim naval, 134; precision, 151, 186

Haig, Douglas, 195

Hansell, Saul, 93

Haynes, Alfred C., 112–13

hierarchy: increased complexity of military, 201–2; workplace, 8–9

Hiroshima, 135, 137

Hirschhorn, Larry, 66

HMS *Dreadnought*, 134

Hollerith punched card, 19

Hollnagel, Erik, 124–25

Homebrew Computer Club, 22, 28

Honeywell Corporation, 64–65

House Armed Services Committee, 164–65

Hughes, Thomas, 70

IBM: and role in mainframe development, 18–19

idiots, invisible, 218

Indian Airlines, 114, 116

individual: empowerment of, 8–9

industrialization: modernist vision of, 7

industry, 123. *See also* computer-aided machinery; inventory control systems; just-in-time systems

Infoworld (periodical), 47–48

innovation: military resistance to, 137–38

Instinet, 80

integrated circuits, 18, 20

Intel, 6, 22, 23, 26, 27

intelligence, 188; aerial, 197; artificial, 17, 211, 216

intelligent machines, 9

Intercontinental Ballistic Missiles (ICBMs), 139, 141

interdependence: reciprocal, 199; sequential, 198

interfaces: human-machine, 3, 24–25, 36, 45

International Stock Exchange, 75

Internet, 4, 6, 43, 48, 51; defined, 228n.28; development of, 44–45; tools, 36; and virtual reality, 214

inventory control systems, 4, 38, 61–62, 212–13

Iran, 154, 155, 158–59, 162

Iran Air Flight 655, 158–59, 160, 161–64, 165, 206

Iran-Iraq War, 154–55, 156

Iraq, 154, 155, 171, 184

Israeli Air Defense Force, 152–53, 154, 205

"jacking in," 94

Japan, 91

Jett, Joseph, 92

JSTARS system, 174, 204

judgment, xiii

just-in-time systems, 4–5, 38, 213, 214; military use of, 183

Kaufman, Henry, 106

Keegan, John, 195–96

Kidder, Peabody, 92

knowledge: experiential, of skilled operators, 110; holistic, 120; tacit, 56–57, 68

Kobe earthquake, 4–5

Korb, Lawrence, 169

Korean War, 139, 140, 170, 199

Kuwait, 169, 171

Landau, Martin, 189

Landauer, Thomas K., xii, 32–33

Lanir, Zvi, 153–54, 162

learning, 215; and computer mastery, 31; trial-and-error, 126, 128–29, 213

Leeson, Nicholas W., 91, 92

libertarianism, 21–22, 28, 43

librarians: enhanced role of, 36, 37–38, 49

libraries, 4, 35–37; use of Internet by, 45

library catalogs: card, 35, 36–37; online, 4, 35–37

local area networks (LANs), 38, 42, 45, 46–47, 98

logistics: of Gulf War, 177–80; history of military, 188, 191–92; of World War II, 198–99

London, 74, 82, 91; Big Bang Transition of 1986, 95; City of (financial district), 74, 75, 77

London Stock Exchange (LSE), 74

machine guns, 133, 134, 248n.11

mainframe computers, 6, 8, 43, 47; early history of, 18–19, 21; social-organizational legacy of, 19–20; and standardization of workplace, 7; use of, in banking, 76, 77

Malone, Michael S., 60

management: as analogous to military command, 188, 189–91; closed systems model of, 58; gains greater control of workers, 46, 47–48, 49–50; and impact of informated workplace, 63–66, 69, 72; middle, 58; open systems model of, 58,

management (*cont.*)
59; scientific, 13, 50, 54–56, 57, 58, 59, 62–63, 65, 232n.47; versus skilled operators, 112
management information system (MIS) staff, 47, 49
markets: derivative, 107; global, 82, 87, 96–103, 104–5; primary versus secondary, 94–96, 104; virtual, 215
market transfer systems, 4
Massachusetts Institute of Technology (MIT), 39, 40; Sloan School of Management at, 60
Mazlish, Bruce, 6
McPeak, Merrill, 169–70
Metcalfe, Robert, 40
Michener, James, 185
microcomputers, 43; development of, 22, 23
microprocessors, 22, 26, 221–22n.15
Microsoft, 25; DOS, 26–27, 36; Windows, 26–27
military: computer transformation of, 190–91; and modern management, 190–91; and sponsorship of computer development, 17, 18, 20; technical conservatism of, 132, 133, 134, 150–51; virtual, 215
military-industrial-complex, 138–39
MILNET, 44
minicomputers, 20, 43, 46, 47; development of, 21–22, 23, 25
missiles, 139, 141, 156, 163, 172, 204; Patriot, 174–75
models: econometric, 190; military, 190. *See also* cognitive maps
Moltke, Helmuth von, 188, 194, 201
Morgan Stanley Corporation, 93
Morison, Elting, 151
Morton, Michael S. Scott, 160
Mosaic, 36, 45
Multics, 39, 41

Nagasaki, 135, 137
Napoleon, 192–93, 194
Napoleonic Wars, 193, 205
NASDAQ, 87–88
Netscape, 36, 45
Neuromancer (Gibson), 94
New York Stock Exchange (NYSE), 75, 78, 83, 87, 88
New York Times (newspaper), 93
North Atlantic Treaty Organization (NATO), 187, 201
NSFNET, 44
nuclear power plant operations, 110, 119, 123, 124, 127, 127–28, 215
nuclear weapons, 137, 139, 140, 148, 170, 200
numerically controlled machine technology, 138

office, networked, 46–48. *See also* Local Area Networks (LANs)
Office of Naval Research, 138
Office of Technology Assessment (OTA), 85–86, 101–2, 103
officers: conservatism of, 134, 138, 147, 170; innovation supported by younger, 155; and modern management, 190–91; navy, 150–51, 162; and promotion of technological innovation, 186
open systems management, 58, 59
operations research, 59, 190
operators, expert, 110, 111–12
Orange County (California), 92, 106
organization: changes in industrial, 53–54; changes in managerial, 51, 63–64; changes in military, 201–2; virtual, 13. *See also* command

Passell, Peter, 105
Patton, George, 197
Pearson, Bob, 113

Persian Gulf, 154, 156, 159

Persian Gulf War: 149, 173, 258n.30; lasting lessons of, 185–86; and problems with smart weapons in, 174–77; and quality versus quantity debate, 172–84

personal computers: Apple, 22; applications for, 27–29; and changes in managerial structure, 63–64; demand for, 29–32; development of, 6; IBM, 22–23, 25–27; ubiquity of, xi, 5, 6, 7

pilots, 99, 108, 112–14, 117, 127; and cognitive framing, 154; errors made by, 112–14, 115–17; expert, 113–14

power, distribution of, 9–10

Precision Guided Munitions (PGMs), 140

process control, computer-aided, 125

product displacement cycle: 259n.46; and military technology, 182–83

programmers, 20, 21; and need for user-centered design, 33–34

program trading, 81, 82, 83–84, 85, 86, 88; regulation of, 104

Project MAC, 39, 40

quality versus quantity debate: 140–44, 169, 170, 255n.3; and Gulf War, 172–84

radio communications, 151, 197

railroads, 193, 194; used in World War I, 205

RAND (think tank), 137, 138

Reagan Administration, 143–44

redundancy: of resources in Gulf War, 178; technical, 127

regulation, 96–98, 102–3; government, 79, 80–81, 82, 85, 86–87, 89–90; institutional self-, 93

representation, 109, 111; in air traffic control, 120, 124, 126; of battle in Franco-Prussian War, 194; and failure of electronic cockpit, 166; of libraries, 36; on virtual battlefield, 206–7; of work, xiii, 12, 51–52

Reuters International, 80, 100

Rheingold, Howard, 210

Rifkin, Jeremy, 210

rifles: repeating, 133; single shot, 133; Spencer, 133

rigidity: in automated systems, 4; of command, 135–36, 195, 197; increased by military automation, 202

Ripley, James, 133

risk, 241–42n.12

Roberts, Ed, 22

Roberts, Larry, 18–19

robotics, 6, 211

Rogers, William C., 159, 161, 164

Rohatyn, Felix, 84

Romans, 191

Sabre (airline reservations system), 3

San Francisco Bay Area, 21

satellites, vi, 77–78, 88, 176, 180, 181, 186, 206

Saudi Arabia, 173, 177

scenario fixation, 165

Schwartz, Peter, 95, 96

Schwarzkopf, Norman, 173, 188

scientists, academic and research, 137

Second Self, The (Turkle), 14

Securities Exchange Commission (SEC), 82, 86, 87

securities trading, computerized. See computer trading

Sherman, William Tecumseh, 193

Silicon Valley, 22

Singapore, 91

slack: need for, 127; reduction of, 55, 63; and redundancy of military resources, 183; and standardization, 212–14

smart bombs, 140, 172

smart machines, 6, 217–18; and expert personnel, 146

smart weapons, 169–70, 187, 200, 201; and problems in the Gulf War, 174–77; and smart systems, 169–70, 186; social effects of, 131–32, 140, 143–47

"sneaker-net," 46

soldier, 170; changing role of, 141–42

Somme, Battle of, 195, 205

Soviet Union, 139, 142

spreadsheets, 27–28

standardization, 53; of computer operating systems, 28; contribution of Internet to, 43–44, 45; employed by Frederick the Great, 192; through mainframes, 7; and slack, 212–14; of workplace through networks, 38, 46–50

Stock Market Crash of 1987, 83–85, 86, 99, 100–101

Stock Market minicrash of 1989, 101

Stoll, Clifford, 43, 100

Strassman, Paul, xii

Strategic Computing Initiative, 200

stress, 163, 164, 165–66; and skilled operators, 129

submarines, 151, 171, 197

Sullivan, Gordon, 203

surge production, 174

surveillance: military, 12–13; of workers in computerized office, 48

synchronicity, 7, 8

systems analysis, 59

tanks, 151, 176, 187, 197

Taylor, Frederick W., 54–55

Taylorism, 10, 14, 55–56, 58, 62, 62–63, 64, 65, 196, 203

technicians: ascendancy of, 57

technology growth: and social change, 29, 30

telegraph, 53, 71, 72, 76, 79, 188, 194; in

World War I, 193, 194–95

telephone, 52, 53, 71, 72, 76, 79

TFX Fighter, 140–41

tight coupling, 94, 199, 200, 201, 202, 203, 207

Toffler, Alvin, 6

Toffler, Heidi, 6

"tooth-to-tail" ratio, 132, 144–45, 147, 191

Top Gun School, 117

translation, computer-aided language, 217–18

Turkle, Sherry, 14, 43, 210

United Airlines Flight 232, 811, 112

U.S. Air Force, 136, 138; and increasing specialization of personnel, 145

U.S. Army, 133, 138, 145–46, 148; conservatism of, 169, 170

U.S. Congress, 85, 102, 138, 164–65, 200

U.S. Department of Defense, 149, 172, 180

U.S. government: regulation of computerized trading by, 79, 80–81, 82, 85, 86–87, 89–90, 101–2; resistance of, to military innovation, 136

U.S. Navy, 109, 129, 136; and bureaucratic resistance to change, 150–51; and Gulf War, 173; Hearing Boards, 151, 162, 168; and ties to intellectual community, 138; and USS *Stark* incident, 154; and USS *Vincennes* incident, 160, 161–66; and USS *Wampanoag*, 150, 151

University of California at Berkeley, 35, 41

University of Chicago, 216

UNIX operating system, 20–21, 40–41

user-centered design, 32, 33–34, 49, 225n.50

USS *Coontz*, 154

USS *Elmer Montgomery*, 156, 157–58

USS *Sides*, 156, 160

USS *Stark*, 154–55, 156, 161, 167

USS *Vincennes*, 149, 153, 156–58, 159, 160–

62, 205; investigation of, 162–65; and role of stress, 165–66

USS *Wampanoag*, 150, 151, 152

Vietnam War, 117, 146, 170; and techno-logical innovation, 148–49; uncertainty in, 199

virtual reality, 214; and financial markets, 96

Wall Street, 75, 76, 77, 100

Wall Street Journal (newspaper), 84

Wal-Mart, 212

war: industrial, 193–97; nonlinear, 185–86; techno-industrial, 197–98; total, 193

warfare: attrition, 149, 170, 186, 199, 200; maneuver, 200, 209; transformation of, 185–86

Waterloo, Battle of, 195–96

Weick, Karl, 115

Wellington, Arthur, 195

Westmoreland, William, 200

Wieckert, Kären, 225n.50

Wilson, James Q., 103

Windows 95, 27

Winner, Langdon, 15, 146

Wired (periodical), 43

WNET, 106–7

word processors, 22, 28

workers: alienation of, 52; blue-collar, 57; computerized surveillance of, 48, 210; defunctionalization of, 66–67; deskilling of, 52–53, 56, 57, 61, 64, 65–66; displace-ment of, 61; empowerment of, 60; ideal Taylorist, 55; as "operatons," 65–66; training of, 69; white-collar, 57

workplace: informated, 63–66; textualiza-tion of, 66

workstations, personal, 8

World Trade Center bombing, 98

World War I, 133, 134, 135, 136, 170; Battle of the Bulge, 197; Battle of the Somme, 195, 205; as caused by technology, 205; communications in, 195, 196–97; role of telegraph in, 194–95

World War II, 16, 58, 59, 117, 133, 135–36, 139, 158, 170; logistics of, 198–99; and personnel allocation, 145; use of rail-roads in, 205; and use of technical inno-vations, 197–98

World Wide Web, 45

Wozniak, Steve, 22

Xerox, 6, 23–24, 25, 42–43

Zuboff, Shoshana, 64–65, 66, 125, 167